845563

Books by Max Hennessy

THE CHALLENGING HEIGHTS
THE BRIGHT BLUE SKY
THE IRON STALLIONS
BLUNTED LANCE
SOLDIER OF THE QUEEN
BACK TO BATTLE
THE DANGEROUS YEARS
THE LION AT SEA

The Challenging Heights

MAX HENNESSY

The
Challenging Heights

NEW YORK

ATHENEUM

1983

Author's Note

For many of the details contained in the last part of this book, I am indebted to the account of a similar operation in *Wings Over Kabul*, by Ann Baker and Air Chief Marshal Sir Ronald Ivelaw-Chapman, Kimber, 1975.

Part One

I

There was no wind and in the damp stillness of the winter day the trees were motionless. Falling leaves spiralled down to stir the surface of the pools of water in the road that picked up the daylight like fragments of polished steel. As the taxi in which he rode headed towards Brooklands aerodrome, Nicholas Dicken Quinney reflected that the year 1919 seemed as empty as the landscape.

Not very long before, he had been sitting in a hospital ward staring out at the frosted garden. With him there had been several other RAF men, all casualties of the greatest war the world had ever known, and all equally lost with its ending. For a while at the end of 1918 they had all been certain that the Germans would denounce the Armistice and that there would be a flare-up of the fighting so that the Allies would have to batter their way to the Rhineland for a final ending in the coming spring. But, even if the German generals had wanted to continue, the German soldiers did not. They had had enough and had gone home, leaving the whole of Northern France silent, with a mist in the valleys and a stillness over it like that of the grave. Even in the hospital, knowing that the great guns which had rumbled for four and a half years had finally stopped, it was like being buried alive. It was as if the ghosts of everyone they'd known for the last four and a half years were rising to remind them of the past, so that the only thing they could be certain of was that the world would never be the same again and that they could never live like those who had been too old or too young to have been part of the tragedy.

Several of the pilots, some of them with wounds, had talked together.

'What are you going to do now it's over?' someone had asked.

Coetzee, the South African, was the first to decide. For him it had seemed simple. 'I'm going back to my job in Durban,' he said. 'Weekends on the beach. A garden. A wife. Kids. That's the height of my ambition.'

Williams, who was an American and had joined the RAF because he was young and adventurous and wanted to fly in action, disagreed. 'I'll stay in,' he announced. 'I want to. I can't imagine being out.'

'Not me.' Noble had been flying RE8s and had spent most of his time in hospital lying on his face because his backside had been nicked by a piece of anti-aircraft shell. 'I'll get a job flying, but a *civil* job.'

'Same here,' Charley Wright was a snub-nosed red-faced man who had found a back exit from the hospital within a fortnight of arriving and slipped out regularly after dark to head for the nearest bar. 'I can't imagine living without aeroplanes.'

They had looked at Dicken for his reaction. They had always been a little overawed by the number of decorations he wore, but even more by the fact that he had been flying as long ago as 1914 and had contrived – by what supernatural lottery there was no telling – to survive without much harm until only weeks before the Armistice when he had been shot out of the sky with four wounds and a lot of broken bones.

When he didn't answer the talk had turned inevitably to girls. Coetzee had a girl in South Africa and Williams, the American, one in Houston. Wright had a woman in the town whom he visited whenever he could get out of hospital and wasn't going to a bar. Dicken had listened to them quietly. There had been only three girls in his life – Annys Toshack, his first love who had turned him down; Zoë, her sister, to whom he had transferred his affections but who had put the Atlantic Ocean between them by disappearing to Canada on almost the first ship that had left England after the Armistice, searching for a man called Casey Harmer who had promised her a job in flying and even, he suspected, the chance of a marriage; and Nicola Aubrey, whom he had met in Italy, where her father had been a member of the Diplomatic Corps. He frowned at the thought of her. She had meant a lot to him but she also had disappeared.

He had barely been old enough to have a girl when the war

4

had broken out but, like most young men about to face the possibility of death in battle, he had suddenly become aware of their importance as he had felt he might well die without knowing anything about them. He had suffered agonised pangs over Annys Toshack but had grown out of them as quickly as he had slipped into them. Zoë Toshack. She was an enigma to him still. He had never been in love with her but there had always been something between them, shared secrets, a mutual love of flying perhaps, and always a frankness that was unusual in girls of her generation, who were more given to a greater delicacy of expression. Nicola Aubrey. His heart sank as he thought of her. Her family had wholeheartedly accepted him into their midst and, despite their being Catholics and of a different religion, had even seemed to encourage him. Perhaps being in Italy, surrounded by the romance of nearby mediaeval Venice and its adjacent towns, had had something to do with it, but no other girl had touched him as deeply as she had. Like the others, however, she too had disappeared from his life. He had written to her but there had been no reply from any member of the family except a blotched and ill-spelled letter from her youngest sister, Marie-Gabrielle, postmarked Genoa and devoid of any address, saying they all missed him and that she, Marie-Gabrielle, would love him all her life. Since Marie-Gabrielle had been no more than nine years old at the time it had not meant much. Nicola had vanished. Her father, he had heard, had been posted to Delhi, and she had been placed totally beyond his reach.

He was still thinking of her as the taxi rattled along and only a slash of squally rain on the windscreen brought him back to the present. He could see his reflection in the glass behind the driver's back, a strong-featured young man but of no particular distinction save a straight nose and a firm chin. A few months before, he wouldn't have given himself a dog's chance of ever flying again, but once they had told him he wasn't going to lose his sight he had recovered quickly. Though his legs were still stiff, they worked and, so he had been told, would eventually be as good as new. But the squadron he had been promised had not materialised; with the end of the war, views had changed and nobody seemed now to know what to do with the RAF.

As the taxi drew to a stop, the driver handed him his walking

5

sticks and, moving slowly, he hobbled into the mess. Several young-old faces looked round at him. There were Americans, Canadians, South Africans, Australians, New Zealanders, to say nothing of Frenchmen and Italians and two disconsolate Russians who had been learning to fly Camels when the Revolution in Russia in 1917 had removed the whole point so that now nobody knew what to do with them. There were a few faces from the past: Archard, who had flown BEs with him and then gone on to RE8s and was still, like himself, miraculously alive; Griffiths, who'd flown 1½-Strutters; Almonde who'd started as an observer but had ended the war as a pilot; Tom Howarth, who'd served alongside him in Italy.

'It's funny flying now the war's finished,' Howarth said as he handed over a drink. 'The wind seems to deal with you more gently than it used to. There's no crackle of bullets, no need to celebrate at the end of the day because you're still alive when so many others are dead. One day I flew to the Rhine and round the cathedral at Cologne. But I found it dull. I was the one who brought the squadron home. I hear now that the machines are to be reduced to produce.'

'Which is a Service euphemism for scrap,' Dicken commented.

Howarth shrugged. 'I reckon the Government's betrayed us all. Demobilisation isn't working and there are cases of last in, first out – because, they say, industry needs 'em. In December I only got the chaps on parade by threatening to withhold their wages. They weren't mutinous, just fed up. What are you doing here?'

'Looking for Willie Hatto.'

When Hatto arrived, he grinned at Dicken with unrestrained pleasure. Like Dicken, like Archard, he was one of those who had survived the long months of aerial fighting and, after four and a half years of the bloodiest battles in the history of the world, was one of the few friends Dicken had left. They had come together from the opposite ends of the social scale: Dicken, brought up by a divorced mother in a row of terraced cottages in a Sussex village, had joined the army in 1914. Hatto, with Eton and Oxford behind him, part of a titled family with a crumbling country seat in Northamptonshire, was a regular officer. He was tall, monocled and languid and, despite his uniform, seemed always to be clad in the clothing of the cavalryman he had originally been. Somehow, he seemed undressed without leather patches on his elbows, a cravat and a riding whip. To the astonishment of everybody in the mess, he grasped Dicken's hands and they went into what they had always called their gloat dance – a solemn ring-o'-roses they had always performed in France and Italy with Foote, the American who had formed with them an anarchical trinity dedicated to the pricking of balloons, the reduction of pomposity and the deriding of inefficiency in senior officers. They had performed it whenever they had been successful at anything not permitted by King's Regulations or the chances of war, whether it was obtaining unofficial leave, routing some difficult officer from Wing, dodging a more than normally aggressive group of German aeroplanes, or merely simply surviving when by all the law of averages they ought not to have done.

When they had finished, Hatto slapped Dicken's shoulder and grinned. 'For a man with a pair of perforated legs,' he said, 'you perform remarkably well. The last time I saw you, you were lying on your back full of holes put there by Ernst Udet and his gang of graverobbers. I thought you'd be out of action for at least a year. I expect you're now badgering everybody to let you fly.'

'Carlin flew with a wooden leg.'

'Not four months after he lost the original. Heard about Diplock? He fixed himself up with a job at the Air Ministry.'

They smiled at each other. Cecil Arthur Diplock, from the next village to the one where Dicken had been born, had married Dicken's first love, Annys Toshack. There had never been much affection between them and what there was had disappeared when Diplock had turned up in France on the same airfield. His inability to screw up his courage to facing the enemy had removed him very rapidly from the scene but, a crafty and resourceful young man, from being appointed personal pilot to the Wing Colonel he had advanced to become his aide. Turning up again as squadron CO in Italy, he had managed to get rid of Dicken, Hatto and Foote, the American, every one of them men who knew his past history, and – though he knew he could never prove it – Dicken even had a suspicion that Diplock had sent him up for his last flight in the knowledge that Udet and his staffel were in the vicinity.

'He's applied for a permanent commission,' Hatto said. 'So have I. What about you?'

'If there's an air force.'

Before 1914 there had been no flying service and even now the RAF, the successor to the Royal Flying Corps and no more than a year old, had still not been provided with any plan for an establishment of regular officers. There were even ugly rumours that, with the politicians eager to cut expenditure now that the war was won and with the Navy and the Army fighting for funds, the RAF might even not survive.

They both avoided the subject. 'How's your wife, Willie?'

Hatto smiled. 'Fine. How about that girl of yours?'

'Which one do you mean?'

'Either of 'em 'll do.'

Dicken managed a smile. 'One's in Canada,' he said. 'T'other –' he shrugged.

'No ties?'

'None.'

Hatto smiled. 'Because the war isn't over, old son. It's still going on. In Russia. When the Russians opted out of the war in 1917, the Czechs who'd been fighting for them set off across Siberia to join the Allies in France. They were still armed and started fighting the Bolsheviks. They now practically control the whole of the Trans-Siberian Railway and it's encouraged a lot of other people to set up anti-Bolshevik governments. Now the French, the British, the Americans, the Japanese and a few more are making it official. We're going in.'

'Where?'

'A number of places. They say it's to relieve the distress of the Russian people but my brother, at the Foreign Office, says it's because everybody in Western Europe's scared stiff of Communism.'

Dicken looked dubious. 'Isn't it a bit cold in Russia?'

'We won't be going to the north. We're going to the south round Yalta. That's different. It's where all the Russian princes and princesses have their holiday palaces. There are a lot of them down there still enjoying life, and countesses are a penny a hundred. My brother's been there and he says it's beautiful.'

Hatto grimaced. 'It's either that or the awful bloody anti-climax of the Army of Occupation in Germany. Can you imagine it? People like Diplock in charge, and the Germans wishing you'd drop dead or break out all over in warts.'

Dicken grinned. Hatto was a forceful persuader. 'Are you going?'

'Not half.'

'All right. Count me in.'

'How about the old legs?'

'You sit down to fly.'

*

Hatto vanished almost overnight and, as soon as he was discharged from hospital, Dicken expected to follow him. But the commanding officer at the camp to which he was posted was an ex-Royal Naval Air Service type transferred to the RAF who still retained the esoteric salute used by the Navy and liked to make everyone aware of his seafaring background by referring to 'decks', 'going ashore', 'the ship's company' and 'running a tight ship'. Free time became 'off watch' and the bus into town from the main gate became the 'liberty boat'. He disapproved of people under his command going off to fight minor wars and, when he heard of Dicken's decision to do so, threatened to court martial him if he tried. It seemed to call for strong measures and Dicken simply packed his kit and arranged for a taxi. As he hobbled from the officers' mess, he was stopped by the adjutant, another ex-RNAS type.

'Are you going ashore?' he demanded.

'Yes,' Dicken snapped.

The adjutant smiled. 'The CO thought you were. He saw you from his window.'

'He must have nothing better to do.'

The adjutant's smile faded and he frowned. 'He instructed me to point out to you that the liberty boat doesn't leave until five o'clock.'

Dicken gave him a look of contempt. 'Tell him I don't need a boat,' he said. 'I'm swimming.'

Turning up in the office of Lieutenant-Colonel Joshua Rivers, who had been his CO while flying 1½-Strutters in France and was now in charge of Personnel and Postings, he

9

was welcomed and provided with coffee. Rivers was a moody man. He had crashed badly early in the war and now had a metal plate in his skull which, in France, had always been rumoured to be affected by rust or the heat of the sun and accounted for his changeable moods. This was one of his good days.

'That was a splendid show you put up against Udet's lot,' he said. 'What's going to happen to you now? Are they going to ground you as they have me?'

'No, sir. They've passed me fit for flying.'

'Have they, by God? And now, I suppose, you've arrived here expecting me to do something for you.'

'Yes, sir.'

'Where are you wanting to go?'

'Russia, sir. They say there are lots of opportunities in Russia.'

Rivers looked amused. 'There are supposed to be lots of countesses going spare out there, too,' he pointed out.

'That's what Willie Hatto said, sir.'

'Is he going?'

'Yes, sir.'

'God help the Russians! What about that mad American you two were always with – Foote?'

'He's safely in America, sir. Going in for law, I heard.'

'Well, America's big enough for him not to be able to do much harm. All right, I'll see what I can do.'

Dicken was so pleased at Rivers' reaction that when he bumped into his old enemy, Diplock, in the corridor, he didn't turn a hair.

Diplock hesitated as he saw him emerge from Rivers' office and seemed doubtful about his reaction.

'Quinney,' he said uncertainly.

'Diplock,' Dicken replied.

'You working here?' Diplock seemed worried in case he was.

'No, thank God,' Dicken said. 'I hear you are.'

'For some time now. It's the sort of work that suits me.'

'It would be,' Dicken commented, but without enmity. His suspicions about Diplock had never been confirmed and never would be now so there was no point in harbouring a grudge. All the same, the observation was true enough. Diplock was never one to risk his neck when someone else could do it for him. 'How's Annys?' he asked.

'Very well. She does a lot of work for charity. Airmen's families. That sort of thing.'

She would, Dicken thought. She went with Diplock. She'd make a good chairman of a branch of the Red Cross or something of that sort. He was glad she hadn't wanted to marry him.

They stared at each other for a moment longer, both of them uncertain how to conclude the conversation. Diplock, Dicken noticed, was fatter than he had been and his face was beginning to develop a jowly look.

'Well, I'd better be off,' he said.

'Yes,' Diplock agreed. 'Where are you these days?'

Dicken told him and for the first time Diplock managed a trace of a smile.

'I know the CO there. Ex-Navy type.'

'That's right. He'd have us all in bell-bottoms and seaboots and sleeping in hammocks if he could.'

Diplock frowned. 'He's a friend of mine.' he said stiffly.

He would be, Dicken decided. 'He disapproves of me wanting to go to Russia,' he said.

'Russia? Are you going there?' Diplock shuddered. 'That's a dreary place to go to. They say nobody knows whose side he's on. I should hate to go to Russia.'

Three days later, much to his ex-naval CO's disgust, Dicken was ordered to be prepared for a posting to Russia and to go on immediate leave. The CO, who had been trying to arrange for him to be put under arrest, gave him an angry look.

'It's an offence to go over a senior officer's head,' he snapped.

'Yes, sir.' Dicken picked up his cap. 'But sometimes it pays dividends.'

Dicken's mother found it as difficult as Diplock and his CO to understand his anxiety to get involved in someone else's war. 'Why Russia?' she asked. 'That's a funny place to want to go. It gets cold in Russia.'

'Not in the south, Mother.'

She shook her head. 'It might have been better,' she decided, 'if you'd gone to sea.'

Considering that, when he'd qualified as a marine radio operator in 1914 while still under age, it had been his mother who had refused to sign his papers so that he had joined the RFC instead, it seemed a bit unfair.

'*Why* are you going?' she asked. 'Because they shot the Tsar?'

'The Tsar doesn't mean much to me, Mother.'

'Because you don't like Bolsheviks then?'

'I've never met one.'

'There must be a reason.'

But there wasn't. The struggle going on in Russia meant little to Dicken beyond that he'd be able to go on flying when the Armistice in France had almost ended flying everywhere else.

Near the end of his leave a letter arrived from the Air Ministry telling him to hold himself in readiness. There was little else to do because Zoë Toshack was still in Canada, and a few days later a telegram arrived instructing him to report at once to the *SS Horatia*, due to sail that same midnight from Hull.

'They don't grow more efficient with the years,' Dicken snarled as he flung his belongings into a valise. 'I'll have to catch the afternoon train to London and the first one from there to Hull.'

Promising to write, he headed for the station and scrambled aboard the train. Passing through London, he snatched some food on the way north, and arrived in Hull late at night. Finding a taxi, he hurried to the docks and, with two hours to spare, scrambled aboard the *SS Horatia*, a high-decked steamer with a smoke stack like a cigarette. Shown to a cabin, he immediately fell asleep and woke up the following morning to find the ship moving down the river.

There were a few soldiers – mostly NCOs going as instructors – in the ship. The captain in charge, a man by the name of Baird, had wound stripes all the way up his arm, seemed a little mad and appeared to spend most of his time holding up the bar. As the ship finally left the river and turned north, Dicken frowned. With the sun behind them, it seemed a strange direction to be taking.

'Are we picking up more people?' he asked the first mate. 'At Tyneside or somewhere like that.'

The mate looked puzzled. 'I've heard nothing of it,' he admitted.

Dicken stared up at the sun. 'Then aren't we going the wrong way?'

The mate grinned. 'Well, I've always prided myself on my navigation,' he said, 'and it seems all right to me. Which way were you *expecting* to go?'

'South. Through the Mediterranean. Where are *you* going?'

'Riga.'

Dicken's jaw dropped. 'Where in God's name is Riga?'

'Latvia.' The mate grinned. 'Any good to you?'

'Aren't they Germans there?'

'Well, sort of. And sort of not. It was Russian before the war but it was invaded by the Germans and under the Treaty of Brest Litovsk the Russians renounced all claim to it. Actually, you're lucky you're not going to Murmansk, which is where I went last trip. That's bloody awful. Riga's much better.'

'What's happening there?'

The sailor smiled. 'Well, it's a bit confusing,' he admitted. 'During the war the Letts fought for the Russians but, when the Russians threw in the sponge after the Revolution, they fought for us. Then a group of Germans, who call themselves the Baltic Barons and want Esthonia and Latvia to be part of Prussia, liberated Riga from the Bolsheviks. Now, the Bolsheviks are back and the Letts, with allied blessing, have declared themselves a republic. Not that it does them a fat lot of good, because the Russian Imperial Army, the German Army, the Bolshevik army and finally the guerilla army have all fought across the bloody place and laid it waste. Our troops there are largely German Territorials run by a chap called Von der Goltz, but the Latvian Government wants to be independent and doesn't want 'em, while the Bolsheviks hate the Poles and the Poles are opposed to both.'

'So who's fighting who?'

The sailor grinned. 'As far as I can make out,' he said, 'everybody's fighting everybody.'

2

The North Sea was grey and ugly-looking but they managed to get ashore at Oslo and Copenhagen, where Captain Baird, in command of the soldiery, was carried back on board drunk and speechless. Because Riga was at the moment occupied by the Bolsheviks they landed at the minor part of Libau, which was supposed to be the seat of the provisional government of Latvia. To Dicken's surprise, the man standing by the Crossley tender on the quayside as they came alongside was Flight-Sergeant Handiside, who had introduced Dicken to the RFC in 1915. He was wearing only three stripes on his arm.

'Handiside!' Dicken said. 'What the hell are you doing here?'

'Same as you, I imagine, sir. Wondering what the hell's going on. I volunteered for South Russia and this is what I got. Minus my crown, of course, because I dropped a step in rank, like a lot of us. You were a major when I last saw you. You'll be pleased to know Mr Hatto's here as well.'

'He is?' This was unexpected to say the least, because Hatto was supposed to be in Yalta.

'He's in Riga with the Navy at the moment, but he'll be back soon.'

'There are Germans here, too,' Handiside went on. 'They're flying Siemens-Schuckerts, which is against the armistice rules because they're not supposed to have anything at all, and the Allied Control Commission's constantly after them.' In Handiside's grin was all the sympathy and understanding of one flying type for another. 'They operate from a field near the frontier and, when the Commission arrives, they fly over the border where they can't be caught and the mechanics remove the spark plugs of the Commission's cars and let the tyres down while they're arguing in the office with the CO. There are some

14

White Russians, too – anti-Bolsheviks – pilots, but they've got no aeroplanes so they just hang around looking sad and hoping someone will take them up for a flip.'

As they drove from the docks they passed Russian infantry officers swaggering along the streets, a grotesque sight, their chests ablaze with meaningless decorations they'd resurrected for the benefit of the local girls. According to Handiside, they were as unamenable to discipline as their troops and were frightened of being shot in the back if they ever left the protection of the British and the Germans. With them were their priests, dressed in red or blue gowns, with greasy curls, shaggy hair and whiskers. The airmen alone were different because most of them had flown in action and their commanding officer, a major called Samonov, wore the British Military Cross.

Though the war had been over for months now, it had left a hundred and one controversial areas of territory. The one thing that was needed was food but nobody had any to give, and the idealistic foundations of the new post-war world were already being built on dubious, much disputed foundations. The area where they were operating had been fought over half a dozen times and the houses, built of wood and more Russian than German, had a battered look, while the fields had all been denuded of their animals and crops.

'The poor sods are practically starving,' Handiside explained. 'They've been living on dried fish and bread made of rye-straw for nearly two years.'

The squadron was flying from a field near the port but there were no hangars and no perimeter fence. It looked like a pocket handkerchief and the machines were DH4s which required not less than 550 square yards to get down if every landing was not to be a squeezing sideslip, while, because of the surrounding pines, taking off meant yanking the machine into a climbing turn immediately the wheels left the ground. The mess was in an old house which had once belonged to a Baltic manufacturer and Dicken was given a vast room with a floor of polished wooden tiles so warped by damp that, as he stepped inside, a ripple ran along them right to the window while the cupboard door swung slowly and dolefully open. As he unpacked, he heard the sound of an aeroplane engine and soon afterwards a

DH4 appeared over the trees. It was sending out puffs of black smoke and its engine sounded like a can full of stones.

'Mr Hatto's,' Handiside said as he went outside. 'It's got a Liberty engine. They say it was designed in a New York hotel in three and a half hours. This one sounds like it.'

Hatto climbed from the cockpit as the propeller jerked to a stop. 'I'm thinking of donating it to a museum,' he informed Handiside. Then he saw Dicken and yelled with delight.

'A gloat dance is called for, I think,' he said. 'We should celebrate.'

'Should we?' Dicken asked as they caught their breath. 'I thought we were going to South Russia. Vines. Sunshine. Palaces full of grand duchesses and princesses. This is some bloody place neither of us had ever heard of before.'

Hatto grinned. 'I nearly *did* go to South Russia,' he explained. 'There were two ships in Southampton Water and they took me off the one I was on and put me aboard the other. And that one brought me here.'

'I think somebody's got it in for us, Willie.'

'I think somebody has. And I think I know who.'

'Not Diplock?'

Hatto was studying him with a rueful grin. 'I got in touch with Tom Howarth who made a few enquiries. We were due to go to 47 Squadron in South Russia but the appointments were changed at the last minute.'

'What's it like here, Willie?'

'Chap called Cuthbert Orr's in command. Flew SEs in France. He's as mad at Diplock and the Air Ministry as the rest of us. The aircraft are old – procedure for take-off is start up, cross all disengaged fingers and let her rip – but there aren't many, anyway, so we have to take it in turns to fly 'em. And that's when the weather permits because the climate's horrible.'

'What about the fighting?'

'Still trying to work it out.'

When Orr appeared, he turned out to be a pale-faced man with a large black moustache and icy eyes. He couldn't speak German and was largely dependent for his information on Hatto who could. Most of his days were spent trying to work out what to do with the admiral in command, a fierce little man whose chief wish seemed to be to get to grips with anybody who wanted a fight, no matter whose side they were on, and with the army, which was being raised to deal with the Bolsheviks under an urbane Irish Guardsman called Harold Alexander.

Dicken's arrival brought the number of pilots up to twelve, but the need for observers seemed to have been overlooked and the pilots had to double up with each other in that capacity. Most of the flying seemed to consist of reconnaissances to find out where the Bolshevik forces were so that the mixed force of German Landeswehr, Letts, Poles and White Russians that formed the anti-Bolshevik army could operate against them. Occasionally, because the Navy were operating light craft along the River Dvina, it consisted also of shooting up or bombing their opposite numbers in the Bolshevik naval forces further inland along the river.

As they worked, the White Russian flying officers under Samonov, sad-eyed and despondent, their shoulders wearing great epaulettes like boards, watched them gloomily, and when the army finally captured several truckloads of equipment and found aeroplanes among them, in spite of their age and shocking lack of care, Samonov fell on them with delight and began to assemble them at full speed. They had originally been captured by the Bolsheviks after the French had evacuated Odessa in the Ukraine, transported north across Russia, and recaptured by the British near Archangel, to be finally brought south to the Baltic. There was a German Rumpler, a British DH4, two German Fokker DVIIs and a French Nieuport.

'The Bolos have exactly the same aircraft,' Hatto pointed out. 'So it'll be a good idea to move warily when you're up.'

The Latvian government was run by a man called Ulmanis who, because he had been chased out of Riga and didn't trust the Germans under Von der Goltz in Libau, was at that moment in Windau. His government didn't seem to do much more than issue proclamations and publish pamphlets and there was remarkably little sign of order because the streets of Windau were muddy, shabby and full of the refuse of the four armies which had passed through it.

Near the aerodrome was a meadow full of wild pansies, violets, cornflowers, clover and buttercups, with, on the far side, a lake where they could bathe, though as the weather grew warmer the midges were so voracious that the only way they could do it was to drive to the water's edge in a tender, fling off their wraps, plunge in and remain up to their necks until on a signal, they all rushed out, grabbed their wraps and drove away as fast as possible. One day as they were swimming, a small and ancient Caudron looking like a box kite dropped into the field. The pilot was a Bolshevik who had had enough of fighting and, still dressed in bathing suits and fighting off the midges, they took him prisoner with his own pistol. He had news that the Bolsheviks were trying to advance near the village of Milorad-nyi and the order to bomb them was given by Orr.

The attempt to get everybody off the ground was farcical. The mechanics had stripped down three of the troublesome DH4s and only two managed to get away, one of them turning back within ten minutes. Excited at the chance of action, the Russians rushed to their battered machines but they had not yet been properly serviced and two of them conked before they had even left the ground and in the end, flying as Hatto's observer, Dicken found he was in the only machine in the air.

They found the Bolsheviks among the forests near the solitary eastbound railway line but, with bombs in short supply, they had had to load up with hand grenades and a lot of empty beer bottles which made a whistling noise as they fell. Flying low through a scattering of fire that put holes in the wings, they tossed out the hand grenades but, as the Russians dispersed, the DH's engine began to falter. It picked up again almost at once but for safety Hatto swung west. As he did so they realised one of the thick fogs which infested the area had come down and the ground beneath them was completely obscured.

'Best keep going west,' Dicken yelled.

'The bloody compass is dud,' Hatto shouted back. 'I don't know which *is* west.'

'That way!' Dicken pointed.

'I think it's that way.'

'You're wrong!'

'No, I'm not.'

Staring downwards, Dicken was convinced he was right. In the observer's cockpit was a spare joystick which he unfastened and brandished in front of Hatto's face. 'It's that way,' he yelled in a fury. 'And if you don't turn I'll knock your brains in.'

With the faltering engine, they struggled on, only to find, as the fog lifted abruptly, that they were both wrong and west was at right angles to the course they were flying. They were still laughing at themselves when the engine cut completely.

As Hatto glanced round, Dicken saw the alarmed look in his face. 'Bet you a quid you can't land without crashing,' he yelled.

Heading for an open space in the forest, they just failed to clear the trees and Dicken was shot out of the rear cockpit as the machine came to a full stop, wedged firmly in a vertical position between two giant pines. Dazed and stupified, he sat up to see Hatto climbing from the pilot's cockpit. The ground around them was littered with empty bottles.

'They'll decide we were drunk,' Hatto grinned. He stared about him, rubbing his shoulder and looking for the Bolsheviks they'd just been bombing. 'Strikes me,' he went on, 'that we'd be wise not to hang about here.'

Following the single railway line, they headed west along the edge of the forest. The sun was out now so that they had to stumble along in the heat in their heavy flying clothes, plagued by midges that seemed to come in millions from among the trees and lakes. After a mile or two, they came to a clearing where sleepers were stacked and among them they found a small rusting hand-driven trolley. Using pine branches, they levered it on to the track but as they clambered aboard, they heard shouts and saw men on horses appearing among the trees.

'Christ,' Hatto said. 'The Bolos! Look slippy, old fruit!'

They began to pump the handles but the trolley was old and tired and it was hard work, though, once they got the handles moving, they began to move faster and faster. A few shots whistled over them but nothing came very near and, surrounded by the squeaks of the handles and the oil-less wheels, they managed to make their escape.

A few last shots whistled overhead as the horsemen dropped behind and disappeared, and they stopped the trolley to get their breath back, sitting on the platform, smoking and enjoying the sunshine.

'Not bad here,' Hatto remarked.

'I've seen worse,' Dicken admitted. 'But not much worse.'

Hatto smiled. 'Old Parasol Percy Diplock would enjoy this

place. All those midges. People who shoot at you. Lots of non-comfort.'

'Pity we can't get him to join us.'

'Fat chance of that. I expect he's got all his anchors out to make sure nobody moves him far from London.'

It was Dicken's turn to smile. 'It would be a triumph if we *could* get him here.'

'Perhaps we should bend our minds to that end. Nothing vicious, mean or vengeful. Just something to take that smug look off his face.'

They were still enjoying the sunshine when it dawned on them that the trolley they were sitting on had started vibrating and that the vibration was coming from the rails beneath, and finally that the Bolshevik horesmen had disappeared not because they had grown tired of the chase but because there was a train approaching and they were in the way and likely to derail it.

'Good God,' Hatto yelled. 'The bloody thing'll flatten us!'

As they struggled in a panic to lever the trolley from the rails, they heard the shriek of an engine whistle and the engine hurtled at full speed round the bend towards them. Alongside the driver his moustache bristling with ferocity and clutching a revolver as big as a cannon, was Orr coming to their rescue. The truck behind was filled with men with rifles.

*

They had good reason to celebrate that night because news had come in that the White Russian armies were closing in and the Bolsheviks were on the run everywhere.

'At the moment,' Orr said, gesturing at the map, 'General Denikin's heading up from South Russia, General Kolchak's heading west from Siberia, another force is pushing down from Archangel, and there's a force here under a chap called Yudenitch who's aiming for Petrograd. The idea's to meet in Moscow and restore the status to quo so that Europe will be freed from the Red menace for ever and ever, amen.' He paused, sucked at his pipe for a while and studied the map, measuring the distances in hands' breadths. 'I hope they pull it off,' he added. 'Because if the Siberian lot really do manage to join the Archangel lot it'll only be at the expense of a lot of hard slogging, and that crowd at Archangel are in no state to restore 'em. All this victory talk needs taking with a pinch of salt because nothing's what it seems out here, and to make matters worse, they all speak some bloody awful Slav language no one's ever heard of, let alone studied at school.'

Hatto glanced at Dicken and smiled. 'What we really need here, sir,' he observed cheerfully, 'is an officer who's a good linguist.'

'I can imagine them sending us one,' Orr growled.

'Oh, they would, sir,' Hatto said. 'Especially if this chap, Ulmanis, who's running the show here, requested it. He needs a good liaison officer. After all he's head of the Provisional Government.'

'And at the moment hiding from Von der Goltz who's behaving as if he's commanding an army of occupation.'

'All the same, sir, if we get his signature on the request they'd have to take notice of it in London.'

Orr wasn't convinced. 'We'd probably get some wet type from the Foreign Office with a face like a hen's arse.'

'Then we should request someone by name, sir, and get Ulmanis to ask especially for him. Make it seem important. Have him claim he's heard of him and wants him very particularly. If it becomes a political thing they can't refuse.'

Orr scowled. 'Who *would* he want?'

'There's a Squadron Leader Diplock, sir. He was studying for a degree, specialising in European languages when the war broke out. Surely what they speak here's European. He's very good, sir. He also speaks French, German and Italian. There's nothing he enjoys more than a job like this. What's more, sir –' Hatto smiled '– he's the chap who was responsible for sending me here – probably you, too, if the truth were known.'

Orr's head jerked round. 'He is, is he?' he said. 'Very well then, Willie, let the bugger have a taste of his own medicine. How do we get Ulmanis' name on the damn thing?'

Hatto beamed. 'Leave it to me, sir. He's here in the city keeping his head well down because Von der Goltz and the Baltic Barons are trying to capture him.'

'Think you can find him?'

'Shouldn't wonder, sir. I hear his Minister of Commerce and a couple of other Ministers are aboard the destroyer, *Seafire*. They'll know where he is and I happen to have made my number with *Seafire*'s captain. Chap called Andrew Cunningham. Rather hot stuff for a sailor.'

*

Seafire lay alongside the breakwater in the inner harbour, just ahead of her a merchant ship laden with arms.

'Her engines have broken down,' the officer on the gangplank told them. 'And the Old Man's scared stiff someone will decide to board her, seize the weapons and start a revolution.'

Beyond the merchant ship was a large barracks containing German soldiers and behind it a tract of pine forest. As they went aboard, Cunningham, a tall round-faced man bursting with self-confidence and salty language, was conducting a ferocious argument with a wild-looking man with a bushy black beard, partly in Latvian, partly in halting German and partly in English.

'The bloody man's claiming the Germans have captured the Latvian GHQ,' he pointed out. 'I'm going along to see what's happened. Fancy joining me?'

As they headed into the forest, they met German soldiers staggering back with beds, pots, pans, chickens, ducks, blankets and various other forms of loot. A house in a clearing was burning fiercely, alongside it a battalion of German soldiers forming up ready to march off. Seeing the British uniforms, Latvian officers, their faces bruised, their uniforms torn, rushed up, waving their arms, to explain that the Germans had arrested all their senior officers, seized their records and started the fire. As they finished, a German band at the head of the column blared out and the column began to march off. Cunningham frowned.

'It's obviously no time for a ship full of arms to be alongside the jetty,' he said. 'We'd better shift her.'

Returning to the ship, the tow was made fast and they began to head down the narrow canal that led to the commercial harbour.

'The swing bridge's supposed to open to my siren,' Cunningham growled, staring ahead. 'If it doesn't, we'll have to ram it and put a landing party ashore to shoot anybody who objects.'

As they reached the outer harbour and made fast again, German troops were visible on both sides of the canal and in a lot of neighbouring buildings, and they could see the black

22

snouts of machine guns near the lock gates.

'This is bloody ticklish,' Cunningham admitted. 'One destroyer against the whole of Von der Goltz's army. We'll go in stern-first, Number One, in case we have to come out in a hurry.'

Backing and filling in the narrow waterway, the ship turned round. The Germans began shouting insults but, as the destroyer's guns were lowered and trained round, ready to fire at point-blank range, the shouting died. In a deathly silence, they waited for what would happen, but as Cunningham rapped out a series of crisp orders, all of them quite audible to the Germans on shore, the machine gun parties at the ends of the wharves quietly picked up their weapons and disappeared. Almost immediately a couple of Latvians, who claimed to be ministers of the deposed government climbed aboard and claimed asylum. They said Ulmanis and other ministers had taken refuge with the British Mission.

When they found him, Ulmanis looked tired and ill but he was more than ready to append his signature to anything that might bring help, and two hours later the request for a linguist and for Cecil Arthur Diplock in particular was in the safe of the captain of a naval trawler heading towards England.

3

Stuck away at the north-eastern end of the Baltic, there was a depressing feeling of being out of the world – especially when they heard stories of men in America preparing to fly the Atlantic. Only a few short years before when aeroplanes had been little more than powered box kites such a thing had appeared impossible but from the newspapers they received it now seemed that Harry Hawker, the famous test pilot, and a companion, with a huge specially-built Sopwith powered with a Rolls Royce Eagle engine, two other men with a converted Vickers Vimy bomber with *two* Rolls Royce Eagles, and a squadron of American naval men in flying boats were all virtually on their way.

The uncertainty of the situation in the Baltic remained, however, and the White Russian forces were totally unreliable. The conscripted Russian peasants had had enough of autocracy to last them for ever and had no intention of supporting any move to restore the Romanovs. The Poles were working for an independent Poland and their interest was only in getting rid of their traditional enemies, the Russians, White *or* Red. The Letts wanted a free Latvia and were only too willing to fight with the British whose idea was to set up buffer states in Latvia, Esthonia and Lithuania to keep back the tide of Bolshevism. The German leaders were interested only in preserving their own estates by keeping East Prussia German and, if possible, adding to it while no one was looking.

It was always difficult to get the separate forces to operate together, and the White Russian officers remained terrified of their men. When one of their battalions mutinied and shot their officers in the back on parade, the Russian generals responded by rounding up a whole host of wrongdoers for punishment, and everybody had to face the business of the execution of the ringleaders. The Russian officers clearly intended to make an example and the court martial was a hurried affair with only lip service paid to justice. There was no appeal and the sentence was to be carried out almost immediately.

After a visit to a tent, where they were blessed by priests, the guilty men were sprinkled with holy water and kissed, then marched under escort to where Russian, German, Polish and British troops formed a hollow square. Some of them were weeping but one of them, a fine-looking sergeant, stood proudly erect as the stripes were torn from his sleeves. A small dog appeared and began to sniff the legs of the condemned men and for a while the affair seemed likely to descend into tragi-comedy because it refused to get out of the way. The officer in charge, a pale-faced young man wearing pince-nez and the enormous epaulettes of the Imperial Russian Army, timidly shooed it aside only for it to return again and again. In the end, a Russian colonel with an iron-grey beard, stamped across and snarled at him to get on with it, lashing out with his boot at the dog which bolted, yelping, so that even the men waiting for execution managed a faint smile.

As the machine guns chattered, the men tied to the posts stiffened and slumped but, as the smoke cleared, the sergeant was seen to be still alive. He had somehow shed his blindfold and, though his face and clothes were smeared with blood, he was shouting 'Long Live Bolshevism.' As the officer in the pince-nez moved up to him to administer the coup de grace with his pistol, the sergeant spat at him. As the officer hesitated, the sergeant went on shouting. In the end the colonel did the job and the young officer promptly turned aside and vomited up his breakfast.

It was a depressing business and seemed to symbolise the uselessness and waste of the operations along the Baltic. However, the generals had finally decided that doing nothing was dangerous and a menace to morale and the following day news came that the army was to move forward. Several of the units passed the aerodrome, the Germans well-fed and well-equipped but the rest wearing only old torn uniforms without greatcoats, cast-offs from the war in France. Most of the fighting seemed to be left to them where possible while the

25

Germans remained in the barracks near the river, arrogant, self-important and behaving more like a victorious army than a defeated one allowed to retain its weapons only because of the local political situation.

The flying went on, for the most part pointlessly because they were short of ammunition and had few bombs, and for a lot of the time only half the aircraft were serviceable through lack of spare parts. Eventually they heard that the allied intervention in Russia was falling apart, and that the British and the troops in the north around Archangel were to be withdrawn during the summer when the sea was free of ice, though they were hoping first to make a swift drive south to link up with Kolchak's drive west from Siberia. Within a week, however, they heard that Denikin's White forces in the south had been driven out of the Ukraine and the great plan to capture Moscow was dying on its feet.

Soon afterwards, the Russian pilots received instructions – God alone knew where from because they seemed to have no senior officers – to fly north. The Finns, as worried about Bolshevism as everybody else in Europe, were also standing with teeth bared in case the Bolsheviks came, and since the fighting round Murmansk appeared to have died down, they had agreed to give the Russians refuge. The airmen gathered their battered collection of machines together for departure and gave the most tremendous dinner, for which they hired a gypsy orchestra, and put on a display of Russian dancing and drinking that left everybody breathless. In turn they were hilariously excited and full of gloom, and the Russian major, Samonov, went round saying goodbye with an intensity that was heart-breaking, growing slowly more drunk as the evening went on. The party continued until dawn and was just breaking up when the roar of an aeroplane starting up came over the by now blurred strains of the orchestra. Rushing outside, they saw one of the Fokker DVIIs just lifting off the ground.

'Who is it for God's sake?' Orr asked.

'It's Major Samonov,' one of the Russians said. 'It's his way of saying goodbye.'

Banking steeply over the end of the field, the Fokker came hurtling towards them with a roar that set the windows shaking. At the top of its climb it turned and dived again and they all flung themselves flat as it howled past, its slipsteam blowing stinging particles of grit in their faces. As they lifted their heads, it banked over the trees at the other end of the field and came howling back once more. Watching it narrow-eyed, they were convinced Samonov was trying to kill himself. As the Fokker came thundering towards them yet again one of the lorries was just coming in from the town and, as the Fokker flashed towards it at a height of nought feet, they saw the driver jump out and run. The Fokker leapt over the lorry and turned again at the end of the field for another run, but this time as it banked, standing on its wingtip, they heard the engine splutter and cough.

'Oh, Christ!' Handiside gasped.

A wing touched the ground in a puff of dust and, as they all started to run, the aeroplane banged down and began to slide sideways across the turf, shedding undercarriage, wings and tail in flying fragments until it finally hit a parked farm cart. As it disintegrated the pilot flew out of the cockpit to hit the ground several yards in front with a thud that sickened them.

As the tender slewed to a stop, Dicken dropped from the running board and fell on his knees alongside Samonov. The Russian's skull seemed concave, one eye was missing, his nose was punched in and his lips were pulped, while his legs lay at impossible angles, as though the bones had been reduced to fragments. He died in Dicken's arms even as the others panted up.

*

The funeral was held the following day, green-robed, bearded and ringleted priests circling the coffin, holding lighted candles and chanting in deep sonorous voices. Sprinkling holy water over the dead man, they bent to kiss his shattered forehead. His medals, which included his British MC, lay on a cushion at the foot of the coffin. It added to the feeling of waste.

The following day several DFCs were handed out as well as several Russian decorations.

'You can get a gong out here,' Hatto said dryly, 'for things which were considered all in a day's work in France. As for the Russian gongs, you can buy 'em in the shops without any trouble at all. Shows what a ragtime affair it is.'

*

As the Russian pilots vanished towards Finland, they heard that several battalions of White Russian troops had deserted, and immediately, as though they had prior knowledge of it, the Bolsheviks to the east began to become aggressive and the army sent up a wail of protest and demanded news of their whereabouts.

Flying with Hatto as his observer, Dicken forged eastwards over countryside that was flat and uninteresting with patches of forest and lakes and rivers steely in the harsh light. They found the Bolsheviks just north of a village called Mizchaikya. They were cavalry, fur-capped men on small shaggy ponies, their bodies festooned with ammunition belts. They seemed not to know how to behave against an aeroplane and remained in a solid phalanx, swarming along a dusty track that did duty as a road. Hatto fired at them with the machine gun from the rear cockpit, so that they scattered across the plain, but after only a few shots the gun jammed. Swinging away, they headed north until they found several Bolshevik batteries whose position Hatto marked on the map. On their return, with the gun working again, they bumped into the same group of cavalry crossing a wooden bridge. They were in a long file, hurrying now, and they caught them in the middle where they couldn't escape. As the gun roared, men and horses crashed into the water and Dicken could see the splashes of bullets pursuing them along the surface of the river. An animal slipped and fell and, as the other horsemen began to bunch he saw the frail structure collapse, throwing them into the water. The rest of the cavalrymen tried to turn round but the other end had been blocked by fallen horses and stalled carts and in the end most of them spurred their mounts into the river and tried to escape by swimming.

They had no wireless and as they landed, the Crossley was sent off with a hurried message to the Navy, who were in touch with the army, to inform them of the position of the Bolshevik forces. It was a ridiculous situation and, in an attempt to improve communications, they were moved to a field alongside a river nearer the port, everybody living on barges moored to the bank.

It was a squalid area of mean evil-smelling streets filled with refuse, the inhabitants not yet recovered from the deprivations of the war years, and Orr shot off in a fury to see the senior RAF officer, leaving Hatto in command. He had no sooner vanished than a crowd of civilians appeared on the bank, begging for food, the women half-clothed and sick, the children ragged little scarecrows with pale faces and hollow eyes lifting their bony arms to ask for bread. The cooks promptly organised a soup kitchen and started handing out army rations and soap.

'I reckon,' Handiside growled, 'that when the Almighty was doing His stuff at the Creation, He realised He was going to be in a bit of a hurry to get it all finished, so He saved all the boners, blunders and blobs and shoved them down in one place for quickness – here! They do everything backwards and, as far as the Russians are concerned, titles are far more important than guts, and my strongest impression of the place got into my head through my nose.'

The following day the children were back again, this time with bowls, pleading for food, and in no time the cooks were handing out thick slices of bread and jam. One small boy, on a raft made of wood and old oil cans, appeared downriver and moored alongside. For his daring, Handiside lifted him aboard and saw him stuffed full of rice pudding.

Late in the afternoon a truculent young German officer appeared on the bank demanding to see the commanding officer. The sentry shouted to the sentry on board the officers' barge. 'There's a bloke here wants to see the Old Man!'

The German scowled and, as he came on board, he complained in English of the rudeness of the sentry.

'You're bloody lucky you didn't get a boot up the backside,' Dicken pointed out. 'That chap was fighting your lot for four years and he doesn't like you very much.'

The situation ashore was still delicate, the Germans and the Letts still at each others' throats with the British in between trying to persuade them to kill Bolsheviks instead of each other, and the German had arrived to register a protest that, under the terms of the agreement between the Allies and the Germans, civilians should not be permitted close to military establishments. Hatto told him what he thought of the complaint and within an hour a line of German sentries appeared to restrain the crowd from approaching. The adults did as they were told but the children were indifferent to the threats and when a small girl, clutching a slice of bread and jam, was knocked flying by a box on the ear, there was a roar of anger.

Dicken reached the deck just as the airmen were about to swarm over the rails ready to heave the German into the river.

'Stay where you are!' he roared. 'Give the kid another slice of bread and jam and escort her to safety. And next time keep your heads. An incident could provoke fighting and that's the last thing we want.'

The Germans watched sullenly as the child was escorted through their ranks but the following morning Dicken was wakened by the sound of hammering and sawing. Scrambling to the deck, he found Hatto placidly watching a large force of carpenters erecting a high wooden barricade on the bank by the barges.

'What's going on?'

Handiside shrugged. 'I think we're just about to find out.'

A German officer appeared, and, stopping in front of them gravely explained that General von der Goltz had heard the RAF were being troubled by the populace and that the fence was being built to ensure their privacy.

'There will be a door in the fence, of course,' he explained. 'With a sentry.'

Hatto listened politely and watched throughout the day as the fence was erected.

'Blighters don't like us fraternising,' he murmured. 'That's the trouble.'

Two days later, he strolled from the barge to the officer in charge of the building.

'Finished?' he asked.

The German beamed and saluted. 'Yes, Herr Hauptmann!'

Hatto smiled, returned the salute and climbed back on board. 'Handiside,' he said solemnly. 'I've decided our berths here are becoming too fouled with tins and empty bottles. I think we'd better find new ones further along.'

Watched by the furious Germans, the mooring ropes were unfastened and the barges dragged along the river, where the children began to appear again at once, grinning and holding out their hands for bread and jam.

*

Libau was not a place where there was a lot of life but it seemed it was the only area where the Allied attempts to bring order along the border of Russia and prevent the spread of Bolshevism was having any success. The army was steadily pushing the Bolshevik forces back and Riga fell to the Germans but, even as it did so, the Allied intervention was collapsing about their ears. In the south the White forces were in retreat and they were also withdrawing from Central Asia, Transcaucasia, Baku and Archangel, and an ambitious project for the formation of a Slavo-British legion in the north ended abruptly when two of its companies mutinied and murdered five British and four Russian officers in their beds. There didn't seem a great deal of future in the plans for intervention.

With the summer hot and the midges almost unbearable, once more the feeling of being cut off prevailed. With the better weather, football matches were played between the men and the officers, and the officers and the NCOs, but it was unwise to go into the town where the Germans were in large numbers, arrogant and domineering and spoiling for a fight. Mail was slow arriving and out-of-date newspapers turned up only when a ship appeared. When they did, the news for the airmen was electrifying.

Hatto whirled round, his eyes alight. 'Great Ned,' he yelled 'They made it!'

'Who made what?'

'The Atlantic! It's been flown!'

'It has? Who by? Hawker?'

'No, he came down fifteen hundred miles out. The Americans. A whole squadron of flying boats going by the Azores. They shed aircraft with every step but they made it! One of them landed at Lisbon.'

'That's one in the eye for the people who said it couldn't be done.'

Hatto's eyes were still glued to the newsprint. 'There are others preparing in Newfoundland, too. A whole crowd of them. Somebody's bound to do it non-stop now the Americans have shown the way.'

The news made them feel more than ever isolated. The flying was monotonous and they rarely saw enemy troops and never another aircraft, though they heard from agents that now that

31

the White Russian campaigns in the south had collapsed, the Bolsheviks had brought north machines which had been flying on that front.

When Orr returned he brought news received by wireless from the Navy.

'They've done it,' he announced. 'Non-stop Newfoundland to a bog in Ireland. Jack Alcock and a chap called Brown. With a Vimy. It could carry six tons for almost twelve hours and they'd fitted extra tanks to give them a range of 2440 miles.'

The mess was noisy with the celebrations but behind the merriment they were also all aware that flying, even the world, had changed abruptly. With the Atlantic crossed in one hop, they knew that from now on flying *must* be regarded as having a future. If it had come to adulthood in the forcing house of the war in France, it had come of age with this new feat. Aircraft were no longer the toys of airminded sportsmen. They had joined ships and trains as a reliable form of transport.

They had finally decided that the personal request for Diplock was either going to bring no response or that Diplock had managed to fight it off when bombs arrived – not very many and not very big ones – and with them orders to use them on Bolshevik gunboats patrolling the Dvina.

In poor flying weather with a lot of low stratus they found the Bolshevik gunboats – sleek black vessels more like motor boats than anything – heading down the Dvina in the direction of Riga and, circling in worsening weather, they dropped their bombs. One of the boats ran aground and ended up partially capsized, while the other, sprayed by machine gun fire, turned and bolted for home. The return fire from the banks was heavy however, and to add to their misery as they swung round to head back for Libau it began to rain.

As they landed with the rain coming down in squally flurries out of a leaden sky, Orr appeared.

'I'm glad you're back,' he said. 'You've arrived just in time to pack your bags.'

The capering stopped at once. 'Where are we going, sir?' Hatto asked. 'South?'

'Yes,' Orr said. 'The Empire's falling apart elsewhere and we're needed. It seems the Government's having second thoughts about this part of the world. Especially now the White Armies are on the run. A destroyer's taking us home.'

Hatto grinned. 'Just think,' he said. 'Duty free gin.'

*

Because the Letts had no pilots and because under the Armistice agreements of 1918, the Germans weren't allowed to have any aeroplanes, they solemnly pushed the DHs together and set fire to them. Nobody was very sorry and they stood watching as the column of black smoke coiled into the sky. On Orr's barge, they lined up for a Latvian Minister they'd never seen before to hand out medals and make a speech none of them understood, then, without speaking, they tossed the last of their baggage on to the lorries and began to scramble aboard themselves.

When they took their last look back as the lorries turned on to the road, they saw an ancient cab appearing down the road from the city. As it came alongside, a head appeared.

'Hey!' A man in RAF uniform thrust his head out and started yelling. 'What's going on? I've been ordered to report to a Major Cuthbert Orr. Is he here?'

Hatto grinned at Dicken. 'It's Parasol Percy.'

Thrusting his head out, Dicken recognised at once the plump pale face and protruding ears of their old enemy, Diplock.

'Just down there,' Hatto yelled, pointing. 'Just packing up the office!'

Diplock had recognised them immediately and was frowning. 'I've just been ordered out here,' he snapped, his expression suspicious as if he already suspected who was behind his unexpected posting. 'What's going on? Where's everybody going?'

Hatto beamed. 'Well,' he said cheerfully, 'I don't know where you're going, but *we're* going home.'

33

4

'Berlin's no place to visit,' Dicken's mother insisted. 'It's full of Germans and full of wickedness.'

To Dicken, Berlin seemed more like the edge of a volcano. Nobody there seemed to be aware of the fact, however, and if they were it seemed doubtful that they would shed any tears, or even that their tears would extinguish the flames. Truncated, impoverished and with an economic crisis that had sat on their shoulders like a vulture ever since the Armistice, after the war the Germans wanted only to enjoy themselves and Berlin seemed like a city gone mad.

Dicken's mother was right, of course. Berlin *was* wicked and it *was* full of Germans. But there were others there, too. Because it had become what it had, it was also full of Frenchmen, Americans, Englishmen, anybody who had money to spend and needed something to spend it on. The fact that the Germans had been their enemies mattered not a jot. The men who had fought in the late war were always more in sympathy with their enemies, the German soldiers, sailors and airmen, than they ever had been with their own politicians who seemed nothing but sanctimonious spouters backed by financiers and businessmen who all seemed to have done remarkably well out of the fighting.

In Germany, it had left a legacy of bitterness. The returning soldiers had inherited a sick economy, and Europe was shaken and weak and lacked stability. Three empires had collapsed, imposing burdens on other countries which were bearing them to the ground, and the cry of 'Back to normal', by which was implied that serene world of pre-1914, meant as little to the demobilised soldiers as Lloyd George's promise of 'a land fit for heroes to live in.'

With high prices and the sudden drying up of jobs as the industrial backlog left by the short-lived post-war boom began to fade, unemployment increased and, with unscrupulous war profiteers unloading their new factories as fast as they could before they lost money, Europe was operating at a disadvantage and a depression was quite clearly just over the horizon.

Suddenly the only thing that seemed to have a future was the brand new industry of civil aviation. The boost given to it by the war and the crossing of the Atlantic had proved beyond all doubt that there was a future in flying. From being regarded as something like high-wire walkers operating without a net, airmen were now being seen as men of the future. But there were ugly rumours about the RAF moving around London, because between them, the army, the navy and the Treasury seemed determined to destroy it, and its officers were wondering what was to happen to them. Even at this late date, no plan had yet appeared for the establishment of regular officers and Dicken wasn't even sure he would enjoy wearing a uniform in peacetime.

Life was uninspiring and his thoughts were unconstructive. The idea of settling down to an earthbound life seemed impossible, yet as he tried to make up his mind what to do, he realised his only qualifications were that he could fly and was still keen to do so. Since service life in peacetime had ceased to appeal, why not become a civil pilot? Merely flying from one place to another also seemed dull, however, and he wondered instead if he might become a test pilot and wrote to several firms with that end in view. But there were thousands of unsettled young men like himself who felt they had a future in aviation, and the ones who had not been involved in the war against the Bolsheviks had got in first.

The unrest he felt was an uneasiness of spirit that many men were feeling. It defied analysis and he even felt he was run down to a state when he was approaching a standstill. Like many others, he was unnerved and humiliated by his lack of success and for a time even thought of emigrating to the United States. Foote, who had flown with him in Italy, had offered him a job until he could fix himself up with what he really wanted to do, but he wasn't sure that he wanted to emigrate and Foote's letter contained a warning that even in the United States the economic world was unstable and could collapse at any time.

'Things'll change,' Hatto advised. 'And you're far too good to disappear from the RAF.'

'It's different for you, Willie,' Dicken protested. 'You're a regular officer. You can wait with patience for confirmation of your appointment.'

Hatto let his monocle fall from his eye. 'Let it be recorded,' he said slowly, 'that, even so, that patience is wearing very thin. All the same, I've heard that Trenchard's to be appointed Chief of Air Staff and he's got Churchill behind him. They really are going to organise a permanent Royal Air Force.'

Dicken shrugged. 'I'm not sure I can wait. I read the report of the House of Commons. It's enough to make you go out and cut your throat. They've savaged us from 30,000 officers and 300,000 other ranks to 5,300 officers and 54,000 men. Surgery like that makes a man prefer to take a chance in Civvie Street. I'm getting out, Willie. I can't afford not to.'

'In that case,' Hatto said. 'Perhaps I can help. Ever heard of Lord Ruffsedge?'

'The newspaper proprietor?'

'The very same. A friend of my Old Man's. Hamer Quinton before he got his title. His son did a bit of flying during the war and since then the whole family's become dedicated birdmen. He travels a lot about Europe and he wants a pilot to run his plane.'

*

And that was how Dicken came to be in Berlin in October, 1920, contemplating the wickedness of the German capital but not entirely without a degree of pleasure.

Despite the excellent pay, the job had turned out to be far more dull than he had anticipated. Ruffsedge wasn't a difficult man to work for, but he was pompous and it involved a great deal of listening to his outpourings on his finances, his politics and himself.

Within a fortnight of the offer, Dicken had obtained his licence as a commercial pilot and two days later was flying Ruffsedge and a friend to Manchester in a converted DH9a on to which had been built a tiny cabin. But then Ruffsedge had a new idea of flying copies of his newspapers to European capitals for British readers there and within four months, instead of passengers, Dicken was flying London-printed *Daily Globes* to Paris where he refuelled before continuing, with another refuelling stop near the border, to Berlin. Lord Ruffsedge seemed to have come to the conclusion that air travel was not as comfortable as train travel and Dicken found he had become nothing more than an aerial transport driver.

There was still a certain lack of respectability about private flying, however, because of the dozens of restless young men who had bought up the old Avro trainers after the war and were putting on shows about the country, risking their necks because they'd been doing it for so long they had no qualms about continuing to do so and could see it only as a means of earning a living with the skills they'd acquired. As the fun went out of Ruffsedge's job, it grew monotonous, and Dicken began again to feel that restlessness which had driven him out of the RAF. He wasn't depressed, but he was perplexed and seemed to be suffering from a hangover from the fighting. The war had been a new kind of war with new methods of waging it and there had been an astonishing distrust between the military and political minds and an astonishing state of muddle and confusion. But more importantly, as Hatto had warned, the way in which life as they had known it before the war had disintegrated left him in a void of bewilderment.

He was in a state of mind he couldn't fully understand. Conditions were different from what he'd expected them to be and it was hard to adjust. Some men clearly hadn't. Griffiths had also left the RAF but Archard and Almonde and Tom Howarth had decided to stay in, and of the four who'd debated the subject in hospital on Armistice Night, Coetzee had gone back to South Africa all right but he'd been unable to put flying behind him after all and had killed himself flying into Table Mountain; Noble's civil flying job had not materialised because he hadn't had enough experience to command one and he had gone back to his old job and was now already beginning to climb the ladder in a finance house in the City of London; while Charley Wright had bought two old Avros from surplus wartime stock and was among those touring the country putting on displays. Williams had done nothing. On his first venture from hospital he had been attacked by the Spanish flu which had been raging throughout Europe and had returned to die with all his hopes unfulfilled.

For so many men things hadn't turned out as they'd expected and when the long-awaited list of RAF officers to whom permanent commissions were to be granted finally appeared it was baffling. First class men with distinguished fighting careers had been left out while men with little or no active service had been included. Men who had been captains during the war were senior to men who'd been majors, while lieutenants were senior to captains. Diplock's name on the list made Dicken shudder.

*

The Berlin hotel where he was staying provided plenty of comfort but he was bored with it and, feeling the need to take his mind off his problems, he telephoned a girl he'd got to know by the name of Janzi Lechner, who lived at Spandau and worked at the American Embassy. She was petite, dark-haired and spoke excellent English and they decided they'd try The Pinguin, a night club she knew. But as they pushed into the smoky atmosphere they found the place in an uproar. A man wearing a flying helmet and leather jacket was riding a motor cycle round the tables and women were standing on their chairs, screaming, while the men were shouting with laughter.

'Oh, Gott,' Janzi said. 'That Erni!'

'Who's Erni?'

'He's a flier. He calls it dogfighting on the ground.'

The manager, his assistant and the waiters finally cornered the motor cyclist and persuaded him to let them have the machine, but, far from subdued, he picked up a pile of plates from the nearest table and began to juggle with them.

Janzi began to laugh again. 'They say that during the war he once sprayed petrol under the tail of the dog of a general who was inspecting them. He caused as much uproar at the inspection as he does nowadays in nightclubs and at airfields. The girl with him's Lo Zink, his wife. During the war he used to have her name painted on the side of his machine.'

Dicken's ears pricked at an old memory. 'What's his name?'

'Udet. Erni Udet. He was second only to Richthofen at shooting down planes. But he hates the kudos it gives him. He pretends he's forgotten all about it and says his reputation will rattle after him for ever like a chain.'

Suddenly, beyond the smoky atmosphere of the nightclub, Dicken saw heavens reddened by the evening sun and a whole sky full of Fokkers, Albatroses, Triplanes, Pfalzes, everything, it seemed, that the German Air Force had possessed, with one Fokker DVII – outstanding among them for the skill of its pilot – with red and white stripes painted like a sunburst on the top wing, the words 'Du doch nicht!' – Certainly not you – on the tail surfaces, and letters, LO, on the fuselage.

'I'd like to meet him,' he said.

'He's too busy by the look of him.'

'He'll meet me,' Dicken said.

'Why?'

'Because he once damn near killed me. That's why.'

Udet was a small man with a broad grin and he shook Dicken's hand warmly. He spoke good English but with a marked accent.

'Quinney! I hear of you. How are you? I thought ve had killed you in the var. And I was damned sorry too. You frightened us to death – all forty-two of us – before we downed you. You got two of my boys. Only liddle kids. They were so young they cried for their mother in their first fights. You forced another to land mit his engine stopped and another had to take to his parachute. He kill himself two months after the Armistice, flying into an electric cable, so it doesn't do him much good. They said that evening that you also knock down a Rumpler. How about you? I was sure we hit you.'

'You did,' Dicken said. 'Four times.'

Udet grasped his arm. 'Und now?'

'Recovered.'

'Wunderbar! Wunderbar! Killing's no pastime for a decent man even if flying is.' Udet seemed to have forgotten his companions, his motor cycle and his juggling, and took over a table in a corner. 'Here we can talk,' he said. Janzi Lechner joined them with Udet's wife and one or two other men and girls but Udet seemed not to notice them.

'Dicken – I call you Dicken, hein?' Udet smiled. 'Call me Knägges. Everybody calls me Knägges. It means Titch. I'm not exactly a giant, you see. Come to that, neither are you.

39

What are you doing now? Still flying?'

'Private pilot to a newspaper proprietor.' It sounded better than aerial transport driver. 'Are *you* still flying?'

'Displays at Oberwiesenfeld in Munich. Sometimes mit Robi von Greim. He also flies in the war. How did you come out of the fighting?'

'Alive!'

'I mean medals. They make it worthwhile?'

'I got a few. So did you, I heard.'

Udet grinned and patted his wife's arm. 'When they give me the Pour le Mérite, Lo here make me walk her past the home of the King of Bavaria because the guard there always has to turn out for any man mit the Blue Max. She make me do it again und again.' Udet's face grew sombre. 'But there are a lot whose crosses are only made of wood. Broken propellers in a grafeyard mit their names on them. Richthofen – the Rittmeister himself. Wolff. Löwenhardt. Voss. Boelcke. Immelmann. Many of your friends, too.'

Dicken's mind flew back. Finding the carpenter in the hangar working on such a headpiece on his return from leave, he had asked 'Who's it for?' and got the laconic answer, 'The next one.' It had seemed to sum up the inevitability of the whole tragedy of war. If it wasn't today it would be tomorrow.

'These people –' Udet's hand gestured at the other people in the night club '– they haf not seen the same things. Once when I am flying I see a man fall out of the clouds above my head, legs and arms going. Yet there is no sign of a falling aeroplane, or a fight, or any wreckage. He must haf been thinking of what it was going to be like when he hits the ground every bit of the way down.' He frowned. 'Once I shoot down a Bristol und the observer's map wraps itself round one of my struts and stays mit me all the vay home. Often an aeroplane goes over my head so close I feel the draught and smell the engine fumes.' The hand gestured again. 'These people don't understand.'

There was a lot of movement round the table as the band started. Udet shrugged and began to scribble on the menu. 'Is different now,' he went on. 'Nowadays we only get killed doing stupid things. Robi von Greim and I do dogfights at exhibitions. He has an old DVII, I haf a Fokker Parasol. Because we haf both the Blue Max we get the crowds, of course. But it makes me feel ashame, doing something to entertain that we once did in earnest. Besides, the crowds only really look for excitement. Vhen Robi hits a high-tension wire und falls into a lake, they think it is part of the act. I decide to give it up. I'm building aircraft now. Mit an American called Pohl. We call it the *Volksflugzeug* – the people's aircraft. Cheap. Easy to fly.'

'I thought under the Armistice terms Germany was forbidden to build aircraft.'

Udet grinned. 'You going to tell on us?'

'Good God, no! But how do you get away with it?'

'They think we are building locks. The aeroplane looks like a goose mit epileptic cramps, but it flies. I hear Tony Fokker vent to America. He manage to get all his half-built machines out of Germany before the end came so they are not destroyed like the rest and he has enough to start again. When it finish, they saw up and burn every German aircraft they can find. Only a few vhich are hidden are saved. The hangar at Schleissheim vas filled mit destroyed machines. They make a bonfire of superb aeroplanes.'

'It wasn't very different in England.'

Udet shrugged. 'They call these days the Golden Age of Flying.' He sounded bitter. 'The only thing golden about them iss the spirit of the pilots. We fly because ve love flying. I once meet Guynemer, the Frenchman. You know of him? Und when my gun jams he just salutes me and lets me go. Now it's all politics. The whole of Germany iss politics. They jaw so much a flier can get toothache.'

He tossed across the menu he'd been scribbling on. On the back was an expert caricature of Dicken sitting in a miniature aeroplane wearing RAF rondels facing a caricature of Udet himself in another miniature plane wearing the German cross.

'You could earn a living at this,' Dicken said.

Udet grinned. 'I prefer flying. Und shooting. Not at men. At targets. You fancy a flip? We haf an old Rumpler. Dual controls. I could fly one half. You could fly the other.'

What time they left the night club Dicken had no idea. Udet's wife and Janzi Lechner had both disappeared with most of the other customers, and the waiters were standing in the doorway yawning and waiting to close the place. They had drunk a lot of what Udet called 'sekt' – sparkling Rhine wine – and Dicken woke up on a settee to see the numbers of aeroplanes decorating the walls with British and French cockades.

Udet appeared soon afterwards. 'Some grossstadtbummel,' he grinned. 'Some pub crawl! Lo goes to stay mit a friend. She often does when I am out on the tiles. Let's get out to the airfield. We'll pick up coffee there.'

The German pilots made Dicken welcome, then they went outside to watch Udet perform stunts in an old Fokker DVII marked D-UDET, trailing his wing tip inches above the ground as he howled across the field.

He seemed to have sobered up when he reappeared – even become sombre. 'One of these days,' he said, 'Lo will leave me. She says she cannot stand my bad habits.' He stared round. 'You're unlucky today. Lothar von Richthofen – the Rittmeister's brother – comes in occasionally. Also Bruno Loerzer. He's around a lot mit Goering, who takes over the Richthofen Circus when the Rittmeister iss killed. The Iron Man, he called himself. All discipline. But he vasn't a Richthofen, you know, despite what he think. He has gone into politics. Fancies himself as Reichschancellor or something. Let's haf a drink.'

Like so many flying men who had survived the war, Udet was restless, edgy, itching for excitement in a world that had suddenly become dull. 'Born in the war; died in the war,' he said. 'That's us flying men.'

That night he took Dicken on another round of the night clubs, this time without his wife or Janzi Lechner. At one point, Dicken remembered him shooting a cigarette out of the mouth of one of his friends, who seemed quite confident that he wouldn't get the bullet through his head. Whatever else could be said of him, he wasn't dull and, as he landed back in England, aware that the two nights spent in Berlin with him had been the most interesting he'd passed in almost a year, Dicken realised he was hankering after the lost community feeling of being in the RAF. Disillusioned with the whole commercial scene, he needed to leave Lord Ruffsedge, yet he knew if he did he was probably cutting himself off from aviation altogether. Then, as he was walking down the Mall, he realised he was approaching a tall moustached figure he recognized. It was Sir Hugh Trenchard, by this time firmly in his seat as Chief of Air Staff. To Dicken's surprise, he stopped in front of him.

'Quinney, isn't it?' he said.

'Yes, sir, it is.' It surprised Dicken that the great man even knew of him.

'What are you doing now?'

'Flying for Lord Ruffsedge, sir.'

Trenchard peered at him searchingly. 'Bit dull, isn't it? Chauffeur to a millionaire.'

Dicken smiled. 'Yes, sir, it is.'

Trenchard eyed him from his tremendous height, shaggy somehow despite his immaculate civilian clothes and bowler hat. He looked Dicken up and down.

'I was sorry to lose you,' he said slowly. 'The RAF could do with men like you. Why not come back?'

5

'You must be mad!'

Clad in surprisingly short shirts and a smart hat, her dark hair done in kiss curls, Zoë Toshack looked more beautiful than Dicken had ever seen her.

'Fancy wanting to go back to that stuffy lot,' she said, her contempt enormous. 'All they're good for is saluting on parade.'

'They do a lot of flying,' Dicken pointed out gently. 'Good flying. Better than some of these people who're getting flying a bad name going round the country giving exhibitions to make money.'

She stared at him angrily. She had returned from Canada full of excitement. She had found Casey Harmer, who noticeably had not given her the job she'd hoped for, and for a time she'd belonged to a group of wildcat young men who had flown round the country barnstorming in the ballyhoo atmosphere of a circus. Since returning, footloose and eager for a challenge, she had drifted into the same background in England and, equally inevitably, since she lived in Sussex and Charley Wright operated along the south coast, had thrown in her lot with him. On the table, for Dicken's perusal, were Canadian posters she'd brought back, billing her as Zoë Toshack, the Zip Girl of the Sky. The praise she had expected from Dicken had not been forthcoming, however, and she was argumentative and defensive.

'There's nothing wrong with making money out of flying,' she said.

'There is if it's dangerous.'

'I'm not afraid.'

'*I* am,' Dicken said quietly. 'You forget I know Charley

Wright and I've seen some of his machines. They're badly serviced and badly maintained because he's neither the money nor the time for anything else.'

She didn't answer and he looked at her under his eyebrows. She had grown more attractive as age had fined off the roundness of her features and he suspected now that, instead of her envying her older sister, Annys, she might well be envied herself.

'How's Annys?' he asked, trying to change the subject.

'Finding Arthur Diplock a bit of a bore, I suspect,' Zoë said shortly. '*I* would.'

'Annys is different from you. She goes with Parasol Percy.'

She grinned at the name they'd given her brother-in-law. 'I think he feels uniform and what goes with it suits him,' she said. 'He's a squadron leader now and a bit peeved because he feels he ought to have been a wing commander.'

'He should grumble,' Dicken said. 'I'm only a flight lieutenant and the amount of war flying *he* did was virtually nil.'

'He has several languages,' she pointed out. 'And he had the Wing Colonel for his best man and as godfather to his son.' She smiled, her manner suddenly different, and crossed to Dicken to kiss him. 'I'm sorry I was sarcastic with you, Dicky Boy,' she said. 'I didn't mean to be. You bring out everything that's bad in me. And knowing you were back where there are aeroplanes – *real* aeroplanes – makes me mad, because that's where I want to be. That's the only thing I want to do. And the only way I can do it is flying with Charley Wright. It fetches the crowds when they learn a woman's flying. They still don't believe it possible. Male pilots are rare enough to be a curiosity; when a woman flies it makes news.'

'And when she crashes and kills herself,' Dicken said dryly, 'it's naturally more regrettable and better news than if she were a man.'

She made a gesture of dismissal. 'In the States there are plenty nowadays. Laura Bromwell was one.'

'And she's dead,' Dicken pointed out quietly.

'There are plenty more. They're flying all the time over there. They're famous. I want to be famous, too. Not just somebody's wife.'

Dicken didn't try to argue her out of her ambition. He knew it was impossible. Instead he tried to change her course because he knew that if she stayed too long with Charley Wright and his air circus she'd kill herself. Charley Wright, careless, noisy, hard-drinking, resentful of authority yet curiously attractive to women with his lunatic humour and a flowery manner that could charm the ducks off the water, obviously appealed to her but she was wrong about his skill. She wasn't even right about Dicken's proximity to aeroplanes because so far he'd done little since his return to uniform except act as adjutant at No.2 Flying Training School at Duxford. It had come as a shock that the RAF didn't want him even to demonstrate his skills to newcomers as an instructor.

'You have to be good to become famous,' he said gently. 'Are you good?'

'Yes, I am. I'll show you.'

From the field where Charley Wright was operating, she took him up in one of the old dual-control Avros, performing tight turns, loops, spins and stalls for him. Though there were parts of her performance – an apparent inability to hold her height in a tight turn and loops that were sloppy at the top – which were lacking in precision, he found he never had to consider grasping the dual controls to help.

'Any good at navigation?' he asked as they clambered from the cockpit.

'Who's worried about navigation?' she demanded.

'Flying's more than just doing stunts. Suppose you want to get from one place to another?'

'Follow the railway line,' she said. 'You can come down at every station to read the sign and check your position.'

This kind of flying – what was known as flying by Bradshaw, after the name of the railway guide – was looked on with contempt by skilled navigators. He tried to interest her in the subject, even contrived to teach her some of it, but she either didn't grasp it or was uninterested, though she was willing enough to fly him about the countryside.

'Know where you are?' he asked her through the speaking tube as they came to the coast.

'Hastings just coming up,' she said.

'If you take the trouble to look down there', he replied, 'even you ought to recognise Brighton.'

She was sulky as they landed, and he tried again. 'If you want to become this famous flier you're aiming at,' he said, 'then learn navigation. The future of aviation's in long-distance flying. Now they've crossed the Atlantic, people are going to find ways of flying to Africa and India. They'll want to open up the Empire and the people who do it will be those who can get from one place to another without making a mistake. There aren't any railway stations in the middle of the ocean.'

She gave him a sideways look that was full of reproach and affection at the same time. It jerked at his heart and left him full of guilt that he had not pursued her as ardently as he felt he should; remorse that, because of it, she had drifted into the wrong company; and doubt – tucked away at the back of his mind – because she had never seemed over-eager to rationalise their relationship.

'Marry me, Zoë', he said abruptly.

Her head turned quickly. 'Why do you ask me that?'

'Why does any man ask any woman that? I've known you since 1914. We've been more than friends. You suggested it when I was in Italy in 1918. "Come home and make me an honest woman," you said. I love you.'

Even as he spoke, he wasn't sure he was telling the truth. While they'd still been in their teens they had clutched each other in the Toshacks' summer house on warm summer nights and had finally become lovers during one of his leaves during the war. But little had come of it because shortly afterwards he'd been sent to Italy and had barely seen her since until now.

'I didn't mean that,' she was saying slowly. 'And I think you're just asking me to get me away from Charley Wright.'

He realised she had hit the nail on the head. There had always been something between them but, though he had a feeling it had never been more than a deep friendship linked with a strong sexual attraction, he couldn't bring himself to admit it. Not now.

'No.' He shook his head. 'I expect eventually I shall get posted abroad. They say in Egypt or India you can live like a lord with hordes of servants, so that wives have a wonderful time. You'd get a chance to fly, too, because quite a few people have private aeroplanes and you can pick up war surplus Avros for a song.'

47

'What about until you get your posting to India? Would you let me fly with Charley Wright?'

'If you could manage to give his aeroplanes a pre-flight check that's more than just a kick at the tyres, a slap at the fuselage and a twang on a bracing wire.'

She laughed and put her arms round him. 'All right, Dicky Boy,' she said. 'If that's what you want.' She paused then gave a little laugh. 'You realise, of course, that we shall have to ask Annys to the wedding, and if we ask Annys, we'll also have to ask her husband, Poisonous Percy.'

'We'll balance that out,' Dicken said, 'by asking Willie Hatto. His wife, the Hon Caroline, comes from one of the best families in the country so she ought to more than balance out Percy.'

*

The wedding was held in Zoë's home village, Deane. Diplock arrived at the last minute, looking faintly embarrassed and trying to pretend he'd been held back by an unexpected appointment. Dicken wasn't deluded. Diplock was wary of him and Hatto, because he knew they were well aware of his cowardice and trickery during the late Great War, and he even seemed to be looking round him for Foote, the American, the third member of the triangle of anarchy that had plagued him during that period. Annys, looking beautiful and self-satisfied, almost as if she wore the rank as well as Diplock and was aware that it was higher than that of the man her sister was marrying, was inclined to be condescending to everybody but the Hon Caroline, to whom she tended almost to touch her forelock.

There was a vague feeling throughout the reception that Diplock might try to introduce some alien and uncomfortable note as Hatto, quite unnoticed by Annys, had at Diplock's wedding, but he seemed to prefer to stay well in the background.

'After all,' Hatto murmured between the congratulatory telegrams, 'Parasol Percy hasn't changed. He was never the type to face up fair and square to anything that might be difficult.'

Nevertheless, it probably seemed odd to the other guests that two of the three RAF officers present – all in dress uniform and wearing their medals – should totally ignore the third.

48

Charley Wright, his red face matching the red carnation in his buttonhole and the red of his eyeballs, insisted on kissing the bride. 'You haven't got away with her completely, my old friend and comrade of the desperate years,' he told Dicken. 'She's promised she'll still fly for me on the days when I'm handy. In fact,' he added, 'I rather hoped she'd marry me. But then, what has William Albert Charles Wright got to compare with Dick Quinney, who holds every gong in the book except the ultimate, to get which you have to be dead.'

*

'I meant it, you know,' Zoë said as they lay in the dark in the hotel in Cornwall where they'd gone for their honeymoon. 'Love, honour and obey. All that rot.'

'I always thought you wanted to be a liberated woman. I thought you'd insist on leaving that out.'

'I lost my nerve at the last moment. I do want to love, honour and obey. If I don't always manage it, you'll try to forgive me, won't you?'

'It shouldn't be difficult.'

'I'm looking forward to Egypt and India. It should be fun. Charley Wright's got nothing to offer like that.' Zoë paused. 'There's just one thing, though.'

'What's that?'

'No children.'

'Never?'

'For a while. I haven't done anything yet, except run Pa's garage while he was away during the war.'

'You've learned to fly. Not many women have done that. You've been to Canada and the States.'

'That was a disaster, Dicky Boy. I went to find Casey Harmer, you know. I thought I was in love with him but when I got there I found he was married.'

'So you married me on the rebound?'

She slipped warm soft arms round him. 'I just realised that there was something about you that Casey couldn't claim.'

'What's that?'

'Honesty. I don't think you'd ever lie to me.'

Dicken wasn't so sure. He still hadn't plucked up courage to tell her that he'd once discarded her for Nicola Aubrey, whom

49

he'd felt was everything a man could wish – shy, gentle, kind, well-brought up, all the things his mother insisted a man needed in a wife. Yet his own mother had been like that, and his father had run off with one of his typists. Perhaps men wanted more than just shyness, gentleness and kindness. Perhaps they wanted what Zoë had in abundance – vitality, vibrant enjoyment of living, laughter, strength and reality.

'What are you thinking?' she asked suddenly, her face in the angle of his neck. 'You've gone quiet.'

'Oh, things,' he said. 'Things that happened in the war and can't happen again because, after that one, there can't be any more wars.'

'What was it really like, Dicken? You never talked much about it.'

He thought for a moment. 'A perpetual state of wind-up for most of us,' he admitted. 'Cold. Cracked lips. Better than the infantry, though. All that man-to-man stuff with bayonets. Sometimes it came as a surprise to find there was a man in the plane you were shooting at.'

'What about Arthur Diplock? What was he like?'

'Very warlike until he crossed the lines.' Dicken pulled her closer. 'But, good God, we didn't get married to spend our first night talking about what it was like fighting the Germans.'

'Trust a man to ask for seconds.'

'It seems like a good idea to me.'

'All right. Provided you take me to India and Egypt.'

'Done. They can't keep me in that stupid job I've got now after all the flying and experience I have.'

*

They were both wrong.

With Lloyd George so immersed in the details of peace he had no time for anything else, the dissolution of the RAF suddenly appeared inevitable. German air power seemed to be dead and only called for burial, and the peace treaty to be covering that very efficiently by prohibiting military aviation in Germany. Clemenceau, the French leader, was taking no chances and had demanded that the Germans accept the terms without argument.

Despite Lloyd George's sentence of death on the RAF, however, Winston Churchill had managed to grant a stay of execution and Trenchard was working day and night to make sure the condemned service had a future. But every man who wore the light blue knew the implacable hostility of the navy and the army, even the contempt with which Wilson, the head of the army, held Trenchard's suggested new ranks.

'Marshal of the Air?' he had said. 'Do you want to bring disrepute to the rank of field marshal?'

Trenchard was a jump ahead. 'The word "marshal" exists in a number of contexts,' he boomed. 'Provost marshal, court martial, Marshall and Snelgrove, the London store.' No one had laughed louder than Churchill.

'Even so,' Hatto observed dryly. 'Marshal of the Air's poaching on the preserves of the Almighty a bit, isn't it?'

In the end, the rank chosen was Marshal of the Royal Air Force but, as the story went round the RAF messes, the dislike of the army and the navy increased. Trenchard went doggedly ahead, however, building up his staff courses, training colleges and ancillary services, though his belief that in any future war bombing could force the government into the bowels of the earth caused him to be regarded as a crank. And when he claimed that the RAF should take over the navy's role as the country's main defence because battleships were out of date, he called down the wrath of the indignant admirals on his head. It was only when *The Times* revealed that, while France still retained 126 of its wartime squadrons, the 185 squadrons that the RAF had possessed in 1918 had been whittled down to twenty-eight, of which only seven were in England and only three were allotted for home defence, that the pillorying of the RAF subsided.

Meanwhile, however, the RAF seemed to have forgotten all about Dicken's war record and while he was soon removed from being adjutant at No 2 Flying School, he was given a second administrative job at the School of Technical Training at Manston in Kent. Willie Hatto was flying Bristols nearby.

'Why are they doing this to me, Willie?' Dicken demanded. 'Surely I deserve better than this.'

'Old lad,' Hatto smiled, 'when you join the regular forces you've got to show you can stand every boring job there is before they start giving you the interesting ones. I did my stint before the war.'

'Diplock's at the Air Ministry.'

'Toadying round his old friend, the Wing Colonel, now known as Group Captain George Macclesfield St. Aubyn. Hold your water. Your time will come.'

'Can you guarantee that?'

'I know how regular brains tick. You'll get the hang of it before long. Just enjoy yourself and keep your thumb in your bum. It's considered good for the soul. The idea is that ambitious chaps like you should be able to count beds and knives, forks and mugs, blankets and sheets, without turning a hair while still swotting for the Staff College exams. Are you swotting for the Staff College exam? Because if you're not you ought to be. New as it is, even the RAF will need staff officers. We might even do it together because the Hattos were never known for their brains.'

Accepting that Hatto knew what he was talking about and even had inside knowledge that came from a father in the House of Lords and a brother in the Foreign Office, Dicken got down to work. But, even as he did so and just when it finally seemed to have been established that an air force was needed, an election removed Lloyd George from power and the new Prime Minister made no bones about his wish to divide the RAF between the army and the navy. Only the fact that the toughest old sea-dog of them all, Jacky Fisher, the very man who had built the battleships, had argued that the development of aircraft could render the fleet useless, saved it. He had long since thrown his weight solidly behind Trenchard, and the fact that aeroplanes were cheaper to build than battleships clinched it. True to time-honoured British methods, committees were formed to look into the question but the outcome was inevitable. The RAF had been saved.

*

By this time the war was long past but the haunted-eyed veterans of the fighting were still struggling to find a place in the scheme of things. Survival, which had been the only thought in their minds in the trenches and had given away to the hysteria of realising they were not only alive but likely to go on being alive, was now back in their thoughts as they struggled to find work in a world that was increasingly lacking in it.

Once again Dicken began to have doubts. He had a wife to

support now and the RAF seemed totally unaware of him. He had entered the war ignorant of life and was almost as ignorant of it when the war had ended. He couldn't imagine himself doing anything else but fly and, since his experience seemed to count for nothing in peacetime, he started once more to consider what use he might be in business or industry. The answer was not encouraging, yet the dreams of unlimited flying which had drawn him back to the RAF were finally dispersed by a series of unimportant ground jobs which culminated – due to the fact that he had once trained as a wireless operator – as head of a signals and communications department at Northolt. Since he had sergeants and junior officers beneath him, he didn't even have to use his fading skills.

Although training had ceased with the end of the war, some of the more senior non-flying officers of the new post-war RAF were feeling naked without wings above the decorations they had received during the fighting for working at a desk, and as they set about acquiring them, by a special dispensation they were allowed to qualify on the Avro, the absolute perfection as a non-combat aeroplane. After flying round Northolt for thirty hours they were allowed to put up their wings, and most of them went back to their desks determined never to fly again.

The one advantage his job brought Dicken was that he was able occasionally to fly an Avro from the training and communications flight when one of the mighty didn't need it to put in his required number of flying hours. There followed a period of ferrying Snipes from Rochford, near Southend, to Hawkinge in Kent where Keith Park, who had run up a score during the war flying Bristols, was commanding a dump of surplus aircraft.

The months passed with only the occasional flight but, because nobody properly understood the RAF's function in peacetime, nobody had any work to do and the boredom began to affect everybody. A few old faces appeared occasionally – Hatto, Park, Sholto Douglas, Taffy Jones, Hill, Vincent, all of them men who'd done well in the war but were now as bored with peacetime duties as Dicken himself. Seeing little prospect of promotion, several had gone like Dicken into commercial flying only to find the experience enough to make them change their minds so that, again like Dicken, they had been forced to return with a loss of seniority.

Once Diplock appeared with Group Captain St Aubyn, plumper than when Dicken had last seen him, paler from long hours in his office, his ears, it seemed, more prominent than they had ever been. He was now at the Directorate of Training at the Air Ministry, still working with his benefactor, and so Hatto said, hourly expecting his step up in rank.

Even Zoë seemed to be doing more flying than Dicken, and it was galling to see her building up the flying hours while his own stood virtually still. Charley Wright was operating along the south coast, giving flights at five shillings a time for a single circuit and a pound for a little extra. His pilots seemed to come and go with alarming regularity and he was constantly calling on Zoë to help him out.

It didn't help their marriage. On several occasions, when Dicken had hoped she'd be with him at some mess function she disappeared to help out and he had to go alone, aware of the eyes on him of the other officers, all dogged up in bum-freezer jackets and cavalry type overalls. Occasionally, it even led to high words between them and once she threw the coffee pot at him at breakfast.

She was contrite immediately – 'After all,' she said, 'breakfast isn't meant to be a social meal' – but it happened again and the occasions when they were at loggerheads seemed to come with greater regularity, so that Dicken found he was learning to live without her. While he was at Northolt she was flying at Brighton or Winchester or Exeter, and he even began to wonder if there were anything between her and Charley Wright. He couldn't imagine it somehow, because Zoë, brisk, forthright, modern as the aeroplane itself, somehow didn't go with Charley Wright, with his red face and booze and dirty stories. Nevertheless, it left him uneasy and uncertain, wishing to God the RAF would post him to Egypt or India so they could disappear from Charley Wright's reach and start living with all the happy informality of a foreign station that was so distinct from the rigidity of dress and behaviour which was being stamped on the RAF by people like Diplock and Group Captain St. Aubyn.

His duties didn't vary much but, while he was bored and restless, Zoë was thoroughly enjoying herself. Her father had

54

died and, true to the promise he had made during the war, had left Annys his house and Zoë the garage he owned. It was clear Annys thought she'd got the best of the bargain because the garage consisted of little more than a few wooden sheds and a certain amount of goodwill, but, skilled at business, loving engines and a competent mechanic herself, Zoë had already started to develop it and had even opened a second garage in Brighton.

'It won't be long,' she said cheerfully, 'before I'll be able to buy the house back from Annys at whatever she chooses to ask for it, and never miss the money. Even if I don't manage to be famous, Dicky Boy, I'm certainly going to be rich. Why not come into the business and keep an eye on things for me?'

'I'm not the type to keep an eye on things.'

'Oh, stuff! You men are always so manly and tough. Anyway –' she put her arms round him, wheedling – 'you *will* keep an eye on things for me, won't you, if I happen to be away somewhere.'

'Where might you happen to be?'

She shrugged and planted a kiss on his cheek, leaving a lipstick imprint on his skin. 'You never know. I'm thinking of opening a third garage. It might be anywhere.'

She had her own car now but occasionally Dicken went along to drive her home from wherever Charley Wright was operating. He was always made welcome but there was a vague suggestion of contempt in the friendliness of the civilian pilots.

'The experts welcoming the amateur,' Wright said with a grin. 'After all, we fly all day and every day. You fly when the powers that be let you.'

They had roped off an area round the aeroplanes – 'To stop the spectators walking into a propeller,' Zoë said – and flagpoles had been erected with bunting strung between them. There were a few cars but most of the spectators had arrived on foot and, with the last performance of the day about to start, were beginning to trail homewards.

As one of the Avros started up with a crackling roar the woman who had climbed aboard as a passenger got into an argument with the pilot and whacked him over the head with an umbrella. As he staggered away, the aeroplane began to move and there was a yell of alarm from the crowd as the woman clutched her hat and began to scream blue murder. The pilot turned and started to run after the aeroplane but tripped and fell and, with the crowd watching aghast, the machine took off in a wobbly lift-off and staggered into the air. As it climbed higher and higher, the spectators yelled with fright, then it plunged downwards with a great gasp of horror from the ground. When it appeared on the point of smashing into the earth it pulled up into a perfect loop, then climbed again and began a series of stunts that took the breath away, and the crowd's terror gave way to delight.

'It's Charley dressed up,' Zoë said.

The performance ended with a display of wing-walking, a parachute descent and a Gretna Green elopement with Zoë and one of the mechanics dressed as the bride and groom in an old Model T Ford and Charley Wright, as an irate father, chasing them all round the field in an Avro and bombarding them with bags of flour and rolls of toilet paper.

'It always gets a laugh,' he said as the crowd finally streamed away. Extracting a hip flask, he took a long swig before offering it to Dicken.

'Booze doesn't go with flying,' Dicken said as they drove away. 'Does he put much of it away?'

'Charley's safe as houses.'

'Until the day he puts too much away. Do you go up with him?'

'I've done my share of wing walking.'

'You've what?'

'I have a harness on that you can't see from the ground. I can't fall off. Don't be stuffy. You sound like an RAF wife.'

He knew she disliked the other RAF wives she met and was unpopular with them because she made no secret of the flying she did with Charley Wright, so that they considered she was letting the side down. One CO had even quietly mentioned it to Dicken.

'They're so boring,' she complained. 'They expect me to go along and drink tea and talk about babies. I prefer coffee and I don't know anything about babies.'

'You could soon learn.'

'Babies would stop me flying.'

'You'll have to stop some time.'

'Why will I?'

'Well, eventually you'll want a family.'

'I'm not so damn' sure I will, Dicky Boy. Women in America are beginning to make a business of flying. Ruth Law. The Stinsons. Phoebe Fairgrave. If *they* can make a career in aviation, so can I.'

The disagreement came to an abrupt end two months later. In an attempt to pin her down, Dicken rented a furnished house near the airfield but within two days of signing the contract he received orders for a posting to Iraq.

'Iraq!' Zoë stared at him in horror. 'You said it would be India or Egypt. Good conditions. Lots of servants. Isn't Iraq what they used to call Mesopotamia? All flat and hot.'

'That's about it. The RAF are policing the place.'

She stared at him, pink-faced with anger. 'I'm not coming with you,' she snapped.

He shrugged. 'They wouldn't let you, anyway,' he said. 'Wives are forbidden.'

And rather to his surprise, he found he didn't feel angry about it.

6

The ranges to the north, snow-clad crests rising one behind the other, were serried white bastions of inscrutable majesty. As the Bristol Fighter flew at 8000 feet, on the same level stretched the high peaks of Kurdistan, Turkey and Persia, a breathtaking wall of mountain filling the whole horizon and dominated by the pinnacles of the Hakkari Range which soared up into the thin layer of cirrus that filled the sky.

It was largely thanks to Almonde that Dicken was enjoying the view. He was leading a detached flight of Bristols and his job was to patrol the Iraqi police posts strung along the borders of Turkey and Iran where sabre-rattling Kurdish tribesmen were in the habit of appearing from the hills to kill everyone in sight before bolting back to shelter with whatever loot they could grab.

As Almonde throttled the Rolls Falcon engine back and they dropped down to 1000 feet, they entered an area of disturbed air that came from the buffetings of strong winds swirling among the tumbling mountains. Turning in his seat, Almonde pointed downwards. 'Kash,' he shouted.

Kash was the most northerly of the police posts and, finding it under the lee of a mountain, Dicken spotted the straight red strips of American cloth laid out in the snow in the form of an E to let them know all was well. From Kash they flew on to Haibu and Harzan and other snow-bound outposts before returning to a splashy landing on a field sodden with water after the melting of the winter snows.

After three years on the ground, Dicken had confidently expected a flying job but, once again, had instead found himself riding in worn-out Rolls Royce armoured cars dating from Lawrence of Arabia's operations against the Turks in 1918.

When the League of Nations had handed to Britain the mandate for Iraq, to avoid stationing a large army there, which would always have been liable to ambush as it marched about the sandy wastes, the job of policing the country had been handed to the RAF, because Trenchard had claimed he could do it with a few squadrons of aircraft, a few companies of armoured cars and a few Assyrian and Arab levies.

'Out here,' Almonde had explained, 'Pax Britannica has become Pax Aeronautica.'

The journey from England had been made with 1500 other men on a troopship built to carry 800. Dicken had slept on a settee in a cabin he shared with two other officers who had had the good fortune to arrive first and claim the only bunks, and the conditions were appalling, with hammocks hung three and four deep above each other so that the duty officer making his round at night had to crawl on hands and knees. The smell was nauseating and the outside temperature as they moved down the Red Sea was over a hundred. Having to change into mess kit with stiff collars for dinner every night, Dicken made a habit of slipping out halfway through the evening to change into a fresh collar and place the limp worn one between the leaves of a book for use the next day. From Basra, the journey had been continued by slow train to Baghdad where the group had arrived itching agonisingly from sandfly bites.

The squadrons flew Snipes, Bristols, DH9as powered with the American Liberty engines, or Vickers Vernons, heavy snub-nosed aircraft with twin tails, four wheels, two Rolls-Royce Eagle engines and a forest of interplane struts. They looked vaguely like whales with wings, but in addition to the two pilots sitting in an outside cockpit they had a cabin which could hold ten soldiers complete with their kit. Though their cruising speed when fully loaded was little more than that of the armoured cars, they had an endurance of seven hours.

Everybody likely to come into contact with the natives of the country carried what was called a blood chit, a piece of paper printed in Arabic which offered a reward for the return unharmed of the bearer.

'Known to the coarse-minded as a gooly chit,' Almonde explained. 'Because if you have to come down in their territory and get captured, they hand you to the women who take a delight in making a few modifications on you with their knives – such as rearranging the position of those small spherical appendages which usually mean a great deal to a man. The chit promises that if you're handed over intact, the finder will be rewarded beyond all his dreams, and financial gain usually has the ascendancy over the simple pleasure of mutilation.'

'But not always,' he added. 'The Wahabi are inclined to be a bit fanatical and then the gooly chit doesn't carry a lot of weight.'

Mosul, from where they operated, was built of white houses rather than the mud brick of the rest of Iraq, because the area around abounded with a local soft marble. It was a maze of narrow streets except in the centre where during the war the Turks had cut a road through towards a bridge over the Tigris. Unfortunately, since the river had changed its course during the building of the bridge, it had never been finished and now terminated in mid stream, with a bridge of boats taking over its function instead. The population was largely Kurdish, straight-featured wiry people quick to use their knives, who wore striped baggy trousers, short jackets and brightly-hued turbans. The place was smelly and busy and in ancient days had been an international crossroads. Xenophon had passed by with his Ten Thousand, as had Alexander the Great on his way to meet Darius the Persian. Nearby was the birthplace of Saladin, the Sultan of Egypt and Syria who had defeated Richard Coeur de Lion and his Crusaders, and a group of mounds marked what was left of Nineveh where Sennacherib had ruled.

Among the work of the armoured cars was the guarding of the route across the desert from Cairo to Baghdad and the building of landing areas for aircraft carrying mail. Because the tracks of wheeled traffic could be seen from the air and were used as navigational aids, it had been decided to plough a double furrow the whole thousand miles of the route, with petrol stored at points along it for emergency landings. The country consisted of endless miles of nothing, though after heavy rain it could look green in places and its changing moods had a strange impelling beauty.

Apart from the terrain, the chief problems were raids by tribesmen led by Kerim Fatah Agha, known to the RAF as

KFA, a Wahabi outlaw who could raid a village and be thirty miles away over mountain tracks before word of his depredations could reach the authorities; and Sheikh Mahmoud, who was a Kurdish patriot who didn't care a fig for the League of Nations mandate and carried on a good-natured war with the British without any real signs of ill feeling. Because he gave the RAF so much experience in the planning and execution of air operations, he was known as 'the Director of RAF Training.'

For the most part the raiders were dealt with by aircraft dropping leaflets on to the villages of the chief troublemakers, warning them to disappear, and then bombing the villages to ruins so that the raiders would have no base. Since the villages were easily rebuilt there were no hard feelings, but the Bedouin, who lived in tents and couldn't be harmed by bombing had to be dealt with by the worn-out armoured cars.

Dicken had been in Iraq for six months when Hatto appeared to take Almonde's place running the detached Bristol flight.

'News for you, old son,' he said immediately. 'Diplock's on his way here, too.'

'I'd have thought someone as clever as Parasol Percy would have managed to dodge that.'

'Iraq's the RAF's sackcloth and ashes. Everybody has to do their whack out here to scourge themselves of all vanity. It shouldn't be too hard for him, though. He only leaves the ground these days to climb into a car. We brought mail, by the way. There's a letter for you.'

Zoë's letter had its usual dashed-off look. She was a poor correspondent and most of the time left Dicken only half-aware of what she was doing at home, merely dropping hints as if she preferred him not to know. They left him irritated and frustrated and longing for her to tell him she loved him, but he was beginning by this time to doubt even that and no longer really expected anything more than bare news.

Charley Wright was dead at last, having crashed while trying to fly after having one too many swigs from his flask. Zoë didn't seem too heartbroken, and the sting came in the last part of the letter. Casey Harmer had written offering her a job and she was wondering whether she ought to take it.

Suspecting Dicken's misery, Hatto immediately offered to let him get his hand in once more by placing an aeroplane at his disposal, and he was at last able to get into the air again in control of his own machine. The Bristol was a superb machine, the most agile two-seater in the Service, fast, strong, amenable to as many adaptations, alterations and refinements as the squadrons chose to add. In return, he worked with Hatto on his patrols and it was during one of them that they met Sheikh Tafas Hashim Fitna, a loyal chief whose Shammar tribesmen held the northern border for the British and reported the movements of the murderous northern tribes with messages brought into police posts by camel riders.

When a large force was reported approaching from the direction of the Turkish border. Hatto's airmen identified them as Ikhwani, merciless tribesmen who had thrown their lot in with Kerim Fatah Agha.

'They're not just camel rustlers,' Hatto reported. 'They've got no flocks and no pack camels for the women and children. And since the Shammar tribe's tents are in that area it could well be intended as a massacre.'

The cars sped north, the crews muffled to the eyes against the flying grit. Because the old-fashioned topee caught on doors and turrets and was difficult to keep on in the wind, they had adopted the Arab headgear of a kuffiyah and argal dyed khaki with coffee. It took up no room in an armoured car and didn't catch the wind outside, while it also had a good flap over the neck and back to protect against the sun and could be wound round the nose and mouth against the everlasting dust which was often as fine as flour.

Shammar herdsmen reported the Ikhwani just to the north and eventually they spotted a vast straggling line of trotting camels. Controlling the cars with flag signals, Dicken closed the group into a V-formation and led them at top speed over the hard ground.

'Give them a shot across their bows,' he ordered and the puffs of dust struck up from the ground by the bullets brought the mass of riders to a halt in a confused tangle of whirling camels.

Through the interpreter, Dicken shouted an order and, after a long impassioned argument, the camel riders sent three of their number forward.

'Tell your people to go home,' Dicken advised them. 'Or

we'll destroy them with the machine guns. Remind them that in Transjordan two years ago Transjordan cars killed six hundred out of a force of thousands who were coming from Nedj to destroy Amman.'

Listening sullenly, the three riders returned to the milling mass of men and, after another long argument, which could be heard in the armoured cars, the huge horde reluctantly swung away. As they set off on their 300-mile journey back to the border, the cars followed slowly until the radiators began to boil.

'Makes a change from shooting gazelle for the pot,' Dicken observed.

*

As they headed south again, they reached the Shammar village of Kerchian. It was surrounded by groups of black tents and near them a Bristol Fighter was standing. As the armoured cars drew up Hatto appeared.

'Well done, old son,' he said. 'Co-operation between the services. The old boy here's so pleased we've been invited to take coffee.'

Tafas Hashim Fitna was a large fat man with one eye, the other covered by a black patch. He wore a voluminous turban and the usual baggy Arab clothing with bandoliers of cartridges round his shoulder and waist, and bristled with guns and knives of all sorts. Everywhere he went he was accompanied by his youngest son, a small boy with eyes like raisins and a half-moon smile. His men escorted Dicken and Hatto to his tent where they sat cross-legged on carpets. Three long-spouted coffee pots steamed on the embers of a fire set in a hole in the ground, and the tent was full of the smell of cooking meat.

Despite his ugliness, the old man had enormous dignity. 'Window-in-Eye,' he said, indicating Hatto's monocle, 'says the raiders have gone. Allah's blessing on the heads of my friends. You will share our meal.'

A murmur of approval came from the hawk-nosed men behind him, every one of them armed to the teeth.

When the coffee was ready, Tafas poured it into a nest of tiny cups and handed them round. The ritual was to taste it, roll it round the mouth as if it were a liqueur and show every sign of appreciation. As they finished the traditional three cups, two

63

men appeared carrying an enormous copper tray piled high with steaming rice. On it was a sheep's head complete with teeth.

'The whole lot's in there, I'm told,' Hatto murmured. 'Intestines and all.'

As the tray was placed on the ground, the man motioned to them to draw closer and, at his signal, they plunged their right hands into the mound, searching for a piece of meat and hoping to God it wouldn't be one of the more unpleasant parts of the sheep's inside. The old man nodded approvingly and, fishing among the rice, produced an eyeball.

'For Window-in-Eye,' he said.

Hatto took it gravely and chewed it with every apparent sign of approval. Immediately, one of the other men found a second eyeball which he handed to Dicken. He managed to swallow it whole like an oyster. After the meal, there was a chorus of approving belches, then copper jugs appeared for the ceremonial hand-washing.

'We can stay the night if we want,' Dicken pointed out. 'He even provides you with a woman. You don't see her because she arrives after dark and disappears before dawn. I wouldn't recommend it, though, because, bless 'em, they weren't behind the door when lice and fleas were handed out. I think you'd better offer the old boy a flight and then we'll push off.'

They managed to persuade the old man to remove his turban and put on a helmet and goggles, then the Bristol took off to give him a bird's eye view of his village. On the ground, Dicken kicked at the embers of a fire so that the smoke would give Hatto the wind direction and the aeroplane buzzed low over the ground and swung round to make a perfect landing.

The old man was beaming his delight but when it came to getting out, his baggy trousers prevented him getting his leg over the side of the cockpit to the mounting slot in the fuselage. The problem was overcome by four of his men making a human stepladder, the first against the fuselage with his head down, the second crouched with his hands on his knees, the third on all fours, and the fourth flat on his face. The old man walked imperiously down the steps they formed, watched by the admiring population of the village.

*

With Hatto's help, Dicken found himself back on flying duties at last. With his flight taken from the border patrol and sent to Hinaidi, when one of his officers was found to be suffering from ear trouble through sitting too close to the muzzle of the Vickers guns on the range, Hatto hurriedly arranged a swop.

On the aerodrome were five squadrons and Hatto's detached flight, each in self-contained camps, the one next door, No 45, whose mess they shared, commanded by a ginger-haired aggressive martinet called Arthur Harris who had built himself a record during the recent war. Taking over a squadron of Vernons and objecting to flying aircraft not designed to carry bombs, he had managed to add racks and a bomb sight and transformed a transport squadron into a highly efficient unit with an excellent record of bomb aiming.

Baghdad was smelly, sordid, and very hot. The city of the Arabian Nights sounded romantic but in reality it consisted of dirty mud-brick houses with scarcely a single imposing building and no streets worthy of the name save a single one cut ruthlessly across it by the Turks during the war. Lined with uninviting little shops, the only place of interest was the bazaar where carpets, carved trays and armour were sold over the inevitable Turkish coffee and cigarettes.

The streets were busy with Arabs, Jews, Christians, Persians, Syrians and Sabeans, and there were only a few hotels where it was possible to get a meal with Japanese beer or watered-down whisky. Everywhere, even the RAF messes, was riddled with cockroaches, and there was no air conditioning beyond slow-moving fans in the ceiling to combat the temperature during the hot season when it rose to 120 in the shade. There was riding, however, and plenty of sport, including shooting, which added duck, partridge, pigeon and grouse to the monotonous menu, but there was a lot of resentment against the British and it was never wise to go far from the base unarmed, and even a visit to one of the pathetic cabarets in the city entailed carrying a revolver.

Since the area had recently emerged from a long period of a cholera epidemic, the eating of all fresh fruits and vegetables was banned and the Vernons were used to carry patients from distant airfields to the hospital, even occasionally a victim of the bubonic plague, after which the crew searched themselves scrupulously from head to foot for the bites of the flea that carried the disease, before heading for the mess for a stiff reassuring drink or two.

With the northern tribes quiet, most of the work consisted of carrying passengers between the aerodrome and Baghdad where general headquarters were situated, and landing after a trip to Mosul, Dicken was met by Hatto.

'He's arrived,' Hatto said.

'Parasol Percy?' Obviously, Hatto couldn't mean anyone else because Diplock sat across their careers like blight.

'All set to go up the ladder,' Hatto said. 'Passed the Staff College examination with honours and selected to go at once. Got a good recommendation from the Wing Colonel, of course. All those languages he speaks. He's also got a new gong, I notice. Order of St. Anne with Swords. Given to him by that chap, Yudenitch, for sitting at a desk in Riga. *They* were two of a kind. Yudenitch's campaign produced about as much as Parasol Percy's.'

'What's he doing here?'

'He's taking over this wing and he starts his tour of duty with an inspection with his old friend, St Aubyn. I gather they're out to find fault. Unfortunately, they got off on the wrong foot. There's a big economy drive on so Percy dug up a lot of petrol that's been standing idle for a long time and delivered it round the squadrons. Harris promptly complained it was dangerous because it contains water so it's all had to be withdrawn and, unfortunately, Percy isn't sure where it all went.'

Hatto smiled. 'They tried to get their own back by ticking Harris off over his bomb racks but that didn't come off either because Harris doesn't have ginger hair and a gift for pungent expression for nothing. He informed them that so long as his Vernons do their transport stuff there's no reason why they shouldn't also be good at bombing. There's no answer to that. We're next and I gather they're out for blood.'

The flight was lined up outside the decrepit wooden hangar they'd been given when the Group Captain appeared, trailed by Diplock. St Aubyn acknowledged Hatto's salute but offered no 'Good Morning'. Like Diplock, he had had occasion from the past to remember Hatto and he was in a mood to find fault. He complained about haircuts, polished boots, the way puttees had been wound, even the straightness of the lines.

Putting on his glasses, the great man then proceeded to inspect the machines and, rubbing a finger along the flying wires of the nearest, half turned and held out his finger.

'What's this?'

'Rustless paint, sir,' Hatto said.

'Other squadrons aren't in the habit of using rustless paint. You'd better make a point of visiting them and see how they maintain their aircraft.'

Hatto's face went red. Dicken could see Diplock standing behind the Group Captain, his face smooth and expressionless. Hatto indicated a chalked circle on the floor of the hangar.

'Sir. Perhaps you'll note that circle.'

'What about it?'

'There are fifty-one like it, sir, and each one marks a leak in the roof.' Hatto pointed to the door. 'And that door, sir, can't be opened because if it were the roof would fall in. If you can provide me with a hangar that will keep out the weather, I'll maintain the aircraft as well as any other station.'

St Aubyn looked flustered and turned to Diplock. 'You heard that,' he said. 'Make a note of it.'

Dicken watched them stalk away, convinced that nothing would ever change because, even if by some miracle St Aubyn meant what he said, it would immediately be vetoed by the staff of the Air Officer Commanding as an unnecessary expense because he was being chivvied by the Air Staff in London, who were chivvied in their turn by a parsimonius Treasury.

*

There were a few frosty faces as drinks were taken in the mess then St Aubyn flew off to some diplomatic function in Baghdad while Diplock announced that he had to go to Diana east of Mosul and needed one of the Bristols to fly him there. It was Dicken's turn for duty when he wished to return and as the staff car drew up and Diplock climbed out, Dicken saw he was wearing a beautifully-cut uniform and topee and was carrying a brief case. His face was set in a petulant expression and, as he approached the aeroplane, he frowned.

'Quinney,' he said. 'How are you?'

'Well, sir.'

'And your wife?'

There was a sly look on Diplock's face and Dicken guessed that he'd heard about Zoë's activities. He himself hadn't had a letter from her for two months now so doubtless Diplock knew more about her than he did himself.

'Very well, sir.'

'I heard she'd gone to America.'

It was news to Dicken but he didn't blink. 'That's correct, sir,' he said through clenched teeth. 'She wrote me.'

Diplock looked about him. 'Strange to find you in a squadron in my wing,' he said. 'I thought you were in armoured cars.'

'I was, sir. No 4 Company. I was transferred to take the place of a sick man.'

Diplock said nothing and, handing his brief case to the officer who had accompanied him from headquarters, struggled into a pair of white overalls and flying helmet.

'Shall we go?' he said.

Perhaps it was Diplock's smugness and the fact that he had advanced in the RAF by kow-towing to the right people, or perhaps because he knew more about Dicken's wife than Dicken himself did, but Dicken was in a foul temper as the propeller was swung. Taxiing into position far too fast, he checked his instruments and controls then took off in a climbing turn which was against regulations but which he hoped would frighten the life out of his passenger.

Lifting across the ridge that framed the landing ground, as they crested the last fold of land suddenly there was nothing ahead but the great bowl of the sky. The ridge had ended in a huge precipice with the plain beyond a thousand feet below, and the aeroplane lifted violently to the air that rose against the contour of the ground, then dropped violently as it passed through it.

Fighting the bumps, hoping that Diplock was hating every one of them, Dicken circled to find his direction and turned towards Mosul. As he landed he was pleased to see Diplock looking green.

He didn't even notice Dicken's quivering salute and climbed into a waiting car without even changing out of his flying overalls. Two days later, Hatto sent for Dicken.

'What the hell did you do to Parasol Percy?' he asked. 'Looped? Rolled? Anything like that?'

'No.'

'Well, you must have done *something*. There's a signal. You'd better read it.' He passed the signal flimsy across.

The words on it leapt out at Dicken as if they were on fire.

'Subject: Captain and Flight-Lieutenant Quinney, N.D. This officer is to be returned at once – repeat at once – to No 4 Car Company. He is not to take command of an aeroplane in this wing until he has completed a refresher course in flying.'

7

The Wahabi were on the move again. There were thousands of them in the valleys and behind the hills to the north. As Tafas Hashim Fitna sent warning, the armoured cars roared north and stood in a wide ring round Kerchian, their radio aerials strung out, ready when the raiders appeared to pass the word to Hatto's flight, transferred back to Mosul within two months of the disastrous inspection.

There had been a lot of trouble recently along the border from disaffected tribal leaders pushed on as usual by Sheikh Mahmoud, who as head of the Sheikhs of Barzinja exerted a continuously disruptive influence. But Mahmoud had finally been forced to withdraw from Persia and once again there had been an uneasy peace until Tafas's messengers had brought news of a new horde – this time big enough to wipe all the northern villages off the map – heavily armed and without the camels and tents that proclaimed they had their women and children with them. They clearly intended vengeance on the chiefs who had stood by the word of law, and Tafas was understandably nervous.

'Will Window-in-Eye be ready?' he asked Dicken.

'Window-in-Eye *is* ready,' Dicken insisted. 'His aeroplanes are bombed up and he can come just as soon as I send him word. As fast as an eagle and strong as a tiger.'

'And you?'

'I am watching the north.'

Dicken was looking at the sky as he spoke. It was grey and opaque and threatened bad weather. Soon the winter would be on them and that would bring an end to the raiding.

As the days passed, there was no sign of the raiders but somehow Tafas had acquired the information that they were led by Kerim Fatah Agha, who was not only noted as a vicious, merciless killer but was also related to him and considered Tafas had usurped his rights to the leadership of the northern tribes.

The days grew colder then, on the day that definite news of the raiders appeared in camp, a signal arrived. Hatto sent an aeroplane for Dicken and, handing him the signal across the folding table that did duty for his desk, he sat back.

'We're moving,' he said.

'Who are?'

'You are. I am. The flight. The armoured cars. We're going to the landing field at Shemshemal on the Persian border south of Sulamainiyah.'

'In winter?' Dicken's eyebrows rose. 'That field closes down at the end of the summer.'

'This year it doesn't. They say that Kerim Fatah Agha's up there trying to get across the border.'

'He can't be up there! He's here. Just to the north of Kerchian. Tafas has never been wrong yet.' Dicken's eyes narrowed. 'Whose doing is this?' he demanded. 'Parasol Bloody Percy's?'

'It is.'

Dicken glared. 'Well, what the hell are you going to do? Sit there and let him get away with it?'

Hatto sounded weary. 'Look, old fruit, I know what you feel. I know what I feel. There's nothing we can do about it.'

'You haven't even tried!'

Hatto jumped to his feet and slammed his hand down on the table to send papers flying. 'Yes, I damn well have!' he snapped. 'So you can take that back.'

Dicken shrugged. 'I'm sorry, Willie. I ought to have known. It was a damn silly thing to say.'

'Forget it!' Hatto growled. 'That bastard, Diplock, gets us all on edge. I sent a signal insisting that Kerim's here, but it came back signed by that bastard, St Aubyn. We can't fight both the bastards. Want to see his reply? It says that we leave at once – repeat at once.'

'And Tafas? What happens to him?'

Hatto gestured wearily. 'Christ knows.'

'You know what it's all about, don't you?' Dicken said. 'It's because I shook the bastard up on that flight to Hinaidi. It scared him rotten and when he's scared he bites like a weasel. He's sending us up there because it's the coldest, most uncomfortable bloody place he can find. You and I, Willie, old lad, are going to spend the rest of our careers fending this bugger off.'

'What concerns me more at the moment,' Hatto growled, 'is that before long Tafas is going to be fending off Kerim Fatah Agha. And that won't work, because Tafas has only a couple of hundred men and KFA's got a couple of thousand.'

*

In the hope of proving themselves wrong, Hatto flew north to the border and Dicken pushed the cars forward into the wilderness. All the signs were that Kerim Fatah Agha was near and Hatto came back to report the wadis to the north of the border where they couldn't touch them were full of men, horses and camels.

Another signal was sent to headquarters but the reply was exactly the same. They passed on the news to Tafas, trying to convince him it was none of their doing. The old man was fatalistic and, though some of his young men went in for angry murmurings, he showed no sign of bitterness towards them, asking only that they would give him and his small son a final ride in the machine like a bird.

They took coffee with him and shared the ceremonial *mansef*, and this time Dicken managed to down the sheep's eyeball without a shudder because his thoughts were concerned with the old man's safety. A tent was offered them for the night but they slept alongside the aircraft and the cars. Lying under the cold stars in the silence of the desert night, Dicken found himself reflecting that despite his dirty clothes and vermin, and the hardships of his life, Tafas Hashim Fitna had a finer code of honour than a few white men he knew.

They left for the south at dawn, having first turned over every scrap of ammunition they could get away with, despite the fact that it all had to be accounted for. Dicken even handed over a loaded revolver, putting it down as lost due to enemy action. The old man took it gravely, then looked at his small son. Dicken knew what he was thinking. Rather than let Kerim Fatah Agha get him, he was prepared to shoot him himself.

On the southward trips towards civilisation they normally talked of meals and hot baths but this time there was no talking. A surprising rapport had grown up between the car crews and the Shammar tribesmen, and they were all well aware that if Tafas Hashim Fitna had his messengers going south, Kerim Fatah Agha had his spies who would even now be going north.

Shemshemal was a cheerless place surrounded by hills. The land itself was stony, metallic and brittle, thorn bushes spouting from every scrap of soft sand with stout sword-like blades of grass like marram grass, straw-coloured and knee-high. The cars arrived in a storm to find Hatto already there with the aeroplanes pegged down and shuddering in the bitter wind. With the fitful sun vanished in the rags of yellow air, a brown wall of cloud came down from the hills and wrapped a blanket of bitter stinging dust round them as they fought to get the covers over the engines of the cars. Whorls of sand enveloped them and torn-up bushes clattered and banged against them, and just as they were completely smothered in dust the rain came in torrents to mould their dusty clothes to their body in layers of yellow mud.

The area was one of low ridges covered with slivers of sandstone and slate, ugly, bare, cheerless and inhabited by puff-adders. The local cure was to bind the bite with a plaster and read the Koran to the victim until he died.

The search for Kerim Fatah Agha started at once. Because of the weather, there was little flying but the armoured cars were constantly moving among the rocky hills, slipping and sliding, their crews cold, wet and cursing. As they had expected, there was no sign of the raiders.

In the evenings, there was nothing to do but read, talk, play cards or look at the mist rising from the plain as the sun sank out of sight in a splash of cold fire in a grey-purple sky. Then for three successive days the air was icy enough to freeze them while the wind never let up, flapping their coats and bellying the cloaks of the local inhabitants. The sleet it carried plastered them with mud and when the sun finally appeared there was a white dome of snow on the hills.

'The mountains wear their skull caps,' the locals said, as the camels bent their long necks to sniff at the strange whiteness that covered the ground.

The misty valleys were sluggish streams of melting snow when they heard that Kerim Fatah Beg had finally descended on Kerchian. The whole village had been put to the sword and flame, and Tafas and his sons, even the smallest, were among the dead.

'Just so that bastard, Diplock, could get a little revenge on us!' Dicken snarled. 'It makes you ashamed to be British!'

Soon afterwards a signal came, ordering the cars back to the Kerchian area and the aircraft to Hinaidi. It was signed by the Air Officer Commanding and despite the formal wording had a note of anger in it.

Kerchian was a ruin of shattered houses and collapsed roofs, silent under the scattered ash that lay over it like snow. Among the ruins were silent heaps clutching the ground. A solitary living thing was a small girl who ran from among the ruins, her clothing stained red. The arrival of the cars had frightened her and, as she collapsed, the Arab interpreter, choking with rage, scooped her up and held her to him. Tafas lay sprawled in the charred ruins of his home with all his family, his smallest son held close to his side, and Dicken stood staring down at them, aware of real hatred for the first time in his life.

They buried the dead and left the place for the south. Hatto met them as they arrived, his face grim.

'The AOC's been,' he said. 'He wants to know why we abandoned Tafas and accused me of disobeying orders. Diplock and that bastard, St Aubyn, had got in first with their story, but I'd saved copies of the signals they sent and the signals we sent – complete with times and dates. The AOC didn't say anything but I reckon that Parasol Percy and his pal have put up a bloody great black.'

'Not for the first time,' Dicken growled.

'No,' Hatto said. 'But this time it showed.'

*

The only satisfaction that came out of the episode was that Group Captain St Aubyn disappeared hurriedly back to England – it was made to look as though he'd been given another command but they knew very well that he hadn't – and soon afterwards Diplock handed over to a man from headquarters and also disappeared.

'To Hong Kong,' Hatto said. 'Nearly off the map.'

74

It didn't bring back Tafas and his sons but it gave them a small measure of satisfaction, particularly when Dicken was instructed to hand over his armoured cars and take up his temporary position once more with Hatto's flight, now at Kirkuk and working with the Iraqi army.

Kirkuk was to the north of Baghdad at the end of a wide plain and at the base of the foothills that led to the mountainous country of Kurdistan. Their duties consisted of continuing the harassment of Kerim Fatah Agha's tribesmen, and aircraft took off almost daily in flights of three and five to search them out and drop bombs on the fringes of their column to frighten them over the border.

It was a time when things were beginning to change. The Arab army, its units started by the new King Feisal, Lawrence's comrade in the Arab revolt against the Turks, was beginning to show its strength. It had already occupied Tektak, Sheikh Mahmoud's HQ, and was now set to occupy El Runu from where Kerim Fatah Agha was operating, and aircraft had been busy escorting the columns through the ranges of hills where snipers could have held up an army for days.

Because of the temporary nature of the posting, the squadron was living in tents round the edge of the field, an uncomfortable business when the wind blew because blankets, bedding and clothes became covered with dust and there was grit over everything they ate or drank. As the winter passed the weather grew warmer and eventually a hot dry spell left them fighting for breath.

Lying on his bed, gasping in the heat with nothing on but a towel, Dicken stared at the latest letter from Zoë. As usual, it was brief and hurried and seemed totally devoid of affection, a duty letter and no more. She now had five garages along the south coast of England and had appointed a manager to run them for her so that she had more time for flying. At the moment, she was in the States engaged on some project in Baltimore, and was not only doing more flying than he was but was also flying now with an Irishman called Spud Murphy, who because of the insistence on licences and safety factors in Europe, had moved to the States where there was more freedom.

'Over here freelance fliers are playing a valuable part in

furthering airmindedness,' she wrote. 'Something that the stuffy people in England don't seem to realise.'

Perhaps they were, Dicken thought. But most air circuses, like the late Charley Wright's, were run on a shoestring and there had been a few avoidable accidents which had given flying a bad name. Standing on the wings of an aeroplane – with or without a harness – wasn't flying. In his youth, he had often been tempted himself to fly under bridges – one RAF pilot had flown through the Arch of Ctesiphon and a Frenchman had flown through the Arc de Triomphe – but that sort of thing didn't advance flying, it merely indicated a man's skill.

Zoë, however, seemed eager to be where not only the excitement but the money was and flying was beginning to get off the ground in a big way in the States. Because of the size of the country, people were realising it was the only quick way of moving about it, and Zoë was anxious to get in on the ground floor of what could only be an expanding industry. Dicken hadn't been slow to notice in the flying magazines that littered the mess the references to Harmer Aircraft Incorporated of St Louis. Obviously Casey Harmer was forging ahead, too, as she had always said he would and he wondered more than once if she had bothered to look him up.

Certainly her letter contained no indication that she was pining for Dicken. Indeed, there were references to men she met, casual references as though she had done no more than take a meal with them, but he continued to suspect that she and Casey Harmer had been lovers during the war even while she was professing to be in love with Dicken, and now that Casey Harmer was back in circulation her visit to the States seemed highly suspicious.

He was still frowning, the letter a damp sheet in his fingers, the ink on it smeared by the sweat from his hand, when Hatto appeared in the doorway. Somehow, Hatto always managed to look cool when everybody else looked roasted.

'It's the blue blood,' he explained. 'Takes longer to come to the boil.' He sat in the camp chair. 'I've got news, old son. We've passed the exam for Staff College and eventually we'll be going. God knows when, of course, but I understand the AOC took rather a shine to the way we stood up to Parasol Percy and that bastard, St Aubyn.' As he talked he became aware of the stuffy heat. 'Hotter than usual, don't you think?' he commented.

Somewhere in the camp a dog howled, followed immediately by another, then another. A mule brayed, then another, followed by a donkey, then the birds started filling the air with an agitated twittering. Hatto's head turned and Dicken sat up, conscious of something strange happening and they had just started for the door when the ground suddenly started to move beneath their feet. As they stared at each other, a dog passed the door, bolting for safety in a wobbly run as if its legs were weak.

'Good God,' Hatto yelled. 'It's an earthquake!'

8

The whole area of the Middle East, in particular Turkey just to the north, was a place where failures in the earth's crust often led to minor earthquakes, but it had never occurred to anyone that they might be involved in one.

As they burst outside and stood staring about them, nearby buildings seemed to be quivering, so that their outline looked blurred, and they saw cracks running crazily up the walls and the earth moving beneath their feet.

The shock stopped almost before they had become aware of it but the air was filled with yellow dust like a fog. A roll call was ordered at once and the station commander began to check his buildings, many of which were already being evacuated. Nobody had been hurt and no machines damaged but it was clear that many of the buildings would have to be pulled down and rebuilt. They were just offering up thanks for not being hurt when all aircrews were summoned to the hangars.

'The epicentre was at Zebar,' they were told. 'We got away lightly. There must have been an estimated thousand deaths in the town and a lot more in the surrounding towns and villages. They're desperately in need of help, but there's no radio contact and we want operators flown in with their sets so they can tell us what's needed and where. It'll take the cars days to get there because it's disputed territory and there's a lot of hostility, but the aircraft can do it in a matter of hours and be sending messages back at once. We want reports on the situation.'

The aircraft began to take off in the middle of the afternoon, for various points along the fault where the wrecked villages lay; Dicken's assignment was Jehuddin, a narrow-gutted little town under ths hills. As he passed over the ridges, his engine started faltering, but, as he looked down at the forbidding terrain beneath, wondering what the hell he was supposed to do, the engine started firing again and, as he descended on the other side of the ridge, it began to behave itself once more. The air over Jehuddin was yellow with dust up to a height of three hundred feet as if the wrecked town had expired in a great gasp. The narrow landing strip had been damaged and a great jagged crack ran in a zigzag down its entire length. All the buildings had collapsed and the landing area was full of people and carts.

They flew low, waving frantically to the crowd to clear the field, but the Iraqis gave no indication that they were intending to move and Dicken started climbing again to find somewhere else to land. As he reached 6000 feet the engine started faltering once more, then cut abruptly. He tried diving with the propeller windmilling to start it again but it had no effect whatsoever and, turning off-course in the hope of finding a less cluttered area, he spotted a piece of ground just ahead which looked flatter and was at least clear. It was boulder strewn, but with no engine and the rocky side of a mountain the only alternative, he decided to get in quickly. Side-slipping off his remaining height, he stalled the Bristol on to the ground from a height of ten feet, losing all flying speed at once so that the aeroplane dropped under its own weight and stayed more or less where it arrived. The impact came in a crash and a twanging of wires but the aeroplane was down.

They were several miles from the village and had been warned to expect hostility so, for safety, the wireless operator, a leading aircraftman called Babington, unbolted the Lewis gun, pushed to the top of a small knoll which would give a commanding field of fire, and sat down to wait. The silence in the hills was unnerving.

After a while a group of men with donkeys, all armed to the teeth, appeared. Babington worked the cocking handle of the gun but the men said they were the bodyguards of the headman of Jehuddin and were anxious to help. Cigarettes were handed round, and they made an examination of the machine. The tail skid and several fuselage cross members had been broken.

More men had now appeared and one spoke enough English for them to make him understand what was wanted and, while Babington erected his set and its aerial, Dicken went by donkey into the town. No one showed any hostility to him because they were still dragging half-suffocated victims from the wrecked buildings. There were no doctors and, in no time, he became involved in digging an old woman from what had been her house. Leaving her moaning in the street with two broken legs because there was nothing else he could do until more help arrived, he immediately afterwards found himself crawling under the ruins of another wrecked house where a baby was screaming. Lifting the naked morsel from its dead mother's arms, he carried it to a nearby tent where the village medicine men were doing their best to set broken limbs and cure wounds with things like chupattis or the skin of freshly-killed chickens and a great deal of reading from the Koran. The water supply had disappeared and all there was came from a few stinking wells, already polluted by putrifying bodies. There was no food and no transport except donkeys and one or two ancient carts.

A second shock occurred even as they worked. Immediately, all the rescuers bolted from the wrecked buildings, and it was some time before they could be persuaded to return. By this time the original naked baby Dicken had rescued had been joined by a dozen more, all of them yelling in the heat and all of them without parents to claim them.

The following day a Vernon arrived packed with tents, blankets, and British and Iraqi medical men and supplies. A second arrived during the afternoon with Iraqi army officers and NCOs to bring order to the shattered town, and the worst of the injured were removed. As the dead were buried and the dangerous houses knocked down, the situation began to improve. More food, blankets and tents arrived by lorry and mule trains from undamaged areas, and as the situation was brought under control, Dicken decided it was time to consider the damaged Bristol.

Despite the smashed tail-skid and the broken cross members, he felt it could be flown again and, coming to the conclusion that it could even be got off the ground where it stood if only the landing area could be increased, he persuaded the headman to allocate helpers, and set about clearing it. The trouble had been caused by the fuel, which must have come from contaminated petrol, doubtless part of the drums Diplock had resurrected and then lost.

During the next two days, he carefully drained and filtered it, then, with the aid of the headman's carpenters, the leg of a broken chair and a lot of luck, they managed to get the tail end of the Bristol sufficiently patched to risk a take-off. The following day another Vernon arrived with more supplies, more Iraqi soldiers, a relief wireless operator with a spare set, and instructions for Dicken that he was to remain at Jehuddin and await orders.

The problem was to get into the air again and, staring round him from the small saucer-like depression where they had come down, he began to remove all the stowed items from the aircraft, the spare drum of water, the guns, ammunition and tool kit.

'Think you can do it, sir?' Babington asked.

'Just, I reckon.'

'Then I'd like to come with you, sir.'

Dicken slapped his shoulder, pleased by the show of confidence. 'Under the circumstances,' he said, 'I think you'd better stick around to pick up the pieces if I don't pull it off.'

The area sloped slightly and, between them and with the help of the local people, they made a last search for dangerous stones. What little breeze there was came down from the hills and was blowing up the slope of the take-off area. As Dicken ran the engine up and checked it, Babington, standing on the wing alongside him, held up his thumb.

'Good luck, sir.'

Assisted by the headman's personal bodyguard, huge men armed to the teeth with rifles and swords, their chests draped with ammunition belts, they pushed the Bristol up the slope, then with the aid of an English-speaking Kurd, Dicken explained exactly what he wanted and left it to Babington to give the word when he raised his hand.

Starting the engine, he revved it until he was satisfied then sat for a while in the cockpit, thinking of the down-draughts along the slopes when the wind was coming over the ridges, and the fact that a DH9a had recently flown into a ridge in very similar circumstances while flying to Sulamainiya and Halebja. If he got the aeroplane over and safely back to its base, there'd be a few congratulations and then the incident would be forgotten because it was the sort of thing that was being done every other week. If on the other hand he failed and hit the ridge and was killed, he'd be forgotten equally quickly, but his epitaph would be nothing more than 'Stupid bugger. He should have dismantled the engine and set fire to the airframe, which is only wood and canvas anyway.'

Before he could depress himself further, he opened the throttle, noticing as he did so that the Kurds had all moved down the slope and were waiting close to the spot where they expected him to hit the hill. Raising his hand, over the roar of the engine he heard Babington shout as he yanked away the chocks and the men holding down the tail in the blast from the propeller, their robes whipped tight against their bodies, released their holds and fell backwards. One of them, slower than the rest, was carried forward as the aeroplane began to move but, ducking under the moving wing, Babington grabbed his leg and yanked him off so that they rolled together in the dust as the machine gathered speed.

The tail lifted at once and the Bristol took up its flying attitude. Its speed rose quickly and, immediately, praying that the petrol wouldn't let him down, Dicken pulled back the stick and lifted the machine off the ground in a steep climbing turn. The ridge of hills in front approached at alarming speed but, lightened of all its extras, the Bristol soared magnificently and he scraped over the top with only a few feet to spare.

Circling, he slipped down to the landing ground alongside the Vernons and within an hour Babington appeared, riding on a donkey and towing a string of other donkeys carrying the wireless, spare equipment, guns and ammunition.

That afternoon a squadron of armoured cars arrived, bringing spares and a corporal rigger and two men, who started at once to replace the chair-leg tail-skid and the broken fuselage members. By this time, the situation in Jehuddin was under control. Its injured, sick and old were being moved and the town was safe, and the army was on the move again.

By now Dicken and Babington were shaving with borrowed razors and living on a permanent diet of goat. Their stay had done a lot of good because hostile tribesmen had suddenly become friendly and were swearing eternal allegiance to King George. The repairs to the Bristol had just been completed when a wireless message arrived, indicating that the Wahabi had been driven into the town of Suqeiwiya in the north-eastern corner of the country. The army was in a position either to finish them off or drive them over the border into Persia, and Dicken was ordered to fill up with fresh fuel brought by the Vernons and rendezvous with another Bristol south of Katchi. He was in position when the second Bristol arrived and he identified it at once as Hatto's. As they formed up on each other and headed north-east, the searching column of Feisal's army was strung across the plain in groups of camels, horses and vehicles.

They found the Wahabi heading down a narrow wadi, hundreds of men filling the narrow gorge in a dense mass of camels, and Hatto left Dicken to keep an eye on them while he returned to the plain to drop a message to the advancing column. The camels, the tassels of their headropes swinging, the riders clutching their rifles, their red and green banners fluttering above them, were moving at a racing trot, half-obscured by a cloud of dust. As Dicken flew over them, he saw the riders lifting their rifles. Most of the firing was wild, but a flag of canvas lifted in the wing to show that some of them were on target.

As the other machine reappeared, Hatto pointed downwards and they dived at the head of the column. Hatto's bombs exploded in bright flashes that flung up small yellow puffballs like melting cream buns. Camels went down in a crumpling crash, legs flying, long necks flailing, their riders hurled under the feet of the following animals. With the head of the racing column disrupted, the rest wavered and tried to turn back, only to become a more closely-packed target as Dicken arrived. As the bombs exploded, the tribesmen milled around, then broke free and fled towards the open plain where the armoured cars of Feisal's army were forging ahead. As the machine guns started, more camels went down and the desert was filled with running men and riderless animals.

As they circled over Suqeiwiya well ahead of the army, a strong wind was blowing from the east, sweeping down on the town from a low range of hills that lay behind it, to send the dust flying in clouds with uprooted bushes and bundles of torn grass. Beyond the first range of hills, a second lifted up its peaks, and as they turned over them they hit an area of vicious turbulence.

Hatto's machine was snatched by the currents to lift two

hundred feet then drop again so swiftly it seemed the wings would be torn off. A moment later, Dicken's machine was flung skywards as if it were no weightier than a moth. The first jolt was not severe but it was enough to make everything on the machine rattle and clatter. The next jolt was harder, then they began to come like the blows of giant fists to press them against their safety belts and plummet them downwards so that the altimeter unwound crazily and the airspeed increased to an unbelievable figure before flinging them upwards again, draining the blood from their brains and making their arms leaden. All the time the plane was shuddering and swinging with an exhaustingly violent motion that put a strain on muscles and nerves and set the wires twanging and humming. Babington was being violently sick over the side of the rear cockpit and there seemed no relief from the torment when, below them, Dicken saw a small open space near the town, which seemed empty of Kerim Fatah Agha's men. Moving alongside Hatto, he gestured to indicate they should land. Even the chance of meeting a few of Kerim's followers was preferable to sitting up above the town in the angry sky.

Landing one after the other, they waited at the end of the field, their engines running in case they had to make a hurried take-off, but after a while the motors began to boil and they had to switch off, Babington and the other wireless operator, still green after the circling over the town, staying by the Lewis guns. By this time, a few people had begun to appear and, as they increased in numbers, Hatto flourished his revolver and indicated that they should not approach any nearer.

After a while, five old men arrived. One of them stopped in front of Hatto and began to make a speech. From the few words they had learned, they gathered that Kerim Fatah Agha had vanished and that the old men were anxious to hand over the town. Cigarettes were exchanged and, as someone lit a fire, coffee was produced. When the army arrived half an hour later, they found that the RAF had completed the arrangements and the town was secure.

Hatto glanced at Dicken.

'I think they ought to give us a gong for this,' he said. 'We won the war on our own.'

Part Two

I

'Dear Dicky Boy,
   This letter is being written to you from Baltimore. I am flying
now with Clyde Richards. I left Murphy's outfit because he was
getting serious and becoming involved with mid-air refuelling.
Any goddam fool knows it can't be done but he persists. We do
regular shows, as well as a few other things which are financially good and the weather here is *always* okay for flying . . .'
   Dicken tossed the letter aside. Zoë was not only in America,
she was even beginning to sound American. Not that there was
anything wrong with Americans, but it was a poor sort of
marriage with himself in Iraq and his wife in the States. She
didn't seem to be suffering from missing him but, he had to
admit, neither did he miss her.
   His position with Hatto's flight was still only temporary
when they heard that a nationalist insurrection had broken out
against the Western Powers in China and that Shanghai was
likely to be besieged. The insurrection, led by a man called
Chiang Kai-Shek, had been growing for some time but as usual,
because the politicians in Westminster thought more of economy than safety, the air force had been cut to the bone and
volunteers had to be asked for from men serving abroad who
could be rushed to China to help.
   When the notice appeared on the board, Dicken was immediately reminded of Nicola Aubrey. The last he had heard of
her was that she was heading for China, where her diplomat
father had been posted from India, and he remembered bitterly
that the only show of affection he had received from the family
had been an ill-spelt letter from her youngest sister, Marie-
Gabrielle. Now, suddenly, he saw a chance of finding them
again.

'I'd like to put my name down,' he told Hatto.

Hatto eyed him shrewdly. They had known each other long enough for him to be aware of Dicken's problems. 'What about going home?' he asked. 'You're due.'

Dicken shrugged. 'I don't think it matters all that much,' he said.

*

China was in a state of unrest. With all the foreign concessions and treaty ports that had been set up in the last century in a turmoil, the Chinese had suddenly realised that the western nations who had battened on to them were holding areas of their country with nothing more than a few soldiers and gunboats and, led by Chiang Kai-Shek, they were suddenly aware that there were enough of them to drive out the foreign devils.

The journey was by air to India, in easy stages via Basra, Bushire, and Bandar Abbas, then from Karachi across India to Calcutta. At Calcutta Dicken picked up a ship to Hong Kong, and from there to Shanghai took a Chinese-owned coastal vessel called the *Shuntien*, whose vital areas like the bridge and the engine room were enclosed by pirate-proof grilles. Because another ship had been taken over only two weeks before by men hidden among her passengers and burned out to the water-line, all her officers wore arms and there was a great deal of speculation about each other among the passengers.

Among them was a burly American Catholic priest, Father Bernard O'Buhilly who, with the aid of a group of nuns, ran a mission in the Louza district of Shanghai. He had been to Northern India for a holiday and was returning refreshed and ready to take up the cudgels again on behalf of his faith.

' 'Tis a dreadful country, boy,' he insisted. 'But, sure –' his arm waved expansively '– just take a look at it and you'll know why I always come back.'

The sunset was flooding the heavens with crimson, the sea with amaranth. Bathed in the glare, the whole ship was red, the black hull as if rusty, the white upper works coral, the brass flashing crimson sparks. For a moment they stood in silence as the ship drove through a sea like a field of jewels, scattering flashes of amethyst, garnet and ruby, then the priest sighed.

88

'If only the human element were half as beautiful,' he said. 'And by that, me boy, I mean the white human element as well as the yellow.' He glanced at Dicken. 'You wouldn't be one of us, would you?' he asked, and when Dicken shook his head, he sighed and smiled. 'Ah, well, you can't win every time.'

It was O'Buhilly, an ardent cigarette smoker and lover of Irish whiskey, who explained the situation. 'When the Manchu dynasty was overthrown by revolutionaries in 1911,' he said, 'the first president was Yuan Shih-K'ai but, sure, when his generals rose in revolt and he had to flee, it occurred to the generals that, since they had the troops, *they*, not the politicians, were the holders of power. Since then China's become the sport of the military. At the moment 'tis two governments there are, a ghostly one with no power and few troops, clankin' its chains in Peking, and one in Canton. But, sure, both are controlled by their generals who support or betray for money whichever they represent. They organise the opium trade, sell positions, tax the people and finally retire to Japan or Singapore with immense fortunes. They don't fight – they prefer to accept or offer bribes – and the poor are oppressed while the soldiers are like bandits. The whole of China's become a battlefield.

'However, -' the burly priest held up a finger '– 'tis now all changed. Chiang Kai-Shek is a touch different from the rest. He is educated. Trained in Russia and head of the Whampoa Military Academy. And he's quarrelled with the Russians and the Chinese Communists and wants the whole of China for himself.'

'Will he get it?'

'That, me boy, remains to be seen. But 'twould be a better chance than most he had, I'd say.'

*

They knew they had reached the Yangtze hours before they saw land because of the oozy yellow nature of the sea and eventually they found themselves in the mouth of the river, still thirty miles wide with a thin brown line in the distance that was all there was to be seen of the land.

The Whangpoo, where the ship dropped anchor, was a muddy tributary twelve miles up the Yangtze. The surface of the water boiled with life, sampans moving across it in ones, twos, groups and fleets like swarms of water beetles. Tugs nudged at vessels anchored in midstream, and river steamers, black-and-red-funnelled and looking as if, with their tiers of decks, they had far too much freeboard for safety, trudged westwards into the hinterland, their sirens rumbling indignantly at the junks which swept indifferently across their course on the tide, huge eyes painted on bows and poops that lifted from their decks like those of Elizabethan galleons.

The sun was going down like a burst pomegranate behind the city, the anchored steamers grey silhouettes on a yellow background. The *Shuntien's* arrival alongside set off the most tremendous din, the noisy greetings and farewells of the old China hands indicating that they felt that they, not the Chinese, owned the country. Multitudinous Chinese clerks, compradores and shore workers poured through the ship, high-pitched voices chirruping cheerfully in their own language as they grinned and kow-towed to the Europeans in the hope of a good tip. Ashore, it was even more ear-battering, more dazzling to the eye with the garish Chinese symbols outside the shops and the bright red and yellow banners billowing over the doors, more offensive to the nose with the smell of drains, night-soil barges moving downstream, and the odour of thousands of unwashed bodies. The high-pitched yelling of the street traders and coolies was interspersed with the fretful honking of motor car horns, and the rising and falling song of working gangs unloading sacks from a merchant ship further up the Bund where the junks covered the water like a heaving mat.

The city itself was a strange mixture of Orient and Occident, and more American than European with its big square hotels, huge advertisement hoardings and brash electric signs. There were hundreds of motor cars, many of them large American importations hooting their way in and out of the rickshaws, the wheelbarrows, the flooding pedestrians, the porters carrying importations, hooting their way in and out of the rickshaws, the trams that groaned and shrieked round unbelievably tight corners packed with coolies, luggage, vegetables and live poultry.

The biggest city in China, it was built in two parts, the old city and the modern area built round the International Settlement and the French Concession. Skyscrapers towered above wide modern boulevards where the luxury of the Westerners contrasted sharply with the ant-like life of the Chinese who swarmed through the streets. Surrounded by the cancerous growths of Chinese towns, the city was the centre of all business in the Far East, and occupying it with honest people doing honest business were men controlling piracy, slavery, drugs, and, ironically, all Christian missionary effort. Alongside bankers and businessmen and earnest churchmen were touts, pimps, white slavers, thieves, smugglers and pickpockets and, in spite of the Sikh policemen and a ferociously efficient Customs service, every morning the newspapers carried some new sensation of murder, gang rivalry, smuggling or the sacking of some upcountry town.

With every kind of currency available, the city's constitution had been founded less on law than do-as-you-please-and-no-questions-asked, and the streets stank at night of opium and were filled with the chatter of singsong girls and streetwalkers, many of them White Russians who had found their way south after the Revolution.

The Chinese population was as mixed as the European, consisting of people who had sold their lands and migrated to the city, and the younger sons and daughters from the impoverished countryside of China, in Shanghai to earn money as sweated labour in the factories that had been pushed up by European financiers. As they went about their business, the wealthy had to pick their way between the starved corpses of the poor.

The city had the tallest buildings in the East, but it also had the most scrofulous slums, and running off the finest boulevards were narrow alleys with open drains. The climate was extreme, with sleet, snow, fog and frost in winter to kill off the poor in their thousands, and a humid heat in summer pressing like a blanket over the buildings. The Bund, one of the most famous streets in the East, curved along the river bank for nearly a mile to the British Consulate, with the great trading houses – Jardine Matheson, Sassoon, Butterfield and Swire, the Glen Line, the Chartered Bank, the *North China Daily News* office – stretching in between. The smell was of cooking from the thousands of tiny stalls offering food, and every street held its quota of hawkers, letter writers, boot black boys, sellers of illicit silver dollars and dirty photographs, and blind, deformed or mutilated beggars, among them occasionally even a White Russian driven to poverty and trying to raise the price of a bottle of booze.

With trouble expected, there were soldiers from France, Annamites from French Indo-China, Japanese, Italians, Swedes, Norwegians, Portuguese, United States marines, Punjabis and Gurkhas, and half a dozen famous British regiments. To say nothing of the Shanghai Defence Force, a locally-raised unit comprising every nationality in the East, which had commandeered the rooftops of high buildings on the city's outskirts and placed machine guns and even light artillery up there where they could command the entrances to the city.

The RAF were operating from the racecourse, flying DH4s, and the CO turned out to be Cuthbert Orr. Large in stature, tough, indifferent to authority, he considered his rank gave him the right to run his command the way he felt fit. 'I'm not a bloody clerk answering messages from the brass at the top,' he pointed out. 'And this place's a shambles, with the Chinese internal politics getting rougher by the day. Friendly Chinese warned us long since that an army was being assembled in Canton to capture the place and for once somebody took some notice and there are now about 25,000 troops entrenched round the boundaries. If anybody draws a deep breath, some poor bugger falls into the river.'

He wasn't happy at the situation. There were plots, bombs and arms smuggling, wheelbarrow riots, rickshaw strikes, and regular stoppages in one or other of the local services – taxis, water, electricity, tramway.

'All stirred up by political factions for their own ends,' he said. 'The foreign-educated students have noticed Western methods of getting your own way and they've adopted them. They want independence and I can't honestly say I blame them. After all, the English run their Customs, the French run their postal services, and all foreigners are exempt from Chinese law, while some of the bastards operating out here would be in clink if they tried the same thing back home. It doesn't make it easy for the Chinese to take into account the benefits they receive from European know-how, while the

Russian Communist Party, of course, is fishing in troubled waters for its own benefit.'

He paused and gave a wry smile. 'Half the Chinese generals on both sides are crooks, of course. They're mostly ex-warlords who terrorised the countryside until Chiang's Kuomintang party got going; then, according to their whims, they joined one side or the other. They're still corrupt and still bloody cruel, and the Europeans don't help. During the war, people in other places served in uniform; this lot merely enjoyed themselves, making fortunes and building damn great houses for themselves. The admiral who's running the show hates the buggers and I don't blame him.'

The Nationalist army was expected any day and the troops were lining up for the confrontation that was bound to come. The Peking Government's army was little more than a rabble, but the Cantonese had been drilled by rootless German ex-officers and had some semblance of military appearance. British and American warships were gathering in the river among the swarming junks and sampans, and Western arrogance was tempered by apprehension.

The Chinese had already tried their hands at Hankow and other places up the Yangtze and had found that what they'd been told about there being enough of them to beat the foreigners was right. There just weren't sufficient Europeans to stand against the Chinese mobs and the first refugees were already heading downriver to the safety of Shanghai, their possessions gone, their faces grey with strain, their children wailing with terror.

Life in Shanghai hadn't altered much, however. The navy was being reinforced and a fresh Punjabi battalion had just arrived. By this time, there were eight British battalions, and more were expected, but unfortunately there was no common command and every contingent had different orders.

The British Consulate knew nothing of the Aubrey family. 'They were here,' Dicken was told, 'but that was two years ago.'

Dicken shrugged. 'It doesn't matter,' he said. He was chasing a ghost, he knew, and it looked as though he'd never catch up with it. It was better to let the whole thing drop. For a moment, he had entertained a hope that he might pick up where he had left off, but it was nine years since. Nicola might have married or, because of her religion, even gone into a convent, and if neither of these things, she would be different – nine years different. With her gentleness and naïvity she had been little more than a schoolgirl. Now she would be a woman of twenty-seven, surely worldly-wise, tougher, more know-ledgeable and less sentimental. The Nicola he had known was gone for ever.

There was only one chance left – Father O'Buhilly. His mission rooms were bare-walled and devoid of ornament beyond a few potted plants.

'It is enough to breathe and live – and sometimes to die,' he explained. 'And sure, that's all we need.'

He had won a medal for bravery with the American army in the Argonne in 1918 and seemed to regard China as just another campaign. Nothing put him off what he was doing, neither the disapproval of the British matrons nor the hatred of the Communists who liked to suggest he was a spy for the foreign armed forces. He had no knowledge of the Aubreys.

'I remember them,' he said, offering cigarettes. 'He arrived here four years ago with his family – and what a splendid family they were, every one of them a beauty, male an' female alike. He was disappointed, I guess, because he was still in a junior position and in the end they all went back to London, and the next I heard they'd gone to Baghdad in Iraq.'

'I've just come from Iraq,' Dicken said.

'The Almighty never intended the Via Crucis to be strewn with roses, me boy. 'Tis the way life treats us.'

Despite the tension, the Shanghailanders seemed to have no intention of giving up their pleasures and continued as before, eating, drinking, going to the cinema or the races, and carrying on affairs with each other's wives. Among them were girls who had come out to join relatives on the hunt for husbands and were finding it hard to compete with the Chinese, French, American and Russians who usually had more character and invariably more vitality in the humid heat. The British wives attacked the morals of the Russian women but the Russians, toughened by their wanderings since the Revolution, were quite indifferent. They regarded the British women as 'flat-chested, flat-footed, and worn out by hunting, hockey and golf.' The clash of tempers and the never-ending hostilities they provoked between themselves and their admirers resulted in the area where they lived and plied their profession becoming known as The Trenches.

In contrast, the British-organised affairs were formal enough to be dull, with everyone eyeing their neighbours, weighing up their chances and considering whether they had been put in the right pecking order. Among them, to his surprise, Dicken bumped into Annys Diplock, recently arrived with her husband from Hong Kong. She was still attractive but she had put on weight and she eyed Dicken warily.

Diplock, it seemed, had been appointed personal assistant to the new Air Officer Commanding – who else but Air Commodore St Aubyn, who had newly arrived from England? It was amazing, Dicken reflected, how people like St Aubyn and Diplock managed to take care of themselves. Every reversal of fortune that sprang from their narrow-mindedness and their concern for their own affairs was turned to advantage. The last Dicken had heard of St Aubyn was when, as a group captain, he had been sent back to England with a flea in his ear for failing to protect Tafas Hashim Fitna and his tribe in the north of Iraq, but here he was, turning up again like a bad penny, with increased rank and doubtless increased power, to sweep Diplock back into his sphere of influence.

Carefully, he avoided asking how the two of them were and kept the conversation to safer subjects.

'How's Zoë?' he asked.

'I don't know,' Annys admitted. 'I haven't heard from her for over a month.'

'You're lucky,' Dicken said. 'I haven't heard from her for two. Got the family with you?'

'Just my small daughter. We left my son at school in England. It's better for him.'

The party was all small talk and he wondered what he had ever seen in her. She had always been the placid one of the family, formal, orthodox, lacking Zoë's vitality. Perhaps he should have married her instead. At least he would have known what his wife was up to.

She introduced him to a girl standing alongside her. 'This is Joyce Mahaffy,' she said. 'She's the sister of Arthur's deputy,

James Mahaffy. She's come out here to stay for a while.'

Joyce Mahaffy had good features, a good figure and a lively eye, and she managed to get Dicken to one side.

'Are you as bored as I am?' she asked.

'I don't know how bored you are,' he replied cautiously.

'Very bored.'

'That's about as bored as I am. Shall we sneak out?'

Dicken had already been invited to the Long Bar of the Shanghai Club, without which no man could say he had 'arrived', and eaten at the RAF Club, founded by ex-RFC men. This time it was the Country Club, its name somewhat of a misnomer because, despite its squash courts, tennis courts and swimming pool, the fields which had once surrounded it were beginning to vanish beneath the tide of skyscrapers which had engulfed the city. Drinking the China-sides summer drink of gin, lime and ice with a touch of bitters, they studied each other.

'You've got rather a lot of gongs,' Joyce said.

'Comes of not having enough sense to keep my head down,' Dicken said. 'You married?'

'Would it matter if I were?'

'A bit.'

'Well, I'm not. How about you?'

'Yes. But that doesn't matter much either. I haven't seen my wife for ages. She's in the States. She likes to think herself a liberated woman.'

'Is she attractive?'

'Very.'

'Do you trust her on her own?'

'No.' Dicken answered with a wry smile. 'I never have.'

'So what's the situation?'

'She seems to go her way and I go mine.'

'Leaves you both pretty free. Do you take advantage of the fact?'

'I haven't yet.'

'Does she?'

'I suspect so. How about you?'

'My brother has a flat here but at the moment he's in Hong Kong, which leaves the flat empty except for me. How about coming for dinner tonight? I'm a pretty good cook.'

He knew at once what she was seeking. He'd heard the

expression, 'The Fornicating Latitudes,' and suspected she was not only bored, but also eager for an affair.

'I'll be there,' he said.

2

Within a week, Dicken was deep in an affair which looked as though it might take some throwing off. Joyce Mahaffy was twenty-nine and was after a man, and it didn't matter whose. Her brother seemed to be on permanent detachment to Hong Kong and she was more often than not alone, which suited her down to the ground. She had an attachment to China and, to the disgust of the Service wives, wore cheongsams slit almost to the hip to show a length of splendid white thigh, and went in for chopsticks, bird's-nest soup, shark fins, boiled sea slugs, Peking duck, fillet of snake, and hot rice wine served in tiny china cups.

'Why be in China and try to live as if you were in London?' she said with some truth.

Fortunately the situation surrounding the city meant that Dicken wasn't always free when she expected him to be and that left him relatively safe because when he wasn't about he suspected she turned her attention to other men. There had been trouble upriver at Wahnsien, Kiukiang and Wuhan, and while trying to be conciliatory, the British Government as usual was expecting its underpaid, neglected men in uniform to protect British lives and property. Unfortunately, they numbered only several thousand while the Chinese numbered millions, and more and more British residents were being evacuated downstream and the daily strikes in the city produced banners, parades, chanted slogans and smashed windows. They were well organised and the city was never able to function properly because when one public service was functioning another was not, while threatening crowds waited on street corners to spit at the troops who were trying to get them going again.

There were riots in the Nanking Road and extra companies of the Shanghai Volunteers were raised, even among the White Russians. There were also still pirates to be put down in the China Sea and along the length of the Yangtze, and aircraft took off regularly armed with bombs and machine guns while, outside the International Settlement, the city seemed to be run by a group of ex-warlords who had held control since 1925. Having got rid of all their opponents, they had left one of their number, General Sun Chuan-Fang, to look after their interests and, while everyone waited to see what would happen when he and Chiang Kai-Shek found themselves face to face, the Shanghai Municipal Council simply tried to avoid trouble.

With the city wilting under a massive crime wave, Sun decided to put an end to it by a series of public executions to knock the ambition out of every would-be gangster within miles, and the authorities nervously allowed him to have his head with a couple of dozen condemned men from the city jail. As burly and as brave as Cuthbert Orr, Father O'Buhilly promptly issued his protests.

'I am objecting, me boy,' he pointed out vigorously, 'because, Heaven preserve us, you don't trade men's lives – even criminal men's lives – just to keep a bully boy like Sun from disturbing the even tenor o' life.'

His protests came to nothing and Sun was allowed to organise a parade through the main streets of the city, including those of the International Settlement and the French Concession, while the Municipal Council shrugged its shoulders.

'At least they've drawn the line at having a brass band to head the procession,' Father O'Buhilly spluttered. ''Twould inevitably have played *Dixie, Tipperary* and *There'll Be A Hot Time In The Old Town Tonight*. They're favourites at all Chinese funerals.'

Twenty-five thousand bug-eyed spectators lined the streets, and cars, carriages, carts and bicycles followed the procession. The condemned men had been crammed into open-sided buses, hired for the occasion and still carrying the advertisements of the Grand Garage Français, the Oriental Luggage Factory and a few others. Guarded back and front by Sun soldiers armed to the teeth, they turned out of the Nanking Road to the execution ground where two film units had their

99

cameras already set up on top of grave mounds and a battalion of Sun soldiers was keeping the crowd back with jabbing rifle butts.

A cheer went up as the trucks containing the prisoners and the Ford flivvers containing the guards and executioners arrived. Every prisoner was chained by the wrists and ankles and behind his back, secured to his arms, was a stick carrying a sign proclaiming his misdeeds. Forced to kneel six at a time, they were shot at point-blank range with rifles. Their heads were blown to bits and fragments of skull and warm brains were flung everywhere. As the gravediggers watched indifferently, a great shout of exultation went up from the crowd.

'It was enough for the city authorities,' Father O'Buhilly said later. 'They've begged off from all further public exhibitions.'

Fanned by professional agitators, the strikes began to grow worse and when the agitators were arrested and appeared before the court, it started a riot which brought out every idle Chinese in the city. With twenty Indian policemen to defend the building where they were held, the inspector in charge was obliged to fire on the crowd.

'Part of the Communist plot,' Father O'Buhilly decided. 'They want to force Chiang Kai-Shek to come here and try to take over the city. The idea's to get him entangled with the International Defence Force. He'll come, all right, but he won't do that. 'Tis too clever by half he is.'

The Canton army had been fighting its way north against the warlords and the remnants of the Peking Government's army for some time, the Communists always moving ahead of them, fomenting disturbances at Hankow and Nanking and in Shanghai itself. In the International Settlement, the hope was that the Cantonese would be defeated, simply because they presented a greater danger to the comfort, luxury and ease of the Europeans than the Peking forces. But the Canton column, preceded by political agents who destroyed old loyalties and beliefs ahead of them, toppled one warlord after another and captured city after city. According to reports, for Chinese troops they were frighteningly efficient with smart uniforms and well-cared-for weapons, and had orders not to murder or rape. Their discipline alone appealed to the harassed peasantry and their foreign policy appealed to the jingoistic students.

There was a feeling in the air that it wouldn't be long before all the hated warlords were finally removed from the scene, and that alone was enough to recommend them to the Chinese, because no woman had ever been safe and there were always wailing girls, and the headless bodies of anyone who protested on the garbage heaps along the river bank waiting for the spring tides to wash them away. But – and this was the point – when the last of the warlords had gone, everybody knew it would be the turn of the foreigners.

The Peking army was now retreating past the foreign concessions and it was clear their cause was lost. The soldiers were shabby little men in grey cotton uniforms, ragged, out of step, exhausted and often shoeless. They wore everything from spats to boaters, and flat tweed caps to furs, and their horses were skinny shadows of what horses should be. Their guns were battered and marked with rust, and their officers, as shabby and exhausted as their men, rode on coolie-pulled wheelbarrows or in litters, carrying umbrellas against the sunshine. As they disappeared, the first of the Canton army appeared.

*

Dicken was the first man to see them. He was piloting an old DH9a powered with a Liberty engine, which had been built to do a hundred hours flying but had already completed four times that amount and was still going strong. The British admiral in command had begun to send aircraft up to the fortified areas where the fighting was taking place to find out what was going on and, climbing from the airfield, Dicken found himself crossing a level plain of white cloud, sparkling in the sunshine like new snow, all ivory towers and empurpled valleys crossed by rainbows, with here and there gaps through which he could see the darker tints of the earth. The light was dazzling and for the hundredth time he marvelled that he was held there in space, lifted into the bright blue bowl of the sky merely by the wood and canvas of the wings and the power of the engine.

Below him China looked like a jigsaw of different coloured pieces, an antique land marked by the living of the generations of its people; never improving, never varying, no matter what happened; its people, their sinewy backs bent, their faces reflecting their endless patience, their minute plots washed away by floods, their families destroyed by famine, their homes, their work, their very lives crumbled by the plagues and the wars that passed over them, always on the verge of starvation but always surviving to rebuild and start again.

He was still caught by his thoughts, touched by the never-ending humility and strength of the Chinese peasantry, when to the south he spotted an unexpected movement. Turning towards it, the sun glinting on his wings as he banked, he saw a column of troops, led by officers on small shaggy ponies and followed by a string of guns and heavily laden ox-carts. Going down low, he swept along the column. The troops looked efficient, well-clad in green uniforms and, unlike the Peking troops, not festooned with teapots, umbrellas and cooking utensils. Then he saw that they carried the red Kuomintang banners with the white sun insignia on blue squares in the corners. They all looked young and he noticed that, again unlike the Peking troops, they didn't scatter into the fields or stop to gape up at the aeroplane, chattering and excited, but went on marching stolidly northwards, their heads down, their backs bent under their loads, unmoved by his presence and the threat the aeroplane implied.

They arrived outside the city two days later, confident and fit and without the habitual kow-tow the Chinese had always given to Europeans. But there were no incidents, not even when they tried to enter the International Settlement and were firmly turned back by grim-faced soldiers determined not to budge an inch.

That night, however, when Dicken appeared at Joyce Mahaffy's flat he found her nervous and worried because it was close to the boundary of the International Settlement.

'They've arrived,' she said.

'Yes,' Dicken agreed. 'I saw them.'

'What did they look like?'

'Like soldiers.'

'There've been rumours that they rape the women.'

They ate out and returned to the flat on the excuse that she was nervous and preferred to drink coffee at home. But they were in her bed within half an hour and, as he lay beside her sleeping figure, Dicken tried to weigh himself up. He felt no conscience about what he was doing. If Zoë had been behaving herself, he might have felt guilty but he knew she wasn't. He still hadn't heard from her and suspected she was taking the attitude that if she didn't think about the problem it would go away of its own accord. The thought saddened him. His own parents' marriage had collapsed while he was a child and he had always hoped to do better. He had even tried hard, but the demands of the service which separated husbands from wives had never really given them a chance, any more than had Zoë's avowed declaration that she did not intend to be anything but liberated.

During the night they were awakened by the sound of firing and Joyce sat bolt upright, clutching the sheets to her throat.

'They're coming,' she said.

'Rubbish,' Dicken said. 'They'd never take on twenty-five thousand European-trained troops. Stay where you are and I'll go and make coffee.'

'I'd rather have a brandy. If they're going to rape me, I'd rather be drunk than sober.'

The following morning, when Dicken reported for duty he learned that the Nationalist troops had broken through the cordon on the north side of the Settlement but had been driven out again at the cost of four British casualties and God alone knew how many Chinese. Soon afterwards, another clash occurred at the station yard at Chapei where there were more Chinese casualties. The Nationalists claimed the trouble was being caused by the Communists, who were committing murders whenever they got the chance, and it was hard to know who to believe, because the Nationalists were reported to have got into the Settlement at Nanking, killing, looting and raping. Six non-Chinese had been killed and others wounded, and British and American destroyers had been obliged to open fire. Eventually the Europeans had been allowed to the waterfront where they were promptly bundled on to the ships.

What had originally seemed nothing more than an anarchical movement by groups of disaffected students had become a campaign of hatred against all Westerners, and the whole of South China seemed to be on the march, each riot starting another one in a chain reaction. Upriver, Western-owned property was being abandoned by its frightened owners without even a backward glance, and the Europeans who had so demanded the respect of the Chinese that they had put up notices in their public parks, 'No dogs or Chinese permitted,' were now feeling the backlash of their contempt. Forced from their businesses and homes, obliged to go as refugees to the safer areas of the coast, they were even having to carry in their own hands and on their own backs what few possessions they had left because there were no porters or rickshaw men who would work for them. Huddled in groups for safety, daily growing dirtier and shabbier because their Chinese servants, intimidated by threats, no longer dared appear, they struggled to where the ships awaited them, thankful for the power and prestige of the Royal Navy which was all that enabled them to escape with their lives. They had long since forgotten how to look after themselves, and were arriving in Shanghai in shiploads, hungry, exhausted, frightened and shocked by the change in their circumstances – Europeans, Americans, Japanese, even wealthy Chinese who had made the mistake of doing business with Western-owned companies.

Shanghai noticed the change brought about by the arrival of the Cantonese army in a different way. Almost from the day the Cantonese troops arrived, the city began to step up its night life for them in a manner that would have set the early emperors spinning in their tombs. The South China troops had been in the wilderness too long, on the march through a succession of small towns and empty spaces, and they were looking for excitement and a little gaiety and, with the owners of the night clubs mostly opportunistic young Chinese, the Cantonese officers were soon crowding the foreigners from what they had always considered their own dance floors. And since, as Chinese, they naturally wanted Chinese dancing partners, a group of smart operators speedily filled the gap and plastered Shanghai with a rash of new and garish night clubs which provided Chinese hostesses in place of the White Russians and the French. Girls were rushed up from the south and, keeping up with the trend, Chinese dancing academies sprang up all over the city and sing-song girls hurriedly converted to taxi-dancers while opium smokers opted for the new drug, jazz. The only concession that was made was to the music because it was impossible to train Chinese musicians for waltzes, foxtrots and tangos, while Chinese singers trying to handle 'Charmaine,'

'There Ain't No Maybe In My Baby's Eyes' or other such delights from the West sounded like cats with their heads caught in railings, and orchestras and singers had to be imported from Manila and eventually from San Francisco, Chicago and New York.

Hounded out of their own playgrounds, the Europeans fell back on those night clubs which operated a colour bar and used only Russian or Eurasian hostesses, and Father O'Buhilly, never on the side of the local Whites, crowed that the country was being won for the Chinese by the night club orchestras. He was being optimistic, however, and he knew it, because the clash between the Nationalists and the Communists was bound to come eventually, and when it did no one knew how it would affect Shanghai.

In fact, when it came it was easier than they had expected. With the arrival of the Cantonese troops and the rash of new night clubs, gangsters had moved in and begun to take over. With smuggling, piracy, drug rackets and slavery already being practised, there was no shortage of experts and they began to move round the night clubs demanding food, girls and drink without expecting to pay for them. Behind the small operators were the powerful men who could close any night club they wanted and sometimes did – once with a boxful of snakes let loose on the dance floor while the lights were dimmed for a waltz.

Since Chiang Kai-Shek had no intention of starting hostilities with the Communists for control, instead he left the business to the powerful gang leaders, and their private army of gunmen moved into Chapei and Natao and killed the revolt against the Kuomintang by the Communists within twenty-four hours.

At the height of the disturbances, Father O'Buhilly announced that he was going to Chapei.

'Are you wanting to commit suicide?' Dicken asked.

Father O'Buhilly lit a cigarette. 'There are French nuns and Christian children there, me boy. Somebody has to see them out.'

He was gone for two days but eventually returned with the nuns and the children, every one of them dirty and exhausted but all unharmed. One by one the fires in the disputed districts died down and the reports that filtered into the International Settlement were hard to believe. In a series of grim, bloody, no-quarter fights, the Communists had been swept out of the city. The reprisals, though they had brought no European casualties, had caused a lot of damage and a great deal more bitterness. The authorities, worried by the possibility of more clashes, were anxious to know where the Communists had gone to, and it was finally learned they had been collected together by a former teacher called Mao Tse-Tung and were heading north towards Kiangsi to gather strength to hit back.

More troops arrived, to be quartered on the racecourse and in godowns, even in Chinese amusement centres. For this the Shanghai residents paid nothing other than for the upkeep of their own Volunteer Forces, which had companies of all nationalities, the American contingent wearing British uniforms and cowboy hats, the Russians parading with their greatcoats rolled and slung across their bodies in the manner of the Tsarist armies, the Chinese largely bespectacled clerks who took their soldiering so seriously they won all the inter-unit competitions.

There was an increase of violent crime with armed gangs attacking both police and civilians even in daylight, so that heads and severed limbs were often found in empty places and on recreation grounds. Then a DH9, flying from the racecourse, had to make a forced landing at Kiangwan outside the perimeter and the party sent out to retrieve it came back only with the engine and the fuselage, dragging it along on its wheels without the wings or the crew. In retaliation the Shanghai-Hangchow-Ningpo Railway line was cut and, since this affected the Nationalists' lines of communication, both the airmen and the wings were promptly released.

Late in the year the Communist Russian Embassy was attacked by White Russians and the trains stopped again as armed agitators forced the drivers to go on strike, and finally, a Roman Catholic mission at Yingjao was attacked by Nationalists and Father O'Buhilly, who had already been awarded an immediate Croix de Guerre for rescuing the French nuns, offered his help.

Dicken found him in his study, dressed in a black alpaca suit, a black clerical hat on the back of his head. He had the usual cigarette between his lips and was reading the poems of Robert W. Service.

"'Tis wonderful stuff for the spirit,' he observed quietly.

'This chap General Lee Tse-Liu, who's got these people, is a nasty piece of work, Father,' Dicken pointed out.

'It's what I've heard, me boy.'

'His father was wealthy and he was a student at one of the big universities in England when the war started in 1914. He was violently pro-British in those days and even tried to join the British army. Orr knows all about him. Some clot with red tabs and a loud voice told him they didn't want wogs in British regiments. When he finished his studies he came home, swearing to chuck the British out of China.'

'Sure, so I understand. There are many stupid people in this world.'

Dicken paused. 'Mind if I come with you to the gate, Father?' he asked.

'Why, no, me boy. I'd even like it. Why, though?'

'I don't know, Father.' Dicken was at a bit of a loss. Joyce Mahaffy had been to visit her brother in Hong Kong and was still on her way back, and he was growing tired of the rising tide of complaints from people who had so far suffered nothing from the civil war except inconvenience. 'Perhaps I'm a bit disillusioned.'

'It's no thing for a young man to be,' Father O'Buhilly smiled.

'Were you never disillusioned, Father?'

'Oh, sure, boy.' The priest gestured with his cigarette. 'Often. But it's like measles: it's something you grow out of as you grow older. Sure, you go on questionin' but disillusionment's a thing no man with faith suffers because, o' course, there's always the final reward of Heaven and a place at the Almighty's side. Maybe you should join us, my son.'

Dicken rode with him to the border of the settlement and shook hands as the car stopped at the barbed wire barrier. He wasn't sure what it was that drew him to the priest. Perhaps it was his simple faith. To O'Buhilly black was black and white was white and there were no greys. He had never discussed Zoë with him but he had a feeling the priest, while trying to understand her, would be unable to make allowances for her.

107

The guardpost was built of sandbags and manned by British soldiers and Sikh policemen. Beyond it there was a crowd of noisy students, most of them mere children, among them a few coolies carrying bamboo staves.

'You sure you're going to be all right, Father?' Dicken asked.

'Oh, sure. Look at the soldierly straightness of the troops, me boy. I'll be all right.'

As Father O'Buhilly indicated his readiness to proceed, there was a shouted order and the soldiers fixed bayonets and lifted their rifles. At once the crowd vanished down alleys knee-deep in rubbish and torn paper.

'I have a bottle of Irish whiskey in me cupboard at the Mission.' Father O'Buhilly grinned at Dicken. 'We'll share it, when I come back.' He paused. '*If* I come back, because this time 'tis a touch further than Chapei.'

They shook hands then the priest lit a cigarette and climbed back into the car which drove off into the darkness. As he stood watching the tail light disappear, Dicken heard the distant crackle of musketry.

'Cross all disengaged fingers,' he muttered to himself. 'And hope for the best.'

Everywhere outside the International Settlement the Kuomintang banners flapped against the walls and windows and upriver outrages persisted against Europeans, directed mostly at the missionaries who had been trying to convert the Chinese to Christianity. In Shanghai, however, the situation seemed to have quietened down and from time to time when off duty, Dicken took a rickshaw to the Louza district and called on Father O'Buhilly's mission. Nothing had been heard of him until finally it was learned that the nuns he'd gone to rescue had been released and had made their way to the coast near Fenghsian, and Dicken took off to pinpoint their position so that a gunboat could move in and lift them off.

He found them without difficulty. Clustered on the shore, they looked dirty and ragged and, circling while his observer sent a wireless message, he was able to see a whaler heading shorewards before he was obliged to turn south. The nuns reappeared in Shanghai the following day, overcome by heat, exhausted, shocked and dirty, with sickening tales of their humiliations under General Lee.

They also brought a story that Father O'Buhilly had been taken prisoner but had been turned loose near the town of Yatien, where General Lee had his yamen. The last they knew of him was that he intended to aim for the flat land near Wuhsi where he hoped to be picked up by an RAF machine.

'I'd like to have a go at finding him,' Dicken said,

'He seems to be worth it,' Orr agreed.

They didn't bother to acquaint Air Headquarters with their plan but somehow they found out and Diplock appeared, plump, pink and self-important, to say that the Air Officer Commanding absolutely forbade the attempt.

'The man's American,' he insisted. 'It's not our affair. It's the Americans who should be providing the rescue attempt.'

'The Americans don't have any aircraft here,' Orr snapped. 'And by the time the AOC decides to do something, General Lee will have changed his mind and the damned man will have been recaptured and probably murdered!'

'I'm sorry but the AOC insists. Yatien's outside Concession territory.'

Orr glared. 'Have you ever been a prisoner of a Chinese warlord?' he demanded. 'Well, for your information, neither have I. But I *was* forced down on the North-West frontier two years ago and held prisoner for a month and I didn't enjoy it. The machine goes.'

Diplock glanced at Dicken almost as if he were seeking an ally. 'The AOC will want to know why if the attempt fails,' he muttered. 'We have no authority over the area.'

'We'll worry about it *if* it fails,' Orr growled. 'I'd rather be kicked out of the service for trying than get promotion for sitting on my arse doing nothing. You can tell the AOC that. From me.'

*

With the rear cockpit of the DH9 ballasted with sandbags, Dicken took off the following morning. The land near Wuhsi was well away from the rice paddies by the river and was flat and hard and provided a good landing area and, picking up Yatien, he circled slowly at a few hundred feet, his eyes on the ground. Suddenly he spotted a man in a black suit wearing a clerical hat waving his arms in the middle of the field. Sideslipping in, he touched down without trouble and saw the man in black begin to run towards him.

As the machine rolled to a stop, he swung it round and headed down the field to turn into the wind. Several figures had appeared from a group of trees on his left and he saw that the man in black was running faster. He looked strangely smaller than Father O'Buhilly but it was impossible to see his face under the clerical hat.

Over the low rumble of the engine, he heard feet pounding on the hard earth and, looking round, he saw that the figures who had appeared from the trees were soldiers, Chinese in khaki cotton uniforms. The man in black was coming up behind him, obscured from view by the tail surfaces and, occupied with preparations for a quick take-off, he reached over with his hand to indicate exactly where he should put his feet to climb aboard.

There was the scrape of a foot on the wing root and Dicken looked up and round, just as the wind from the turning propeller caught the clerical hat and whisked it away. He just had time to be aware that the wearer was a Chinese when something heavy hit him on the head and he was vaguely conscious of an arm reaching past him to switch off the DH9's engine.

3

Sitting in the corner of the field, holding his head, Dicken watched the Chinese soldiers lift the tail of the De Havilland and pull it round. He was circled by men holding pointed rifles, all of them obviously eager to be the first to pull the trigger.

The man who had appeared behind him had divested himself of the black alpaca suit now and was wearing the khaki cotton uniform and baggy trousers of a Chinese officer. He was only young but his face was hard, his eyes black as boot buttons.

'Please don't attempt to move, sir,' he said in good if stilted English. 'Or, my goodness gracious me, I shall be obliged to order my men to shoot you dead.' He smiled. 'You must be jolly unhappy,' he went on. 'Because I have you a prisoner and a hostage and I also have a brand-new aeroplane to add to our air force. My name, by the way, is General Lee Tse-Liu, and I shall probably win a medal for this. It is a good job that I once had a flight in England when I was there as a student and knew how to switch off the engine.'

He smiled. 'I shall send to General Chiang for a pilot to come and take it away,' he went on. 'It may take some days but it will give you plenty of time to stare at the twigs and branches camouflaging your splendid aeroplane and to think how sad you will be to lose it.'

'You've got another guess coming,' Dicken growled. 'The RAF will be out looking for me.'

Lee smiled. 'What a pity they will be unable to find you.'

Satisfied that the aeroplane was safely secured to stakes in the ground and covered by foliage from the trees around, he gestured to Dicken to rise and they set off across the field towards the road.

'When I was in England during the war,' Lee said, 'I was

called a wog by a fat man with a khaki suit. But, my goodness me, I am not a wog. I am a Chinese of good breeding and we shall see, I think, what the West thinks of us before very long.'

Dicken was pushed into an elderly Crossley tender, its bonnet red with rust, its canvas hood missing, and they drove through the nearby town. The place stank of incense and was noisy with the hawking and spitting of the inhabitants – what was known to Europeans as the Chinese National Anthem. People sitting in doorways eating coloured sweets, spitting out sunflower seeds or having their ears cleaned by professional aurists, pushed forward to see. Camels and sorebacked mules plodded through the crowded pedestrians, picking their way round heaps of dirt where babies, dogs and scavenging pigs wallowed together. A group of soldiers, slovenly with their festoons of teapots, saucepans and umbrellas, watched from a doorway where they were guarding a group of criminals tied together by their pigtails. Old ivoried men with long whispy white beards and peasants carrying aged relatives on their shoulders all stopped to stare at the European face in the car.

Leaving the town, they pushed out into the countryside beyond, rattling along a road through a plain set with rice and maize and broken with paddies smelling strongly of human manure. Here and there a wooden pump was rotated by blindfolded donkeys or sinewy coolies on treadmills, and from time to time tombs could be seen among the pines with small poverty-stricken farms.

The village of Wuhsi was a place of one-storey buildings with curved tiled roofs. A gutter ran down the centre and rubbish was piled against the walls, and there was a smell of decaying vegetation, ammonia and something else that was probably the odour of unwashed bodies. There was little sound, none of the tinkling of Chinese voices, the honking of cars or the cheerful shouting of the wheelbarrow men. The people here seemed subdued and wary and watched with black blank eyes.

Removing a bar from the door of one of the hovels, Lee kicked it open and a hand shoved Dicken through. As he fell to his knees, the alpaca suit Lee had worn hit him in the face, then he heard the door slam and the bar replaced.

A hand caught his elbow and raised him gently. 'I very much

regret, me boy,' a soft Irish voice said, 'that you should find yourself in this predicament because of me.'

Sitting up, Dicken found himself staring at Father O'Buhilly. He was dressed only in a shirt with a clerical collar, his long bare legs ending in huge laced boots.

'You all right, Father?' he asked, scrambling to his feet.

'Sure, I'm all right, my son. But gasping for a cigarette. I've finished all mine long since. You wouldn't have one about you, would you?'

Fishing in his pockets, Dicken produced a packet. He was about to offer them when he changed his mind, took one out, lit it, drew a deep puff at it and handed it to the priest. 'I think we'd better smoke half each,' he suggested. 'I haven't many and we don't know how long we're going to be here.'

O'Buhilly took the cigarette, drew one or two deep puffs from it, so deep the smoke seemed in danger of coming out of his ears, and handed it back.

''Tis a wonderful thing, the weed,' he said, coughing. 'I'm sorry you're in this mess, me boy. I'm to blame. Sure, they took me clothes while I was asleep, which is why you find me in fancy dress.'

Puffing at the cigarette alternatively, they exchanged questions as Father O'Buhilly dragged on his trousers and reached for his jacket.

'How long have you been here?'

'Six days.' The priest's face was bruised but he managed a smile.

'Did they beat you up?'

'But of course, me boy. They'll probably beat *you* up. Not so much to hurt you as to humiliate you, to make you lose face.'

As they talked, the door opened and wooden bowls of rice and a jug of water appeared. Lee stood behind the man who carried them.

'Kneel,' he ordered. 'Say please.'

'Not bloody likely,' Dicken snapped.

Father O'Buhilly smiled, took his hand, and, with a surprisingly strong grip, pulled him down alongside him as he knelt. Dicken was about to scramble to his feet but the priest clung on to his hand and held him firmly on his knees. As the food was placed on the floor and the door slammed, Dicken scrambled to his feet.

'Damn it, Father,' he said, 'I'm a British officer! I don't go down on my knees to people!'

'You do here, me boy, or you'll go hungry. I've discovered hunger's a wonderful persuader and, sure, nobody'll ever know.'

'It's so bloody humiliating!'

'Loss of face exists only in the mind, me boy, and if you feel you're their master, it is no humiliation at all.'

'It's all right for you –!'

'It is also all right for you, my son. You are no good to your country if you are dead, and while you're alive to pray to the Almighty for rescue there's hope. The Via Crucis is a long one and was never intended to be easy. Besides – ' Father O'Buhilly smiled – 'there's no sense I see in unnecessary suffering. I saw the Calvary in France ten years ago and I have too much to do, me boy, to be ready to die merely to please an egoist like Lee. Besides – ' he smiled '– I have plans of me own that he doesn't know about.' He indicated the window which was covered by a grille. ''Tis typical Orientals they are. Inefficient and careless. And these houses are old. This was once a village jail here, but doubtless it hasn't been used since Kwang-Hsü was Emperor. The bars are loose and I have found a piece of iron under the soil I use as a chisel.'

Dicken's head jerked round. 'They're loose?'

'Keep your voice down, me boy.' The priest's voice was gentle and monotonous, almost as if he were praying. 'I've been workin' on them. We shall get out of here when we wish, and walk home to Shanghai.'

Dicken stared out of the window, thinking of the grounded aeroplane. 'Much better to fly back,' he said. 'Safer.'

'Then we'll have to hurry, me boy,' O'Buhilly said. 'Lee's Chinese pilot will be here soon to take it away. There are plenty of them, I gather, trained by the Russians and Germans. It should take another day or two to get free but it will take longer than that for Lee to find himself a pilot.'

*

The next days were spent sweating in the humid heat in the narrow-gutted little prison. Several times, they heard aircraft and once saw a DH9 flying about a thousand feet above them on a north-south course. It was close enough to see the roundels on the wings and fuselage, but nothing came of it and they could only assume that the camouflaged machine hadn't been seen. Eventually, they became aware of shouts and the capering of excited coolies and, looking out, they saw a lorry towing Dicken's captured DH9 along the road to the field alongside their prison. Then it dawned on them that, because they had no idea how to detach the wings, the Chinese soldiers were chopping down any tree that was in the way and prevented it passing. As it turned towards the field, it proved impossible to manoeuvre it by the tumbledown home of a peasant farmer and immediately the soldiers started knocking the house down. When the farmer, dancing with rage, began to shout his protests, the officer in command simply drew his revolver and shot him, then the house was razed and the aeroplane bumped into the field past the wailing wife and family.

'Pray to St Jude, me boy,' Father O'Buhilly growled, as they watched through the window. 'He is the patron saint of lost causes and, Holy Mother of God, it is surely needing his help the Chinese peasants are.'

When Lee came again it pleased him to see Dicken go on his knees with the priest and thank him for the bowl of rice he was given to eat.

'I am glad you have jolly well changed your attitude,' he said cheerfully. 'For your entertainment, this afternoon we have arranged a little spectacle.'

The spectacle turned out to be the execution of several captured Communists, who were forced to kneel outside the window of the jail.

'No parties *outside* the Kuomintang,' Lee said. 'No factions *inside* the Kuomintang. That is our leader's slogan. As our friends out there will soon find out.'

The kneeling men were dispatched one by one, the peasants by shooting in the back of the head, the officials by strangling or beheading by a brawny headsman carrying a huge curved sword. Held to the window by bayonets pricking their backs, Dicken and Father O'Buhilly were obliged to watch every minute of it. Dicken was shaking with rage but the priest quietly muttered prayers to himself from beginning to end.

'Sure, if the poor heathens are anything at all they'll be Taoists,' he said, 'But I don't think the Almighty will mind a Catholic prayer being offered for their souls.'

Wailing women collected the bodies. Those who had bribed the guards were allowed to have the heads which they then sewed back on to the severed necks so that their menfolk could go to their ancestors without losing face. Those who could not afford the bribes or had refused to pay found the heads were hung from poles with cords pushed through a slit in the ears. Nevertheless, Lee allowed the funerals to take place and there was a procession of lanterns and gongs, and Lee provided a mockery of a military band which played *John Brown's Body* in front of the wreaths and effigies of horsemen and favourite pets, while the local orchestra of hired musicians blew sobs from long intruments like huge garden syringes.

That night Dicken worked all the harder with the scrap of metal Father O'Buhilly had found, digging at the crumbling plaster round the base of the bars in the window. In between, when they rested, he found himself discussing religion.

He had never been a religious man and had always regarded God as a sort of benevolent commanding officer but, falling in love with Nicola Aubrey, listening to her talk about her Catholicism, had made him think about it because she had often worried what would happen to her if she married a Protestant. The priest listened carefully, nodding and saying little.

Then Dicken lit a cigarette, took a puff and handed it to the American. 'How does one become a Catholic, Father?' he asked.

Father O'Buhilly smiled and returned the question with another. 'Are you a good Protestant, me boy?' he asked.

'I try to be, though I reckon I've not always been successful. I seem to have been too busy.'

Father O'Buhilly smiled as he took his turn again with the cigarette. 'Then the first thing to do, me boy, is to become a good Protestant. When I first came east, I, too, had doubts and I once asked a Taoist priest how to become a Taoist. He advised me first to become a good Christian.'

Dicken smiled back. 'Does your religion allow you to escape, Father?' he asked.

'Most certainly.'

'With a Protestant?'

'God's more broadminded than most people give Him credit for, my son. Contrary to what many think, provided you've been a good man – and I'm thinkin' you have – he'd even allow you into the Kingdom of Heaven, whether you've been a Catholic or not, a good churchgoer or not. He couldn't possibly raise any objection to me goin' with you.'

Dicken grinned as he took his turn with the cigarette. 'Even if it meant clocking that sentry over there by the aeroplane? We might have to.'

'Even with that, me boy.'

'How do you reckon He feels about revenge, Father? Because if I bump into Lee again, I might lose my temper.'

'Pride, me boy, is the spring of malice and the desire for revenge. Does your anger spring from pride?'

Dicken grinned and passed over the last of the cigarette. 'No, Father. Just a strong desire to punch him on the nose.'

The priest finished the cigarette and tossed it through the window. 'So long as it is no more than a calm, cold-blooded, non-denominational straight left to the jaw,' he said, 'I feel He would not object.'

4

Two nights later they had the bars loosely held in place in their sockets with mud which they had made by the simple procedure of urinating on the dirt floor. Over it they had sprinkled dust so that it looked like old cement.

'You're quite sure,' Father O'Buhilly asked nervously, 'that it would be unwise to make the journey back to Shanghai on Shanks's pony. I have never flown, y'see, and I have to confess that the idea strains the fastenings of me faith.'

'Listen, Father,' Dicken said quietly. 'It's a waste of time trying to walk from here to Shanghai. We must be a hundred or so miles away and Lee will get his men out as soon as he finds we're gone. They'll have horses and cars and I doubt if we could shelter with the local people. Even if they wished to help us, they wouldn't dare in case he comes down on them with reprisals. It's the aeroplane or nothing.'

'We can start it, me boy?'

'I think so. But it'll have to be quick. And that means you've got to learn what to do. I shall dispose of the sentry –'

'We'll discuss that later.'

Dicken grinned. 'When he's disposed of, we chuck his rifle away so he can't grab it if he comes round, then I climb into the cockpit. Your job will be to swing the propeller. But there's a bit of rigmarole to go through before you do that, and you'd better do it properly or you'll get your head whipped off.'

'It would be a most unusual way for a servant of God to go to his Maker, my son.'

'Right, then. You handle the propeller. I hope you're strong because you have to be to swing a DH9. When I'm in the cockpit and I've checked the controls, I'll stick my thumb up. Like this. Then you call out "Switch off. Petrol On. Suck In," and turn the propeller to get rid of excess petrol, leaving it horizontal. Then wipe your hands – spit on 'em if you like for good measure – scrape your boots on the ground a bit to make sure you've got a good foothold, then lean well forward, with your hands on the blade of the propeller and try your balance. Like this.'

Demonstrating, he waited until Father O'Buhilly had understood. 'All this is a safety measure,' he explained. 'So that when you're fiddling about with the propeller, I don't allow the engine to fire and whip your block off. Understood?'

Father O'Buhilly nodded. 'It is terrible dangerous by the sound of it.'

'Not if you do as I suggest. Right, then, when you're ready, you call out "Contact". That's to let me know *you're* ready and I can switch on. That's when I switch on the magnetos and the engine's ready to fire. Right? I reply "Contact" to let you know I've heard, and then, and not until you hear that word, you heave down and away on the propeller, leaning back as you do so, so that you're out of the line of the blades. Think you can do it?'

'Perhaps a little rehearsal will do no harm.'

'It might not fire straight away, of course.'

'And if it doesn't fire at all?'

'In *that* case we shall be Lee's guest for a lot longer, because it looks very much as though nobody's going to stage a rescue for us.'

*

They decided to go the following night when there would be a slight moon to enable them to see.

'We're going to be taking off in the dark, Father,' Dicken pointed out. 'I'm going to be doing it by the seat of my pants.'

'And I, me boy, will be in the other seat with my eyes tight shut prayin' to the Almighty to make the seat of your pants a good guide to the two sinners who're dependin' on 'em.'

They had rehearsed the rigmarole of starting the engine until Father O'Buhilly had it perfectly, then Dicken had drawn marks on the dirt floor of the cell to indicate exactly where the mounting slots were in the fuselage to enable him to climb quickly into the rear cockpit when the engine was running.

'But not,' he explained, 'before you've yanked the chocks away from the wheels. Those are the triangular wooden blocks which stop the machine moving forward when the engine's running. If you forget them, we might have trouble. Chocks first, then the cockpit.'

The priest nodded. 'I have it, me boy.' He tapped his head. 'Up here. 'Tis full o' nothing else so there's plenty of room.'

'Once you're in the cockpit,' Dicken said. 'You'll find you're probably standing on sandbags. They were for ballast, to trim the machine on the way up here in place of a man, and if they haven't been removed, get rid of them. Toss 'em over the side. But try to do it before we start moving fast. We don't want 'em bouncing off the tail surface. There's no gun to get in your way. Which is a pity,' he went on, 'because we might have put a burst or two into Lee's precious yamen as we left. Can you work a gun?'

Father O'Buhilly smiled. 'I worked one often in the Argonne, me boy, but I would imagine the Almighty might frown on that sort of revenge. So perhaps it is as well we haven't one. Since we finished the last cigarette. I've been harbourin' thoughts in me mind that don't become a servant of God.'

*

The following afternoon, another DH9, bearing Chiang's sunburst markings on the wings, landed and stopped outside the cell with its engine throbbing. A man climbed out of the rear cockpit and headed for Dicken's machine. Climbing into the cockpit, he sat there checking the controls, while the pilot of the new machine worked the propeller. As the engine roared to life, the chocks were hauled away and the machine rolled forward.

With grim faces, Dicken and Father O'Buhilly watched it lift into the air at the end of its run and begin its climb away to the hills.

'Well, that seems to be that,' Dicken said. 'It looks like being Shanks's pony after all.'

When the rice appeared that evening, Lee brought the pilot of the Chiang DH with him.

'I say,' he said. 'This is Captain Hsu. He learned to fly in America. He has come to thank you for the gift of your so splendid aeroplane to his squadron. It is now beyond your reach.'

Hsu was a lean good-looking Chinese who spoke English with an American accent. He wore smartly-cut breeches, a short leather flying jacket and a white silk scarf, with ribbons attached to the top of his flying cap in the manner of the pilots in the American pulp magazines.

As the bowls of rice were placed on the floor, Lee gestured. 'When Captain Hsu goes tomorrow, we shall withdraw northwards. You'll go with us as hostages for our safety. We shall be celebrating our new aircraft tonight with rice wine.'

*

The sun went down in a lemon yellow sky and they could hear a lot of laughter from the big house with the curved eaves where Lee had his headquarters. Dicken was staring through the bars of the cell window at Hsu's DH9. It was a new aircraft but its mechanics had not cared for it and there were streaks of oil along the engine.

'What are ye thinkin', me boy?' O'Buhilly asked. 'Now the aeroplane's gone?'

Dicken was silent for a long time. 'That there's another one, Father,' he said. '*That* one.'

'What are you gettin' at, me boy?'

'Why don't we take it in place of the one we've lost?'

'Y'have terrible thoughts, me boy. Here I was thinkin' almost the same thing meself.'

Dicken smiled. 'If we took Hsu's machine,' he said, 'it would be a fair exchange. It's even probably newer than the one they've pinched. Unfortunately, there are two sentries there now and I couldn't get one without the other raising the alarm.'

'So what's wrong with me tacklin' the other, me boy?'

'Does your religion permit violence of that sort?'

'I've tried to convince you, me boy, that the Almighty's more broadminded than most people think. I'm sure He wouldn't object, if I do a little prayin' beforehand to let Him know what we're about. So long as I report to the Orderly Room, I think it will be all right.

*

121

When it was dark, they quietly worked at the bars in the window until the crumbling cement in the upper sockets fell away. Quietly removing them, Dicken was about to lay them on the ground when he hefted their weight in his hand, smiling at the priest.

'Father, do you think God would permit you to hit the sentry with one of these? It ought to be enough to keep him quiet for a while without killing him.'

O'Buhilly smiled back. 'I don't think the Almighty would frown on a severe headache,' he said.

'Right. You know what to do. Let's go through it once more. It'll be exactly the same with this machine as mine. Can you do it quickly?'

'Did I not see it, boy? Right there, outside the window. Did not Captain Hsu obligingly go through the whole rigmarole for me within yards of me nose? I already had thoughts in me head of replacing our machine with that one and I gave it the utmost attention just in case your own thoughts were the same as mine. I have it clear in me mind.'

'And the sentry? You can fix him?'

As the priest nodded, Dicken stuck the iron bar in his belt and climbed on to his back to clamber into the window opening. Sitting there, he grasped Father O'Buhilly's hand and hauled him up, before dropping quietly through to the other side. Father O'Buhilly followed him, landing alongside him in the shadows.

Quietly they crept on to the field until they could see the wide wings of the aeroplane against the sky.

'It's facing the wrong way,' Dicken said. 'When we've polished off the sentries, we'll have to swing it round before we go through the start-up routine.'

Crouching in the long grass close to the sentries, he whispered to the priest. 'You take the nearest. I'll whistle when I'm ready.'

Working to within two or three feet of the sentry, Dicken whistled gently. Almost at once there was an answering whistle and he saw the sentry stiffen. He was staring towards where Father O'Buhilly was crouching as Dicken leapt to his feet and swung the iron bar. There was a grunt and the Chinese crumpled up, his rifle clattering to the ground. Almost at once, he heard a scuffle where the other sentry stood, then a muffled cry and, hurrying across, found the priest struggling with one hand over the man's mouth. As Dicken's arm swung and the man collapsed, Father O'Buhilly's teeth flashed in the faint light caused by the glow of the moon coming over the trees.

'I think the Lord was holding me hand,' he said. 'I didn't hit him hard enough. Heaven be praised for unbelievers like yourself.'

Dicken gestured at the aeroplane and, together they lifted the tail and swung it round. 'Chocks,' he said. 'Otherwise she'll jump forward when the engine starts.'

Pushing the chocks back into place, he climbed into the cockpit, wriggled himself into the seat, checked the controls and looked at the instruments. He could just make out in the faint light what he was doing.

As he stuck up his hand and waved, Father O'Buhilly's face turned towards him. 'Ready?'

'Yes. For God's sake, Father, get on with it!'

'Right, me boy. Switch off. Petrol on. Suck in.'

Dicken repeated the phrases after him and Father O'Buhilly turned the propeller as he'd been told. Then he wiped his hands on his trousers, scraped his boots to make sure of his foothold and leaned forward with his hands resting on the blade.

'Contact,' he said.

The magneto switches clicked.

'Contact! Heave, Father!'

As Father O'Buhilly pulled out and down, the engine coughed to life, seemed in some doubt, then caught and began to roar. The sound was the most exciting thing Dicken had ever heard. Inside the cockpit, his head down, he watched the revolution indicator and the pressure gauge. As he looked up he saw the priest climbing on to the wing.

'Chocks, Father! For God's sake, the chocks!'

'Sorry, me boy! I forgot!'

Scrambling down, the priest reached under the wing for the chocks. In the half-light, Dicken was quite certain he'd be hit by the propeller but he remembered to back away instead of moving forward and a second later he was scrambling on to the fuselage. As the machine began to swing into wind, a screech came from the rear cockpit. 'The sandbags! Where are the sandbags, boy?'

'There aren't any! This one came with a passenger.'

By this time, they could hear men shouting and shots being fired. The first figures emerged from the darkness as Dicken opened the throttle. Slowly, maddeningly slowly, the DH9 began to move forward, rolling across the uneven turf. As it began to pick up speed a man ran out and tried to grab the wing but he was knocked flat on his back as the aeroplane passed over him. A rifle exploded and Dicken heard the whine of the bullet. As he lifted the tail, a few more figures appeared dead ahead, waving their arms, and there were flashes as rifles were fired. Praying none of them would run into the whirling propeller, Dicken lifted the tail and glanced at the air speed indicator, but it was too dark to see it and he had to make a guess. Yanking at the control column, he felt the nose rise and all the figures in front fell away beneath and behind, then they were in the air and, holding the machine close to the ground until he had built up sufficient speed, he hauled on the stick and swept into the air in a steep climbing turn.

5

Joyce Mahaffy welcomed Dicken back with open arms.

'I thought I'd lost you for ever,' she said. 'And I was going to Wei Hai Wei to mope. How about coming with me and making it a holiday? We can celebrate. Can you get away?'

It was easy enough to get leave after being a prisoner and the island was wooded and beautiful with no traffic beyond rickshaws. The hotel was a long wooden bungalow divided into what looked like horse boxes set on a green rise over the harbour, where lights shone from warships anchored on the swaying water. Pomegranates glowed among their spiky leaves and white acacias dripped petals like snowflakes in the fading evening light.

It was an idyllic place to be but Dicken was curiously unsettled. He knew his affair with Joyce Mahaffy was going to produce nothing and he wasn't sorry when the time came to return to Shanghai. As he walked into Orr's office, Orr rose and tossed down a file.

'You're for England,' he announced at once. 'Staff College. The way to the top. A few years from now I'll be saluting you instead of t'other way round. And that's how it should be, because you're young and I'm not.'

Joyce bade him a tearful goodbye, though he suspected the tears were laid on for his special benefit and didn't have a great deal of meaning. She promised she'd follow him home but he doubted if she ever would, and he said a maudlin goodbye to Father O'Buhilly in his stark little room over a bottle of Irish whiskey.

'I don't suppose we shall ever see each other again,' Dicken said.

'Ach, it is most unlikely that we will not,' the priest retorted.

'Two people who met and defeated General Lee, as we did, me boy, are bound to cross each other's paths again before long.'

It was strange to be back in England where the girls had taken to applying a lot of make-up and wearing their skirts higher above their knees. In addition the motor car had been discovered and horse traffic was beginning to show signs of disappearing.

Halfway through the course Dicken received an unexpected letter from Zoë's sister Annys, Diplock's wife, who, it seemed, had followed him home on the next ship. She was concerned about Zoë's business interests. The single small business she'd received under her father's will was now a chain of garages operating along the south coast and was making money hand over fist. The recession that had hit industrial England had barely touched the south and according to Annys, the manager Zoë had appointed was suspected of fiddling the books.

He turned out to be an ex-captain of the RASC, called George Peasegood, smooth-tongued, sleek haired, and given to wearing yellow spats, and as he talked to Dicken it was obvious he was being very careful what he had to say. It didn't take Dicken long to decide he was indeed helping himself to the profits and he wrote his views at length to be forwarded to Zoë when he managed to find her.

Towards the end of the staff course it was announced that it was routine for students to spend a few weeks with the air force of a foreign country. Hatto, on the same course, suggested they plump for America.

'Most people go for Europe,' he said. 'Because it's nearer and cheaper, but the States shows more imagination and initiative. Nobody's ever asked for it before.'

Their request was turned down, but the Under-Secretary of State for Air happened to appear the following day and in a speech commented that he couldn't understand why no one ever asked to go to America. Since a wink was as good as a nod, they promptly reapplied, quoting him, and Hatto persuaded his father in the House of Lords to put on a little pressure in the right places, and the Air Ministry changed its mind. A few weeks later they found themselves on the deck of a transatlantic liner staring at the incredible skyline of Manhattan, and the manoeuvres of a small red and white biplane which had met the ship far out of reach of land and had swooped and dived just above the mast and done delirious loops and half-rolls in the bright sky to the surprised delight of the passengers. Its appearance seemed to imply that in America it had long since been decided that there was a future in the air.

It wasn't long since the Atlantic had been flown direct from New York to Paris and everybody was now trying to get in on the act. As long ago as 1919, even before Alcock and Brown had flown the Atlantic, a French-born New York hotelier called Orteig had offered a prize of 25,000 dollars for the first man to achieve the feat, but at that time there were neither the aeroplanes nor the engines fit for ocean flying and experienced airmen had preferred to wait. When Orteig had renewed his offer in 1925, however, aeroplanes had changed. The lines were sleeker, their engines more reliable, and finally a young American airmail pilot called Lindbergh had managed it.

The achievement had not been made without loss of life, however, and six men had died, though it had caused no slackening of enthusiasm and since Lindbergh's feat two other aeroplanes had also made it and flying had burst out in the States like an exotic new flower.

The tall buildings of New York shouldered the stars, while girders, stark against the sky, indicated where new ones were still going up. Somehow the place made Dicken feel he had never been so much alive. The streets were crammed with motor cars – Chevrolets, Franklins, Fords and a dozen other makes he'd never heard of, sedans, limousines, roadsters, coupés, all long and cumbersome and swallowing petrol, all fitted with vast headlights like enormous basins with glowing insides, all thundering and rattling and backfiring so that the area between the towering brick and concrete skyscrapers was hazy with smoke and breath-catching with the smell of burnt fuel. In England, motoring had still barely caught the public imagination and there were still as many horse-drawn carts as petrol-driven lorries, but here in America the craze had swept across the country like a forest fire, filling the streets, changing the whole face of the land, and, with the hurrying pedestrians who crowded the sidewalks, giving an impression of immense wealth, power and urgency. As an American on the ship crossing the Atlantic had said, there was a lot wrong with his country – girls with bobbed hair, painted faces and skirts half-way up their thighs, prohibition with its attendant gangsters, bootleggers and hi-jackers, and corrupt politicians with a finger in a hundred and one pies anxious to make a fast buck – but there was one thing that wasn't wrong and that was business. America was booming.

The tabloids brought the same breathless excitement to the news that was obvious in every pulsing movement of the streets, screaming at the top of their voices the latest vice exposure, the latest disgraced name, the latest disaster – and disasters, exposures and scandals all seemed bigger in America than in Europe FILM STAR'S LOVE NEST RAIDED. RACER CRASHES INTO CROWD. BOOTLEGGER SHOT DEAD IN BAR. It was a land of tremendous vitality whose leisure seemed as urgent as its business, yet from the middle of all the violence that was implicit in the foot-deep headlines, middle-class honesty and labour shone like a beacon from the cramped Vermont features of President Coolidge. From shops, offices and hotels, his photograph directed its disdainful stare on the people he represented, his expression implying a total disagreement with all their habits, their enthusiasms and their excitements, everything they enjoyed, but judging by the undiminished vitality everywhere, apparently unable to do a thing to curb a single one of them.

Dicken and Hatto were received with enthusiasm by the American airmen who immediately made up a party to show them the town. Starting at a restaurant, they produced flasks even as they sat down and calmly poured large tots of bootleg whisky into the glasses on the table. Nobody turned a hair because it was clear everybody else was doing the same.

'You have to learn to live with prohibition,' one of the Americans pointed out.

Later they were taken to a teetotal bar which appeared to be almost empty but, after a quiet word with the barman, they were directed to a blank door where a conspiratorial knock opened it into a smoky room packed with respectable-looking men of all ages rapidly knocking back whisky and gin.

'If you want a bottle of scotch,' one of the Americans said, 'ask the bellhop. He knows where to get it. You can also buy kits in the drug stores to distil gin in the bath but I shouldn't try it.'

You can use it as dope on your airplane.'

They were not needed over the week-end so they decided to try to find Walt Foote, who had served with them in France and Italy. Foote was from Boston and the telephone operator looked up a variety of Footes before finally coming up with a Walter C. Foote, in Chestnut Street, off Bunker Hill.

'Best part of town,' the operator said. 'You want I should call him?'

Dicken's voice was greeted with a yell of delight.

'Jesus, Mae! It's Dick Quinney and Willie Hatto! They're here in America!'

The following day a roadster as long as an ocean liner drew up outside the hotel and Foote, Dicken and Hatto started doing a gloat dance on the steps to the amazement of Foote's wife and two children.

'Meet the Feete,' Foote grinned, waving at them. 'How's Parasol Percy? Anybody strangled him yet?' His face clouded. 'I don't think I'll ever forget that guy,' he said slowly. 'I swear he killed my brother with his goddam orders. It's a long time ago now but he still sticks in my craw.'

He was working in the law department of one of the big American firms doing business in China and was interested to hear that Dicken had just come from there.

'What's it like? They're talking of sending me to Hong Kong. Me and Mae and the whole family. It'd sure make a change from here. What are you doing in the States, anyway?'

'Staff course,' Dicken pointed out. 'It seemed a good opportunity to come to America and dig out my wife. She's over here.'

'Bring her round and meet the folks.'

Dicken frowned. 'I have to find her first,' he said.

'America's a goddam big country.' Foote shrugged. 'But we can try. I've got a little Waco I fly so I'll ask around the airfield. Somebody's bound to know something.'

Their duties with the United States Air Force started the following day when they took a train to the army airfield from where they set out in two Curtiss two-seaters for Washington. Dicken's pilot commented that he'd heard of his exploits during the war and, clearly intending to show him that the United States could produce pilots too, took off in a steep climbing turn that was so near a stall it took Dicken's breath away. Flying along Long Island, he dived boldly over the Bronx and into the centre of Manhattan, skimming along Central Park at a height well below the towering hotels and apartment blocks on either side, then zoomed up to roar over more high blocks of offices to look down on the grid pattern of the city, before descending over the Battery and flying at fifty feet above the waters of Upper Bay towards the Statue of Liberty, circling it so closely it was possible to see the faces of sightseers on the observation platform in the hollow head staring out through the open eyes. Holding his breath, Dicken wondered what would have happened to an RAF officer who had done such a thing over London.

In Washington, they were received by the Chief of the Air Staff who offered transport anywhere they wished to go and the following day they flew to an airfield where an experimental station had been set up with an incredible thing called a wind tunnel, which enabled the engineers to watch the behaviour of air as it passed over the wings of aircraft in flight. From there they flew on to the Naval Air Station at Hampton Roads, then over the Shenandoah Valley to Dayton. Dicken's pilot was more than pleased to allow him to handle the controls.

They were given night flights over Dayton in a Curtiss piloted by an Army Air Corps lieutenant called Doolittle, who held one of the low-numbers in the licences which American pilots now needed to pilot a plane. Short in stature but with the build of an athlete and a ready smile, Doolittle already had a reputation as a daredevil and had been the first man to perform an outside loop. He was an expert instrument flier, however, and, despite his smile, was a serious aeronautical scientist, contemptuous of the old-fashioned seat-of-the-pants fliers who relied on their senses to tell them the altitudes of their machines. He had won the Schneider Trophy races in 1925 and no air race meeting in the States was complete without him.

It was in Detroit that they met Rickenbacker, the American pilot who had been most successful in France. A tall, hawk-faced balding man who had originally been a motor racing driver, he had turned his hand since the war to designing cars and aeroplane engines and had produced one of the first ever small planes with landing flaps and a tail wheel, flying it a distance of 220 miles in two and a half hours on twelve gallons of petrol.

'You could land in a cow pasture,' he claimed, 'fold the wings back, disconnect the propeller and drive it off like a car, because it had a two-speed transmission.'

Like other ex-wartime fliers he had since started an airline flying mail at the rate of three dollars a mile per pound.

'We pushed up the income,' he grinned, 'by sending each other wet blotters, but some of the boys began to grow greedy and sent wrapped house bricks and a postal inspector spotted them.'

Also in Detroit, they visited the factory of Henry Ford, who had recently turned his attention from motoring to flying, and had produced an all-metal tri-motored monoplane popularly known as The Tin Goose. He was dissatisfied with the power plants he was having to fit.

'I'm looking for an engine which will do as much for flying as the four-stroke I put in the Model-T,' he said. 'Something revolutionary. Neat. Simple. Without the untidiness of a propeller.'

'Without a propeller?'

Ford smiled. 'You ever seen a blown-up balloon released by a child?' he asked. 'It flies – a bit erratically, I guess, but it flies – because of the jet of air coming through the neck. With that sort of power, we'd need something better than the Trimotor, but give me the power and I'll produce the airplane. Right now, we fly as quietly and as carefully as we can because folk regard flying as dangerous and it's our policy to get 'em to look on it as safe and normal before we offer 'em something exciting.'

They seemed to see aircraft everywhere – some of them new and of original design – and American enthusiasm showed in the gay colours of the Orioles, Wacos, Swallows and Jennies which gave the impression that there were a great many eager young men trying to wrest a living from them. After the more stolid approach of Britain, it was like a breath of fresh air. In the States, even the law was less demanding – perhaps even a little more dangerous – but the freedom to fly and build was implicit in the very numbers, and the newspapers gave flying sensational publicity, making it sound less technical and more exciting than British newspapers.

American air force pilots were bounding with enthusiasm and professionalism but they longed to have an air force like the RAF, freed from the dead hand of the army, which, they claimed with some heat, was even deader in the States than it was in the United Kingdom. From a purely technical point, the trip was an eye-opener, with engine starters, operable from the cockpits, brakes, and night landing lights, none of which had yet appeared in the Royal Air Force, but the pilots claimed their organisation was hidebound and they were lagging behind in radio direction and operational control.

Back in New York, they tried Foote again. He sounded delighted. 'Got her,' he said at once. 'She's still in Baltimore.'

'What's she doing in Baltimore?'

'She's taking part in the air races there.'

'Zoë?'

'Sure. Everybody who wants to be anybody in flying has to have a go at the races. But that's not all. She's aiming to fly in the Dufee Derby!'

'What the hell's the Dufee Derby?'

'It's a repeat of the Dole Derby.'

'And what the hell was that?'

'A guy called Dole, who was president of the Hawaiian Pineapple Company, offered twenty-five thousand dollars for the first man to cross from North America to Honolulu non-stop. A hell of a lot of people died and there was an uproar in the press. Eventually things quietened down some, and now this guy, Ryan Dufee, has started it all up again. Like Dole, he says it's because he believes Lindbergh's crossing of the Atlantic's the forerunner of transpacific air transportation, but I guess he's also got his eye on free publicity, because he's made it a race by offering ten thousand for the second place. They're due off in August.'

'Zoë couldn't find her way round the other side of a hill, Walt, let alone to Honolulu.'

Foote laughed. 'Hell, man, she's not flying alone!'

'She's not?'

'Hell, no! There's a guy flying with her. He built the plane and he's got a lot of experience. Guy called Casey Harmer.'

6

So Casey Harmer had come back into Zoë's life.

It explained her long silences and her eagerness to get back to the States. Casey Harmer had first appeared in England from Canada about 1917 and after the war, Zoë had shot off to Canada as if the hounds of hell were after her in search of the job he'd promised – perhaps also Harmer himself. Now, after nine years, he appeared to be back in circulation.

A bundle of aviation magazines arrived the following morning from Foote. They included articles on women pilots and there was more than one on Zoë alone, together with photographs, invariably depicting her leaning on a wing strut or against a propeller, wearing a flying helmet and the bug-eyed goggles that were so popular. Her normal dress appeared to be jodpurs or white overalls and her name was mentioned in the same breath with Amelia Earhart, Anne Morrow Lindbergh, Thea Rasche and Ruth Elder, though always it seemed, tagging a little behind the others. Male aviation seemed almost lost in the publicity.

Needing to know more about her, Dicken began to enquire round the hangars. The response was predictable.

'Hell,' one pilot said with a grin, 'that one sure is a looker.'

It seemed to be time to look her up and Dicken started making plans to go to the Baltimore air races. There were two clear weeks at the end of the course when they were free to do as they wished and as Hatto had disappeared to Washington to visit his Foreign Office brother who was at that moment with the Embassy there, Dicken persuaded Doolittle to fly him down.

As they landed, in one corner of the airfield as part of the ballyhoo, an air display was taking place and several elderly machines stood in a flag-enclosed area. A man in a straw hat and yellow boots was collecting entrance money near a notice, 'Hank Rabat will positively stand upright without support on the top wing of an aeroplane.'

A machine was just climbing over the end of the field and a patch of undoped fabric rippled in the slipstream. One wingtip looked like a bandaged thumb, and there were several tears in the fabric of the fuselage that had been crudely sewn up, but the pilot wore the usual tight-fitting helmet with fluttering ribbons, and big bug-eyed goggles.

'This is why I spend so much time with the science of the game,' Doolittle explained. 'Rabat loops a Ford Trimotor, though what the hell good *that* does, I don't know. These guys are on their way out. Flying's becoming respectable since they issued licences and they're finding it harder every year now the government's watching. An inspection would finish most of 'em, I guess.'

A band, flat straw boaters on the backs of their heads, their jackets discarded to show red, white and blue sleeve bands, were thumping out a tune and a few people in flivvers were watching, nervously expectant, chewing at chicken legs and cold fried chops and scattering their newspapers and wrappings to the breeze.

'Eventually, I guess,' Doolittle said dryly, 'somebody'll change planes, wing to wing, and if they miss and fall nobody'll give a damn. These guys aren't aviators; they're trapeze artists. Tomorrow, there'll probably be six-inch headlines in the papers, "Plane Plows Into Crowd. Six Dead." That sort of thing.'

With almost thirty events, the programme included several cross-country races terminating over the field, and a woman pilots' race round a course marked by three pylons. Somewhere near the finish Dicken had a feeling he would find Zoë.

As he searched for her, to his surprise, he bumped into Udet, a little fatter than before, a little balder, but smiling as always and clutching a bouquet of flowers.

'Udlinger!'

'Dicken Quinney!'

'What are you doing here?'

'Stunts.' Udet grinned, led the way into a shabby office where his flying gear was piled on a chair and dragged out a flask. 'You must come and visit me in Berlin,' he said as he filled glasses. 'The Tauentzienstrasse isn't as good as the Place Pigalle in Paris but Berlin's always good for entertainment.'

'I'd like to see Lo again.'

Udet gave him a sad smile. 'That is over,' he admitted. 'It vas my fault, I think. Someone once asked her why she left me. She said "*I* left *him*? You don't know what you're talking about. I couldn't ever keep up with him." I am here because in Germany things have changed. All is too much political. It iss bad now. I am glad to get avay.'

Underneath his smiles there seemed to be a worry at the way Germany was heading and he had nothing but scorn for her rulers. Assassination, it seemed, was the order of the day and the political parties contained every creed imaginable, while an ex-Serviceman's party known as the Stahlhelm, largely ex-officers and NCOs, could not forget that they had been chased through the streets after the defeat in 1918 and had their epaulettes torn from their shoulders by the parties of the extreme Left.

'The German people long for a leader,' Udet said, refilling the glasses. '*Any* leader. But they don't know who, because there's nobody who's an obvious choice.'

He made no bones about the fact that German airmen were being trained in secret under a variety of disguises – and had been for years – on the banks of the Voronezh in Russia.

'And, of course, we are building aeroplanes,' he admitted.

The army, he explained, had provided the pretext for a large scale provision of funds by German industrialists: With the French army occupying the Ruhr and clearly not intending to leave, they had said that the only way for Germany to regain its industrial strength was to *drive* them out, and the industrialists, realising what the prizes could be, had found the money. Fokker aircraft – ironically powered by British Napier Lion engines – had been acquired from Holland, and young Germans in civilian clothes were being sent off with forged passports to learn to fly them. For the look of the thing, Russian machines were dispersed about the airfield and Russian soldiers provided the guards.

'But everything comes from Germany,' Udet continued. 'Shipped from Stettin to Leningrad. The machines are in crates, and bombs are smuggled across the Baltic in small boats. Vhen there are accidents and bodies haf to be brought home they come in cases labelled "engine parts".'

He gestured with the whisky flask. 'They tried to get me as Chief Flying Instructor,' he admitted. 'But I'm making too much money in my own vay and I don't like uniforms. On the other hand – ' the old familiar grin came – 'they do vell with the girls.'

'Do the German people know all this?' Dicken asked.

'But of course, my friend. And they are proud of it. Germany is air-minded in a way that the English have forgotten. Didn't ve make a public ceremony of the return of the Rittmeister from his grave in France? Thousands turned up. I was there myself. So was President von Hindenburg, several senior officers and many of his old eagles. There are a lot who would like to see the Richthofen Geschwader flying again. And it will.'

'How?'

Udet shrugged. 'We teach the liddle boys to glide. There's nothing in the Versailles peace terms that say ve mustn't have non-powered aircraft and you can learn a lot about flying in a glider. Enough to move quickly, when the time comes, on to powered aircraft. And Lufthansa, the airline, is run by a type called Erhard Milch, who was a flier during the war. They are good. Even your RAF uses their blind approach system. Goering vorks for them, too, and he and Milch are like that.' Udet held up two fingers. 'They're in it up to here.' Udet's hand went to the top of his head. 'Goering is surrounding himself with fliers und he is telling them "to cherish hatred for the British and the French." Between them, they are picking the cream of the German youth, and civilian air liners can become bombers just like that.' His fingers clicked. He leaned closer. 'Do you know Heinkel has a machine mit a 750-horse BMW engine that is faster than the RAF's latest fighter?'

'I expect we know about it,' Dicken said, doubting it even as he spoke.

Udet smiled. 'You don't behave as if you do. *Our* politicians don't. Only this Bavarian ex-corporal, Hitler, who runs the National Socialists. And him I don't trust. I use his picture as a target for pistol practice.' His smile had changed to a frown. 'He talks already of war. Und how he talks! I've heard him. He doesn't believe in conciliation, understanding und world peace.

Next time, you see, he von't have to do the fighting, and politicians are always good at going in for wars when they don't have to wage them. But his aims are for a greater Germany and, I, my friend, am a German and vill do vhat I can to help. There is something here today you must see. During the war did you never notice that vhen you strafed our trenches you aimed your bombs by aiming the airplane? The American Marines have developed that as a technique. In 1919 they discovered they could hit a target more often by diving low at an angle of forty-five degrees, and they began to use it to deal mit the uprisings in Haiti and Santo Domingo. Last year a detachment was cut off in Nicaragua and their DH4s drove the enemy away by this dive-bombing. Such methods could win a war.'

'Which war?'

'The next one.'

'When will that be?'

Udet gave him a wide grin. 'Sooner than you think, my old friend. If you take the trouble to look, you'll notice that the Nazis are on the move. The streets of Berlin are full of SA men and if you listen carefully you'll hear what they're saying.'

'What *are* they saying?'

Udet gave him a smile that was a mixture of sadness and guilt. 'Deutschland erwache!' he said. 'Germany awake!'

7

By the time they left the hangar the airfield was warming up for the main events. The excitement was obvious and the thump-thump of the band came over the din of motor horns, the shouts of hot dog vendors and the crying of lost children.

An American pilot flew a few solo stunts, then Udet appeared flying a red machine marked D-ERNI. He had been bet he couldn't pick a handkerchief off the hood of a motor car with his wingtip and he had accepted the challenge.

'An aeroplane for an automobile,' he said. 'It is easy.'

He performed ten minutes of breathtaking stunts then the car was driven to the centre of the airfield and a handkerchief arranged in a pyramid on the hood. Flying over the crowd, Udet let them all see the small rod he had fixed to the wingtip, then he hurtled down towards the car in a shallow dive. As the crowd held its breath, half-hoping he'd hit the car, he trailed his wingtip along the ground, then, at the last moment, pulled up over the car. As he roared upwards, the engine screaming, there was a tremendous cheer as the handkerchief was seen fluttering on the end of the rod.

Doolittle watched critically. 'One day he'll kill himself,' he said flatly. 'The crowd want a show and showmanship's the keynote of these affairs. Watching fast planes zip round pylons isn't enough. They want thrills, and thrills for the crowds mean risks for the men providing 'em. Last time I put on a show I flew out of my wings. They folded back five miles from the airfield and I had to walk back with the chute under my arm and ask for another ship.'

Udet was cock-a-hoop as he climbed from the cockpit. 'It vas easy,' he crowed. 'Und now I am richer by an automobile.'

The owner of the car seemed as delighted as Udet. 'That's goddam dangerous,' he said.

'No, no.' Udet smiled. 'I just shut the eyes und pull any handle vithin reach.'

The stunting was followed by a massed parachute jump from a flight of elderly Jennies, then a Cierva autogyro was put through its paces. One had already flown the Bristol Channel and several had appeared in England looking like Avro 504s without wings. It had rudimentary planes, a propeller on the nose and four huge blades revolving by air pressure above the pilot's head. Its chief asset was that it could take off in half the space needed for an orthodox aeroplane and return to earth almost vertically, and the crowd cheered as it settled down like an elderly hen returning to its nest.

As it vanished, Udet tapped his programme. 'Und now, the dive bombing. This, my friend, is what we must watch.'

As he spoke, a flight of stubby-winged single-seaters appeared over the grandstand and began to peel off one after the other. Coming down like swooping eagles, their dives as rigid as if on rails, they dropped their flour-bag bombs inside a target circle painted on the grass. As the missiles burst in splashes of white, they lifted into the air again, their engines howling, in a tremendous zoom that carried them back to their original height in seconds.

Udet grinned. 'Wunderbar! Wunderbar!'

Dicken was staring into the sky at the climbing machines with narrowed eyes. 'Perhaps good enough for those friends of yours who're building up your air force to be interested?' he said.

Udet acknowledged the fact. 'An airplane mit special air brakes and flaps to hold it steady could be magnificent,' he crowed. 'Und vhen I show it off at the Templehof in Germany I shall be better than these men because I am a better pilot. They tell me Curtiss are thinking of developing a special airplane, and that, my friend, will be a *weapon*. Mobile artillery. When you can drop bombs as accurately as that, you can bomb a hundred yards in front of moving infantry. I hope one day to fly one.'

'In battle?'

'Mein Gott, no! I've had enough of war. But that *is* something new and the Americans don't seem to know what to do with it. *I* do. An airplane mit strong vings you can't lose will be excellent for my stunt flying.'

With the entertainment out of the way, the excitement began to warm up for the races.

The main event was a free-for-all military race in which the Army Air Force had entered a standard Curtiss Hawk.

'They haven't the funds to build a new one,' Doolittle said. 'Laird are building a biplane with single interplane struts and streamlined spats. She looks like a bumble bee and she's the fastest racing plane ever. I'm told they can whip round a pylon like a cat down an alley. Next year I'll have one and I'll take the Nationals. Then I'll quit. I've got two growing sons and it's time I took better care of my health.'

The five-mile course was triangular and laid out in such a way that the race could be watched throughout from the grandstand. At each corner was a fifty-foot steel tower at the top of which sat a judge whose function was to report any cheating on the turns.

'They pass within feet of him at over a hundred,' Udet pointed out. 'He bite his nails a lot.'

There were different schools of thought on how to go round a pylon. Some liked to climb between them and swoop down on them for the turn. Others preferred to skim the grass and take the pylon on the climb.

'Benny Howard makes vertical banks,' Doolittle explained. 'They call him the pylon polisher. Me, I prefer to start a slow bank well ahead of the turn.'

The races followed one after another then, in the main race, to increase the excitement, instead of being flagged off separately and clocked as usual, all seven aircraft were to set off in what was called a racehorse start, all lined up to take off together for a twenty-lap circuit. One of them, classed as a mystery aircraft, was wheeled out of its hangar at the last minute. The machine had a huge radial engine with the pilot's seat not far forward of the rudder. There was also a Page, two Travel Airs, a Lockheed and a Cessna. The mystery machine was a parasol type with a single high wing.

'They didn't get the vings bolted on until three hours ago,' Udet said. 'It vas hopped here from the factory field after only a ten-minute test flight and arrived mit ten minutes to spare.'

The Parasol made a faster take-off than any of the other starters and gained visibly at the turns until it had actually lapped some of the other competitors. Watching the machines whip round the pylons, Dicken found himself agreeing wholeheartedly with Doolittle. This was nerve-flying, not scientific flying. Hurling aircraft through narrow spaces, wrenching them round with strut-straining violence was the sort of flying they'd done during the war when there'd been no option, and he couldn't see it adding much to aviation.

One of the Travel Airs was giving the Parasol a close race when its engine started to cough. Its speed dropped rapidly and the pilot had to set it down. The Cessna also dropped out, which left the Parasol and the second Travel Air as the only planes still with any chance. They were squinting into the sun watching the Parasol keenly as it took the home pylon wide and high.

'Something iss wrong!' Udet said shrewdly. 'He iss not as he should be. Hey –' his voice rose ' – he iss out of control!'

For a hideous moment, it seemed that the machine was aimed straight at the grandstand, then that the pilot was making a supreme effort to avoid smashing into the crowd. As the machine wobbled, the screams rose but the Parasol swung sharply, wrenched aside, it seemed, by a pilot fighting for consciousness, as if carbon monoxide from the exhaust had got into the cockpit. People started to run and for a moment the air was filled with shouting, then the aeroplane hit the ground at a shallow angle, throwing up a cloud of dust as it ploughed along, shedding pieces as it went. A wheel flew into the air to land and bounce towards the crowd as if it had a life of its own, a wing flapped wildly, like a chicken taking a dust bath, became detached and leapt into the air in a shower of pieces, then the machine began to somersault, flinging fragments of wreckage about as if a bomb had gone off inside it, before finally coming to a stop in a cloud of smoke and steam at the far side of the field. An ambulance and a fire tender screamed from their positions near the stand and hurtled across the grass, their sirens howling.

For a while nothing could be heard but shouts and screams with, over the din, the iron voice of the announcer on the loudspeaker appealing for calm. Dicken stood gazing at the shattered machine with cold eyes, his mouth a tight line. Udet quickly lit a cigarette then pushed his hands deep into his pockets, his shoulders hunched, almost as though, despite his incredible confidence in his skill as a pilot, the disaster were something he had foreseen a hundred and one times for himself. Doolittle sighed and shrugged. 'That,' he said, 'is why I'm quitting.'

Gradually the hysteria died down and the cries and the sobbing of women faded. To Dicken's surprise the races were not abandoned, and after a while the announcer, his voice shaking a little, informed them of the beginning of the women's race. This had also been intended to be a racehorse start but it had been abruptly changed to a seperate-start race, with the machines taking off one after the other and, pushing to the front, Dicken struggled to get a clear view of his wife. He was half-hoping to persuade her to abandon the race but he was too late and the machines were already taxiing into position. The machine she was flying, a small red and yellow two-seater with the word 'Harmer' emblazoned on the fuselage, was an open-cockpit machine, but it was hard to recognise Zoë with her goggles and flying helmet, and Dicken watched her with narrowed eyes, caught by a strange longing overlaid by sadness.

The race was flown cautiously. The disaster in the main race had had its effect and Zoë handled the Harmer warily, skimming the pylons closely but without taking chances. But her machine had nothing like the speed of the other aeroplanes and as the race finished and the machines landed, zigzagging up the field to the roped-off enclosure, their engines burping and coughing, Dicken broke away from the crowd and began to follow it.

The steward at the entrance to the enclosure, a young man in white overalls and a boater, leaning on a post holding a copy of the pulp magazine, *Wings*, was prepared to dispute Dicken's right of entry when Udet's voice came over his shoulder.

'Listen, my friend,' he said. 'You are a great reader of that magazine you've got there.'

'Sure am, Mr Udet.'

'You read in there about Dicken Quinney?'

'Dick Quinney? Sure have, Mr Udet. There's an article in

this here very one.' He started turning the thick pulpy pages. 'Why?'

Udet grinned. 'You haf just refused him permission to enter your enclosure. That iss why.'

Zoë was just wrenching off her helmet and running her fingers through her hair. To Dicken she looked strained, thin and pale and he suspected that the sort of flying she was doing was taking more out of her than she realised.

As she turned away, he studied the machine she had been flying. There was a saying that if an aeroplane was good to look at it was good to fly and the Harmer had a clumsy appearance with stubby wings and an undercarriage that seemed too tall. It had been built for racing but it looked unstable and Dicken was still studying it when he heard his name called and saw Zoë staring at him with wide eyes from the hangar entrance.

'Dicky Boy!'

To his surprise there was genuine delight in her cry. Running towards him she flung herself into his arms and kissed him enthusiastically.

'What are you doing here?'

'Looking for you.'

'Pity you didn't come yesterday. Casey was here. He had to head back to St Louis. His machine's there.'

Dicken gestured at the Harmer Racer. 'This is a hell of a life for a woman,' he said.

A stubborn, defiant look appeared in her eyes. 'It isn't the sort of thing Air Force wives go in for,' she agreed.

He gestured again at the Harmer. 'And is this what you're doing with your time?'

She gave him a sidelong glance. 'I've got more in the pipeline than chasing other women round pylons,' she admitted. 'This isn't flying. Any more than that.' She gestured at the display area and the band still pounding out *Hail, Hail, The Gang's All Here* in their flagged enclosure.

'You used to think it was.'

'Times change. I change with them.'

Dicken frowned. 'I heard from Annys that Peasegood, the man you've got running your garages, was swindling you right, left and centre. I had a look. He is.'

Zoë gestured. 'Aw, pfui,' she said. 'He still makes me a small fortune, so he's entitled to fiddle a bit if he can. Annys is jealous, that's all. She gave up her share of the garage in exchange for the house. The house was worth two thousand and she thought she'd got the best of the bargain, because the garage was only worth a hundred or two. But it's now nine garages and, with all the other odds and ends, it's worth getting on for sixty thousand. George Peasegood might be a bit sharp but he knows what's good for business. We decided there was a difference between repairing cars and selling gas. Most people can't sell gas for repairing cars, and can't repair cars for selling gas. We decided to separate them. My gas stations only sell gas and you can operate them with a man and a boy. But they sell twice as much gas because they're not doing anything else. And the mechanics in my repair depots are good because they don't get distracted by having to stop to sell gas. People come to us.'

Dicken eyed her warmly. As long as he lived, he knew he'd never be able to regard her as an enemy. As adolescents they'd clutched each other on hot summer nights and shared the same fears and the same ambitions. Whatever she did to him, he knew he could never totally reject her. No matter how much she hurt him, he could never forget the past.

'Why not,' he suggested, 'come home and make yourself a millionaire?'

8

They ate at Dicken's hotel. There was a room off the restaurant where they were able to drink cocktails made of bootleg gin and Zoë led him to it like a homing pigeon to its loft.

'Prohibition doesn't prohibit much,' she said. 'Perhaps the fact that it's illegal gives it an extra zip.'

She was wary and elusive and he knew she was avoiding telling him her plans for the Dufee race. In the end he tackled her about it.

She gave him a sidelong glance then drew a deep breath. 'We're flying to Hawaii,' she said.

'Who are?'

'Casey Harmer and me.' She lifted her hands. 'Now don't start yelling. There's nothing between us. It's purely business. He means nothing to me.'

Dicken frowned. 'He does to me. Especially if he thinks he can haul my wife across two thousand five hundred miles of ocean in one of his machines which, if it's anything like that Racer of his, won't manage one thousand.'

Her brows came down angrily. 'What's wrong with the Racer?' she demanded.

'Everything's wrong.'

He noticed she didn't dispute the fact and suspected she'd guessed it herself.

'And who's doing the navigating?' he asked.

'We're doing it between us.'

'You couldn't navigate round a hill, Zoë.'

'I've studied,' she snapped.

'A lot?'

'Some.'

'Enough?'

She seemed doubtful. 'I can study some more.'

Dicken leaned forward. 'It's all right business men looking for publicity with these air races they promote,' he said. 'Because that's chiefly what they're after. But, Zo, they aren't thinking of aviation or they wouldn't think up such half-baked stunts. You're not flying for *you*, you're flying for *them*. And you're not flying the Atlantic with the wind behind you towards a coastline that's thousands of miles long. You're heading south-west into the weather towards an island that's about thirty-five miles wide. Over the sea every bit of the way. Without railway stations en route so you can check your position.'

'I've progressed beyond that, dammit!' she snapped.

'It's to be hoped so. I've done some checking. There were thirteen entrants for the Dole Derby last year. Several crews were killed before they started and they ended up with eight. Of those only four of them got away and of those four only two made it. The others were lost. The only people who benefit from that sort of flying are the organisers.'

She eyed him angrily. 'We've come a long way since then. A whole year. A year's a long time in aviation.'

There was an awkward silence that lasted until the arrival of steaks the size of bread boards.

'Are you happy about it?' Dicken asked.

'Sure I'm happy.' Zoë's eyes were bright but he noticed that she gave him a lost lonely look.

'What's in it for you?'

'It puts me in with Earhart, Elder and those people.'

'Is that what you want?'

'Yes.'

He studied her for a moment then went on quietly. 'Other women fliers have given it up and settled down to marriage.'

She shrugged, the lost lonely look reappearing momentarily. 'I guess maybe I will, too, Dicky Boy. When I've pulled this off.'

He found it hard to believe. Flying had become a drug for her, a habit that couldn't be put aside.

'And what about Harmer?' he asked. 'What's in it for him?'

The lost look disappeared in the old frank, forthright grin. 'Money,' she said.

Dicken didn't reply. He'd flown because he enjoyed flying

and never purely for reward, and had always accepted the dangers that went with it as part of his profession; and it had never occurred to him – not once since he'd first taken to the air in 1914 – that, as he struggled with the ancient machines it had been his bad luck to fly, he was furthering the progress of aviation. He'd never been able to think of any other way of life and had never considered himself as a martyr and certainly never as brave. But he was a professional and had always believed in taking every possible precaution against disaster.

As they finished their meal, he looked up at Zoë. 'What now?' he asked.

'Back to my apartment,' she said. 'I thought you might like to take me to bed and it's got more mod cons than this place.'

He smiled at her, puzzled at her attitude. She seemed to wish to be his wife, but never to have the responsibilities of a wife.

Her apartment was large and well-furnished and she offered him a drink.

'Bootleg as usual,' she said. 'Everybody gets blotto on bootleg over here.'

They sat listening to the radio for a while, Zoë snuggled against Dicken on the settee. He found himself wondering how often Harmer had been in his place but he didn't ask questions, accepting the strange fact that he had a wife who wasn't a wife.

'What happens after staff college?' Zoë asked.

'Posting somewhere. Perhaps England. More than likely abroad. Coming?'

'No.' She didn't hesitate. 'Air force wives are bad enough in England. I bet they're twice as bad abroad.'

'They're with their husbands.'

'Do you resent me not being with you, Dicky Boy?'

'I've grown used to it.'

They made love pleasurably but without any great passion and Dicken found himself wondering if the coolness came from the fact that Harmer had also been in her bed.

'Don't fly to Hawaii,' he said abruptly.

What made him say it he didn't know. But he'd known Zoë since she was little more than a child and had met her first when he'd fallen in love with her sister. Their marriage seemed to be one largely of convenience, because they had spent remarkably little of it together, but there was still something that tied them

147

together, some strange invisible thread that bound them.

She had turned her head on the pillow to stare at him. 'Why do you say that?'

'Because, unless Harmer's a better navigator than you are, you'll never make it.'

Again she seemed doubtful. 'He's studied it.'

'More than you, I hope. Listen, Zo, I don't want to stop you if you're set on it, but let me check you again. Will you do that?'

She continued to stare at him, then she nodded. 'Okay,' she said abruptly. 'You can check me out.'

*

The following day, they hired one of the elderly Jennies from the owner of the display. It was obvious at once that Zoë's navigation was elementary, and as they climbed from the cockpit, she gave Dicken an anxious look.

'How did I do?'

'Zo, you'll be committing suicide if you try for Hawaii.'

Tears came to her eyes. 'I'd got my goddam heart set on it,' she said.

'Then you'd better get it unset. As my wife, I could probably take out an injunction to stop you.'

'You'd never dare!'

'No,' he admitted. 'Perhaps I wouldn't. But for God's sake, take a month's crash course. If at the end of it your instructor thinks you can do it, then go ahead. You can learn a lot in a month.'

He had a feeling that above all else she would have liked to have settled down to matrimony and all it meant, that she felt that life was passing her by, but, having built up the image of a liberated woman aviatrix, she had to live up to it. Nothing in the world would change her mind, he knew, certainly not argument; yet he also knew that because of the past he could never simply abandon her. He needed her in a curious way and was certain she needed him.

She was studying him again, her expression lost once more, then she snapped abruptly to life.

'Okay,' she said. 'I'll do that. There are plenty of boys around the hangars who'd be glad of a few bucks to give me some instruction.'

'Listen,' Dicken begged. 'Don't go to "one of the boys round the hangars." Go to an expert. Pay him what he's worth. If you learn something you can use it on other flights.'

*

That night they had dinner together again but she disappeared beforehand to telephone Harmer. She was away a long time and Dicken, putting back gin cocktails that tasted vaguely of aircraft dope, wondered what she was having to say to persuade the Canadian. If Harmer had any brains, he would see the sense in the argument. The Pacific was wide and Hawaii was small and good navigation was going to be important.

When she came back, her expression was a strange mixture of relief and anxiety. 'It's all off, anyway,' she said.

'Why?'

'The port engine keeps blowing cylinders and he can't decide why. We'll never make it now.'

'For which,' Dicken said dryly, 'I'm very grateful.'

She gave him an angry look then cheered up again. 'But it doesn't matter,' she said. 'The Japanese are offering 25,000 dollars for the first machine to fly from the North American continent to Tokyo. They reckon they're isolated out there. They've got no civilian flying and they want to encourage it. Casey says he'll change the engines and we'll fly to Vancouver and have a go at that instead.'

'At least,' Dicken commented, 'if you miss Japan, you ought to hit China. It's bigger than Hawaii.'

She hugged him. 'Come upstairs,' she whispered.

Their love making this time was more tender.

'I love you, Dicky Boy,' she murmured.

'You've got a bloody funny way of showing it,' Dicken said.

She was silent for a moment, then she moved her shoulders. 'I can't help being the way I am,' she said. 'I'll never change. You don't as you grow older. Just get more so. But I do love you.'

'It's a funny kind of love.'

She was silent for a moment then she answered in a small voice. 'I know,' she said. 'But it's all I've got.'

'In spite of Casey Harmer?'

'Yes. In spite.'

'He's been your lover, hasn't he?'

She ignored the question and went off at a tangent. 'Will you come and meet Casey?' she went on. 'He says he'd like to meet you and I want you to look at the machine he's built. I want you to approve. We'll go as soon as I can tie things up here.'

*

They flew to St Louis in the Racer and Zoë allowed Dicken to do the piloting, while she practised her navigation. The aeroplane was surprisingly stiff on the controls for such a small machine and responded badly to the movements of Dicken's hands and feet on the control column and the rudder bar. As he flew he watched the stubby wings quivering on either side of him in the bumpy air as they crossed the Appalachians. The machine felt as wrong as it looked, off-balance, awkward and stubborn, and he found himself hoping that the new machine Harmer had built was an improvement. His criticism bothered him but at least he knew he was working from a practical knowledge of aeroplanes, an experience of hard flying that was almost as long as that of anybody alive. He had flown all kinds of machines in all kinds of conditions and wasn't one of those people who criticised aviation from the depth of a club's armchair.

Landing at the city airport, they found a large roadster parked behind the hangars. Zoë drove it with her usual dash, and Dicken reflected that she was – and probably always had been – far better with a car than with an aeroplane.

'It's Casey's,' she said, almost apologetically, as though probing his thoughts and emotions for a safe resting place.

Outside the city there was a second smaller airfield made from a group of meadows with the hedges removed. There was a line of sheds where small aircraft were being wheeled out and at the other side an old wooden hangar stood on its own. As Zoë stopped the roadster outside it, Harmer appeared and Dicken saw at once why he appealed to Zoë. He was taller and better-looking than Dicken, but he had the hardheaded look of a businessman and his features were spoiled by a calculating expression. 'Casey,' Zoë said, 'this is my husband.'

Harmer thrust out his hand. 'I've heard of you,' he said.

'Dicken's come to see the machine, Casey,' Zoë said. She seemed nervous, as if she expected Harmer to resent Dicken, and Dicken to be critical of the aeroplane for purely personal reasons.

Harmer gestured at the wooden hangar. Inside was a huge red and yellow biplane, studied by a group of interested spectators and small boys. It had an open cockpit and, though, with its two huge motors, it had a look of power, it had the same wrong look the Racer had, too heavy, too awkward, and with insufficient thought given to keeping down its weight.

Inside the cabin behind the pilot's cockpit there was even a touch of luxury in a colour scheme of red and gold, and space for two wicker chairs.

'She'll be carrying passengers after we come back from Japan,' Harmer said, pushing the hangar doors back to give them more light. 'People want to fly these days and they'll want to fly in *this* machine.'

'Wouldn't it have been wiser to strip her down to the limit?' Dicken asked. 'Save weight. She's a long way to go.'

'She'll do it,' Zoë said. 'We want to *prove* she'll do it, so people will want to use her. She's called the *Baltimore Bantam*.'

'Bit big for a bantam, isn't she?'

Harmer shrugged. 'Just a name, I guess.'

'She's going to do it to Tokyo easily,' Zoë said, her enthusiasm beginning to show again. 'The hell with the Dufee Derby. We can get just as much money flying to Japan when the new engines are properly installed. What was wrong with the others, Casey?'

'They didn't work,' Harmer said laconically.

They walked slowly round the machine, Dicken touching the elevators and rudder thoughtfully, studying the biplane tail and the four huge wheels. The machine reminded him of the Vickers Vernons in Iraq. Bright-eyed, Zoë waited for his opinion.

'She's superbly instrumented,' she said. 'She's carrying safety equipment, too – two inflatable rubber dinghies.'

'Wouldn't one do?'

'A spare in case of emergencies.'

'Won't it add weight? Lindbergh flew what amounted to a

petrol tank with wings and not much else, and did it alone to save weight.'

Harmer gave him a quick look, as if he suspected resentment of the fact that Zoë was to accompany him, then he went on quickly. 'I designed her myself,' he said. 'The engines are Junkers, the best there are.'

'I've heard Wrights are better,' Dicken said, already aware that he sounded carping and over-critical but anxious to protect Zoë. 'They weigh short of six hundred and fifty pounds and generate two hundred and thirty-seven horsepower. Lindbergh had one.'

'Byrd had Junkers and he made it, too,' Harmer growled. 'He also made it to the North Pole.' He gestured. 'This isn't the first ship I've built. She's going to make us money. She's got to. She cost me over a hundred thousand dollars. She'll knock 'em cold.'

Privately, Dicken didn't agree. The machine was too big, and was over-decorated and over-equipped, and there was no longer much future in biplanes, though people went on building them, despite the acknowledged fact that they caused tremendous drag. 'Built-in head-winds,' they were called.

When he said nothing, Zoë spoke nervously, as if she guessed he couldn't give his wholehearted approval.

'We'll fly it to Vancouver just as soon as the ballyhoo over the Dufee Derby's finished,' she said. 'Hell, in this country people live off publicity and it's no use trying to compete. The newspapers'll lap it up.'

'Once in Vancouver,' Harmer went on, 'we'll get her ready and take off for Tokyo at the first sign of good weather and a wind from the east.'

'Who's flying it up?' Dicken asked.

'Casey and me,' Zoë said.

'You might have to wait a long time for a good wind for Tokyo. The winds come from the west. Why not take her to Tokyo by ship and fly the other way?'

'It'd cost too much money and the Japs want the flight to end there.'

'She'll do around a hundred,' Zoë put in, and Dicken was conscious that she was well aware of his unease. 'We're supporting the tail with a wheeled platform to put her in a flying attitude right from the start. It'll get her off the gound more quickly. It's an idea that's been used before.'

'Fonck tried it when he tried to fly the Atlantic in 1926,' Dicken agreed. 'It came adrift. What's her weight?'

'Two tons,' Harmer said. 'Six fully loaded. She had a housed cockpit originally but – well, we decided it was safer to have it open. There've been cases of leaking exhausts and pilots being asphyxiated, and Davis and Wooster might have been saved when the *American Legion* crashed if their cockpit hadn't been glassed over. She's already flown around two thousand miles.'

'All up?'

'No, of course not.' Harmer sounded faintly irritated, as if he had suddenly noticed, as Dicken had, that in his concern for safety an unspoken doubt was hidden. 'You don't go filling a machine that costs as much as this to the brim until you need it. But we'll fill her for Vancouver and see how she performs. And as for the platform under the tail, we've fixed a mirror to watch our rear end. We'll use the trip north to check that everything works.'

9

Dicken kept his doubts to himself. It seemed to him that if Harmer had expended as much time and energy on the design of the machine as he had on the safety precautions and the colour scheme he might have had a better chance. The distance to Tokyo was four thousand seven hundred miles, longer than Lindbergh's flight to Paris, longer than the Derby flight to Honolulu, but at least the Aleutian Islands stretched almost all the way across the North Pacific and in the event of trouble they might be able to reach them.

The thing that worried him most was Harmer's casual approach. Lindbergh had taken enormous trouble. He had learned great circle navigation and checked time zone and magnetic variation charts, to say nothing of information on the weather ahead of him. Zoë was still not taking her navigation seriously.

'There's no problem,' she insisted. 'God Almighty, Dicky Boy, for a professional airman you sure let your nerves get on top of you. The navy made it across the Pacific to Honolulu. In a Fokker trimotor. Even before the Dole Derby last year.'

'The navy usually does the job thoroughly,' Dicken pointed out. 'And they installed a lot of navigation instruments and had an expert navigator to provide a dead reckoning course.'

'And they were followed by another machine that didn't,' she snapped. 'It landed on Molokai. *They* did the trip all the way with a solid cloud floor.'

Dicken refused to be convinced, but his worries were swamped in the furore that was taking place in the newspapers about the Dufee Derby. Despite the uproar after the disastrous Dole competition the previous year – when the newspapers, which had whipped up the enthusiasm had just as quickly turned their backs on it and claimed no responsibility – the press were plastering their pages with enormous headlines. The United States Navy had more than once indicated that it was not prepared ever again to comb vast stretches of ocean for missing competitors but they were being urged by interested politicians and businessmen to change their minds, while the National Aeronautical Association, which had condemned transoceanic flights instituted for individual publicity rather than scientific progress, were being accused of lacking enterprise.

As the start drew nearer, the newspapers became almost hysterical, all the chances and non-chances weighed up by newsmen who knew nothing about flying, and nobody seemed to notice that the Hawaiian group was only 317 miles wide so that an error of more than three and a half degrees either way could cause a machine to miss them altogether.

The entries numbered twelve, the oddest a big awkward triplane, but while being flown to the starting point at Oakland, in California, it stalled on landing and the three wings had crumpled into a shambles. It had become clear by this time that, despite the disasters of the previous year, there had once again been more enthusiasm than thought in the preparations, and a shocking haste on the part of some of the contestants to meet the deadline.

Dicken, Zoë and Harmer were all in the same hotel and Dicken noticed that now that Harmer was on the scene Zoë showed no inclination to share his room. In the evenings as they listened to the big brown radio with the fretwork motif on the front, she sat equidistant between the two of them, as if she were establishing the fact that she belonged to neither.

As the aeroplanes lined up at the Oakland Municipal Airport, it was noticeable that none of the famous firms had provided entries, as though, after the previous year's casualty list, they didn't wish to be associated with another failure. But the newspapers, despite their complaints that money prizes did more harm to aviation than not by encouraging the unready to take chances, were busy whipping up enthusiasm with questions about which was to be the fastest machine in the race – a Lampert Omega or a Norden low-wing monoplane. Another of the competitors had already been eliminated when a Trewint with a defective fuel system had crashed en route to the take-off, killing the two naval officers who were crewing it.

As they ate a late breakfast on the morning of the start, the newspapers announced that yet another competitor had been eliminated. The Norden had failed on a test flight and the pilot had taken to his parachute too late.

'This isn't a race,' Dicken growled. 'It's another slaughter.'

There was an across-the-nation radio hook-up and everybody in the hotel had crowded into the lounge where the air was full of cigarette smoke.

'There goes the first!' The announcer's voice rose excitedly. 'The flag's gone down and away goes Si Izzard's *Voyager*. He's away, heading bravely for the good old broad Pacific. Now it's the turn of Roy Lewis's *Esperanza*. He has another naval flier as his navigator. There he goes – heading down the field, picking up speed, he's going to unstick at any moment – hey!'

As the commentary stopped in a shout of surprise, the whole room leaned forward, their faces tense for news of an accident.

'He groundlooped!' The announcer's voice was shrill. 'He groundlooped, folks! He groundlooped! Just as he was about to leave the ground, he whirled round and came to a dead stop! From here, it looks as though he might have touched a wing. Maybe his undercarriage collapsed. I can see the ambulance and the fire engine heading down there, but – wait a minute! – yeah, there they are! I can see Roy himself climbing out with his navigator. They're okay. No harm done, except to the ship.'

As it went on, the tension increased. The next machine off, a Knevett monoplane, veered from the runway and had to be towed back to the end of the line of waiting machines for a fresh start. Then the Lampert Omega, as expected, made a beautiful take-off, half an hour after the first machine.

'There goes the favourite,' the announcer crowed. 'He sure looks fine. He's climbing away now at speed and looks set for a fast passage. Now here comes the Thurston, *Muriel of Milo*. She's named after Muriel Nugent, the pretty stenographer from Milo, Michigan. She's not much more than twenty-one years old but she's mad about flying. Her pilot's Art Gaydon, a guy of twenty-four who walks with a limp, the souvenir of a crash. Rooney Savage's the navigator. And there goes the Flying Stenographer! But, wait a minute, the Thurston's backfiring badly! They're turning round and coming back for another go! I guess it's spark plugs!'

Another Knevett, a French-built Lafosse, a Kelly biplane and a Mirac Messenger followed, pursued by the Knevett which had veered from the runway. This time the Knevett groundlooped and smashed a wing. *Muriel of Milo* left for a second time and the commentator breathed what sounded like a sigh of relief.

'Well, there you are, folks,' he said. 'We've now got eight of the entries actually in the air and making for Hawaii. That's a whole lot better than last year. They're being followed at the moment by a crowd of escort and camera planes, but I guess *they*'ll soon be on their way back.'

The commentary went on for a little longer but it was desultory now that the machines had left and someone rose and switched off the set.

'I guess that's that,' Harmer said. 'My money's on the Omega.'

The following day, the radio messages, punctuated by crackling, were being relayed from Honolulu.

'There's a crowd of thirty thousand here at Wheeler Field,' the metallic voice said. 'All ready to welcome the winners. Among them are the Governor and Ryan Dufee himself and there's to be a monster civic celebration in the city when the machines arrive.'

It was clear nothing was happening and the commentator was being pushed to provide something to say. Music started, light music that turned to jazz, then it was abruptly interrupted.

'Here it is!' The metallic voice was high and loud with excitement. 'Here's the first one! Everybody's cheering! It's only a speck in the sky but I guess it's the first!'

There were a few tense minutes until the machine was identified. 'It looks like the Omega! I think it is! No, it isn't! Now, that's a surprise. I think it's either the Voyager or the Knevett. I can't make it out. They've both got the same engine and the same two undercarriage struts up to the wing root. Wait a minute, I can see the name! It's the *Voyager*! It's Si Izzard in the *Voyager*! Si Izzard is the winner, folks!'

A few dollar bills changed hands as bets were settled and

there was a lot of relieved laughter that the machines had made it. Two hours later, news came that the Knevett had landed to claim the second prize, followed soon afterwards by the Mirac Messenger.

'Where the hell's the Omega?' Harmer demanded. 'She ought to be there by now.'

When no more machines had landed several hours later, it was clear that a depressed feeling of defeat had come over the commentators.

Later in the morning the news was flashed that the French Lafosse had landed in the sea three hundred miles out with a faulty fuel feed, but that her crew had managed to put her down close to a freighter on its way to San Francisco which had picked up not only the crew but the aeroplane as well. The delay in learning what had happened was because the freighter's radio had been out of action and they had had to wait until they had spoken another ship with a radio which had passed the message to the shore. Then an hour later news came in that the Kelly had landed on the Mexican island of Guadalupe.

'But that's almost due south!' Harmer said. 'How the hell did she get there? Their compass must have been acting up.'

It helped to relieve the tension a little but by this time the commentators were finding it difficult to unearth something new to say and the information that yet another machine had failed to make it wasn't quite the same as that the other missing machines had arrived. In Honolulu aching eyes were still watching the sky but it was already obvious that the Omega and the *Muriel of Milo* were beyond the limit of their fuel. As it became obvious that there would be no more landings, it was possible even over the radio to sense the exuberance draining out of the festivities that had been planned.

By the following day, despite its statement to the contrary, the United States Navy had mounted an air-sea search and, as if more money could retrieve the situation, Dufee had offered another ten thousand dollars for the rescue of the crews of the missing planes. Other interested tycoons put up more sums.

Izzard, the pilot of the winning *Voyager*, his machine refuelled and serviced, took off again to fly back to the mainland, promising to search for the lost aeroplanes en route. Several hours later a flash message on the radio announced that the plane was in trouble and soon after that it went off the air while only six hundred miles from the coast.

There were no crowds round the hotel radio by this time. Everyone was going sheepishly about their business and all the exuberance had faded. Harmer's face was flushed and his eyes were red, and Dicken suspected he'd been drinking. Like Zoë, he had not changed his plans and it seemed to Dicken that, like so many long-distance fliers, he was impelled along his path less by the wish to go than by the feeling that the great newspaper reading and radio listening public would regard him as cowardly if he didn't follow through with his plans.

That night there was a soft scratching at Dicken's door. 'It's me. Zoë. Can I come in?'

As he opened the door, Zoë slipped into his bed. As he took her in his arms, he heard her whisper. 'Dicky Boy, all those poor people! Eleven of them! All dead! It's worse than last year.'

Dicken said nothing for a while. 'It's all so bloody pointless,' he said eventually. 'We know people are brave. Why go on proving it?'

She was silent for a while, curled up in his arms.

'Zo,' he said. 'Don't go on this trip of yours. You'll never make it.'

'Casey thinks we will.'

'I've been flying a long time, Zo' he said. 'Longer than you. Longer than Casey. I don't think you will.'

She sat up in bed. 'Christ,' she said bitterly, her whole mood changing. 'You're bloody encouraging! Why not?'

'That machine of yours doesn't look right. It's out of date.'

'You're bloody sure, aren't you?' She was angry with him now.

'Yes, I'm sure.'

She was silent for a moment and when she spoke again her voice was shaky. 'We've *got* to go, Dicky Boy,' she said.

'Why, for God's sake?'

'Because we've said we're going. Casey says there'll be a reaction against ocean racing now and it's our last chance.'

There was truth in what she said. The newspapers had once again performed a volte face.

'Before this, half the cities in the US were wanting long-distance flights to end on their airfields,' Zoë went on in a small voice. 'Now they're backing down. San Francisco, Boston. Philadelphia. Cleveland. Tokyo have agreed to hold on because we've announced we're coming, but they're not so keen as they were.' She sighed. 'It's been a hell of a two years.'

'People have been looking at flying with their emotions,' Dicken agreed. 'They've not been *thinking* about it.'

There was a long silence then Zoë's voice came again. This time it seemed almost like an attempt to regain lost confidence.

'Casey knows what he's doing,' she whispered. 'He's built other planes.'

'As big as this one? Why not let him fly it up to Vancouver without you? If it behaves well, then that's that. If it doesn't, he'll soon find out.'

For a moment she stared at him. 'What's it to you, anyway?' she asked miserably. 'You've nothing to thank me for, the way I've behaved to you. Why are you trying so goddam hard to look after me now?'

*

Some time during the following day Dicken heard that, although the *Baltimore Bantam* had been placed in position ready for an early take-off the following morning, Zoë had said she wasn't feeling well and that Harmer had signed on a co-pilot.

'He's a guy from across the field,' she explained. 'He's got a good record.'

Dicken agreed to be present at the take-off to see how the great machine behaved.

'And if the goddam thing flies to Vancouver without trouble, I don't want to hear another goddam word,' Zoë said.

When the taxi picked Dicken up it was raining, the water sliding through the beams of the headlights, straight and silvery and shining. Mist hung in the air and the hiss of the tyres was surprisingly loud.

As Zoë climbed in beside him she sat huddled in one corner of the seat, silent and pale, the collar of her coat turned up, her face turned away from Dicken. By the time they reached the airfield, the rain had stopped and Harmer was waiting by the empty hangar.

'She's out at the edge of the field,' he said. 'I've decided to dispense with the rear undercarriage.'

It was clear that Dicken's doubts and the disasters of the Dufee Derby had worried him and he went on hurriedly, almost as if he hoped to prevent Dicken making any comment.

'It's clearing fast,' he said. 'There's a good forecast and it hasn't been raining long enough to make the ground heavy.'

Zoë was looking at him anxiously. 'It'll slow the take-off, Case,' she said. 'Getting rid of the rear undercarriage.'

Harmer gave an irritated gesture, as if he were nervous. 'It's all right, it's all right,' he said quickly. 'I've decided to go for a ramp instead, like Byrd did. It'll give her the same fast start as the rear undercart. None of that slow build-up of speed as she rolls and nothing to damage the tail like Fonck's rear undercart did. Byrd used one when he flew the Atlantic. She'll be tethered at the top with a rope.'

They climbed into the big roadster and Harmer drove them along the side of the field. The *Baltimore Bantam* had been pushed to the top of an inclined ramp which had been built of earth and sandbags and covered with planks to prevent the wheels sinking into it. A heavy double rope, knotted in several places, ran back from the undercarriage and the tail skid and was secured to two or three iron girders which had been driven at an angle into the ground beyond the end of the ramp.

As she climbed from the car Zoë gave it a worried look.

'It helped Byrd,' Harmer insisted. 'He used a ramp of snow for his take-off for the North Pole, too. One of the ground crew'll cut the rope at a signal from me when the engines are warm and beginning to pull.'

'Unless it breaks first under the strain,' Zoë said in a tight voice. 'Byrd's did.'

'*It's all right,*' Harmer said again, his voice urgent. 'We've also had the runway smoothed and lengthened. We don't want another disaster like Fonck's.'

'Is she fuelled up?' Zoë asked.

'Before she was brought out of the hangar. No chance of water in the gas.' Harmer peered at Zoë. 'How're you feeling?'

'I'm okay. I'll join you by train.'

He leaned closer and Dicken heard him whisper. 'You're sure it's not that goddam husband of yours?'

The word that the *Bantam* was leaving had spread and there was a small crowd of spectators. The press moved forward as the preparations were completed and the flash guns popped and filled the air with smoke as Harmer stood alongside the machine with his new co-pilot, one arm round Zoë.

Surrounded by the mist, Dicken felt the ground with the toe of his shoe. It was soggier than Harmer seemed to think.

About him was the chatter of the spectators. They weren't all aviation enthusiasts by any means and he guessed a lot of them were there in the hope of something more spectacular than a mere take-off.

Harmer was shrugging himself into a leather coat now and winding a red woollen scarf round his neck.

'I gave him the scarf,' Zoë said abruptly, almost defiantly, as though she were challenging Dicken to question her relationship with the Canadian.

Pulling on his helmet, Harmer turned towards the door of the machine. As he did so, Zoë slipped forward and kissed him full on the mouth. As he grabbed at her, the camera guns popped again.

'For luck,' Zoë said as she rejoined Dicken. 'That's all. For luck.'

He didn't say anything and watched as Harmer moved through the cabin of the machine to reappear in the cockpit and begin to move the rudders and elevators.

'She'll do it easy,' Zoë said.

As the propellers were swung the engines started with a crackling roar and a few scattered leaves, chaff and grass clippings whirled away. Moving to one side, Dicken noticed that Zoë was holding a clenched fist to her mouth and guessed that she was as well aware as he was of the doubts that hedged the big machine.

For a while, Harmer let the engines tick over and they could see his head and that of the co-pilot in the cockpit. Then, as the throttles were opened, the machine began to shake and quiver under the thrust of the powerful engines. The wing tips were trembling under the intense vibration as Harmer leaned out of the window to make sure the mechanic was standing by the rope with his axe. The mechanic waved back and lifted the axe above his head. But, as he did so, before he could use it, before Harmer could give him the signal, there was a gasp from the crowd. There was a twang as the rope snapped so that the big machine hurtled forward, lumbering noisily over the planks that floored the ramp, its speed building up at once.

Harmer had been looking backwards at the mechanic as the rope went and he was unprepared for the unexpected start. The rudder was not central so that the machine went down the ramp at an angle. As it reached the level ground at the bottom, it seemed to leap into the air and the knot on the trailing end of the broken rope caught against one of the planks that floored the ramp. Dicken saw the plank lift and bang against the tail of the machine. As it was wrenched out of position by the aeroplane's forward movement, other planks leapt up, clattering against the elevators.

The crowd, which had become silent as the preparations for the start had begun, began to shout. The metallic howl of the engines was echoing from the airfield buildings as the machine gathered speed but the unexpected start had sent it off in the wrong direction and, as Harmer pulled it back on course, it began to swing. The rope with its heavy knots was still trailing behind, slapping up and down between the undersurfaces of the elevators and the soggy ground from which it was tossing up stones and clods of earth. As the machine rumbled over a shallow rise the wings swung again and Harmer tried to wrench the machine straight. As he did so, a small cry escaped Zoë and, glancing at her, Dicken saw she still had her fist against her mouth, her eyes wide and horrified.

As Harmer hauled the machine back on to course once more, it swung heavily the other way, then began to swerve even more wildly. The wheels left the grass and there was a gasp from the crowd – 'He's away!' – but the wheels slammed down again with a spattering of muddy water. Then, quite clearly, where the knotted rope was hammering at the tail, Dicken saw something fall away and he realised the rudder wasn't functioning but seemed to be jammed towards starboard.

The machine began to yaw, lurching awkwardly like some runaway juggernaut under the shifting weight of its huge cargo of fuel. The tail was still rumbling along the ground and it was possible now to see that the tailskid had been damaged and that the rudder was hanging crookedly on its hinges.

'For God's sake,' Zoë gasped. 'Close the throttles! Close the goddam throttles!'

But the big machine was still careering across the field, its wheels still firmly on the earth, trailing a cloud of mist from the rain-wet grass. It was clear that Harmer would never get it off now and Dicken saw fragments fly into the air from the damaged elevators. Then the rudder, which Harmer was trying to use to correct the yaw, swung hard over as if he had been frantically kicking at it and it had suddenly come free. As it slammed over, the machine went into a tremendous turn, still moving at speed, until it was heading back almost on its tracks.

The crowd began to scatter in a panic, screaming and shouting and falling over the barriers that had surrounded the enclosure where they had been standing. Two cars started to move in a hurry, crashed and locked together, their radiators steaming. But the trailing rope, which until a moment before had been behind the machine, was now facing the wrong way and it jammed under one of the wheels so that it locked and the machine swung again until it was thundering in the direction of the old wooden hangar where it had been housed.

A choking sound escaped from Zoë's throat that was just recognisable as another plea to Harmer to close the throttles, but as she covered her face, the sound changed to a thin wail, hoarse as a frightened animal's cry. It was possible to see Harmer in the cockpit. He seemed to be fighting with the controls ,and Dicken could see his mouth open, yelling with fright and fury, but, because of panic or some mechanical fault, he still didn't seem able to slam the throttles shut.

A shock absorber went, a wingtip touched and crumpled and the *Bantam* swerved again, a rattling, swaying monster heading straight for the wooden shed which had seen its birth. As a wire fence vanished under the wheels and stakes pierced the wings and fuselage, the whole machine began to disintegrate into flying fragments of wood, steel and fabric. A long yellow wing whipped into the air like the last agonised throes of a wounded bird, before the machine hit the side of the hangar with a crash that could be heard clear across the field.

They heard the thud as the huge petrol tank went up, and a vast mushroom of yellow flame, edged with black, billowed out, sprays of burning petrol leaping into the air like sparks from a roman candle. The ruined side of the hangar fell in, bringing down the roof, and slowly, as if in slow motion, the two ends followed in a shower of splintered planks, effectively covering the aeroplane. In seconds there was a furnace of burning wood and petrol, the roar of whose flames could be heard all the way across the field.

'Casey!' Zoë's voice was broken and harsh with torment. 'Casey!'

Then inexplicably she turned on Dicken, her eyes blazing, her face pink with rage and despair, her hands flying in desperate swings at his head.

'You killed him!' she screamed. 'It was you who made him do it this way! You killed him! You killed him! Damn you, you killed him!'

Part Three

I

There was a remarkable take-it-or-leave-it attitude in London. Jealousy and ambition were still paralysing promotion and Diplock, back in England, was very much in evidence.

Yet there was no doubt about it, after the houpla in America, aviation had finally stepped from infancy to adulthood. Lindbergh had started the progress with his lonely flight across the Atlantic, a scientific project despite its amateur background, and despite the disasters that had followed, despite the rejection of aviation by nervous people who only the year before had been doing the cheering, the world had begun to think about aircraft. Up to 1927 two wings had seemed the safest thing to fly with but now everybody was thinking of monoplanes, and Fokker, Ford and Junkers were even building them of metal. In England civil flying had even overtaken military flying and the only view of the future seemed to be that of the Supermarine company and the Schneider Trophy machines, sleek-winged planes with which they had pushed up the air speed record to an incredible 300 miles an hour.

For Dicken it was a period of frustration and anger, and London was a dreary place that seemed to be full of unemployed demanding the right to work. The country's share of world trade had fallen since the war, when those nations not involved in the struggle had snatched up what Britain had been obliged to let fall, but according to Foote, effusive at having rediscovered Dicken and Hatto after so long, even in the States the upswing was coming to an end.

The RAF had finally survived the attempts by the navy and the army to do away with it and, like flying itself, was beginning to flex its muscles. In Iraq it had shown it could control a country at half the cost the army demanded and there were now more dissenting voices, particularly in the States, claiming that aircraft had made battleships useless.

Because of the financial crisis, however, the RAF was still doing what it could with aeroplanes which were not only out of date but actually looked out of date. The new Victorias were only an improvement on the Vernons, which were really only an improvement on the wartime Vickers Vimy with which Alcock and Brown had flown the Atlantic. New fighters were due but they were still biplanes, built for aerobatics and, compared with the Schneider Trophy machines, desperately slow. RAF officers, travelling in Germany, saw what was going on there and came back indignant that their country was being taken for a ride.

Germany was in a far worse state financially than England and Dicken had heard that Udet had gone bust again but it was well known that, though the school in Russia had finally closed, its graduates were all over Europe in jobs that gave no clue to their qualifications. Some of them flew little planes advertising factory products, some were actually in mounted regiments, struggling with recalcitrant horses and cursed for their lack of horsemanship.

Of his wife Dicken knew practically nothing and what he knew he learned from his mother. In a way that was almost vulgar in a country that was staggering from one crisis to another in the depths of a depression, she was making money hand over fist from her chain of garages and was still thinking of long-distance flying. The fact that he knew she was quite incapable of it reduced Dicken to fury.

For a long time he wondered whether to ask for compassionate leave to go to America, but, when no explanatory letters came, he decided it wasn't worth it. She'd got the bug in her blood and would never be satisfied until she had at least one record, however trivial, under her belt. It was like a climber looking at a mountain. She had to tackle it because it was there and nothing in the world would put her off until she had.

Then suddenly a *New York Times* arrived from Foote with a ringed story on the front page. GLAMOR GIRL BREAKS RECORD, it said, and there was Zoë's face beaming at him from a centre-page spread. She had flown from Charleston to San Antonio in Texas then back to New York. It had been a safe flight mostly over flat land with an experienced navigator, but she had broken a record. The newspaper seemed more impressed by her good looks than by her skill as an aviatrix, but there was no getting away from it: The bug which had bitten her had finally turned into something real and genuine.

After that, he saw her picture in the newspapers again and again. Because she'd lived in the States on and off for so long, the Americans liked to regard her as an American, but because she was British the London newspapers took her up, too, and her face, smiling and beautiful, was always appearing in reports of receptions for flying personalities. She was a wealthy woman now and clearly intended to use her wealth. She had always boasted that she intended to be a liberated woman and had finally become one. Her days of flying with the likes of Charley Wright, giving flips in soggy-winged Avros was finished. She was a personality and it was clear she considered she was getting more out of life than Dicken.

Her rare letters all harped on the same theme. Why not leave the RAF and join her in business? There was never any question of leaving him. She seemed to think he gave her dignity and somehow, behind the requests there always also seemed to be an unspoken announcement of her need for him so that the question of a separation, despite the fact that they saw so little of each other, never arose. It was almost as if she suspected that civilian aviation hadn't yet quite achieved respectability, that it was still too near to the barnstorming days, and that the men who hung around the civilian hangars, with their too-widely-cut breeches, silk scarves and beribboned flying caps, smacked more of fiction than fact.

Since completing the staff course, nobody seemed to know what to do with Dicken. The old attitude that a man had to have the right background for high rank still prevailed, there was an overweight air staff, and more money seemed to be spent on building luxurious officers' messes than was spent on aircraft, while, amazingly, committees of experts still haggled over such trivialities as whether RAF officers should wear spurs. In the scramble for promotion Dicken seemed to have been overlooked and, as the old bugaboo of his Merchant Navy wireless operator's certificate rose again, he found himself in command of the Signals Section of the Flying Training School at Upavon where he had flown in 1917 before going to Italy.

The pupils, full of the eleven-year-old effervescence of the Air Force, wore an uncomfortable service dress of breeches and puttees and saluted everybody in sight who looked as though he might be an officer. During the morning, the field was always empty of aeroplanes until five minutes to midday, when it was filled with returning machines, each trying to get in first so that the pilots would be at the head of the queue for lunch. At one-thirty they all took off again and the aerodrome was quiet once more until on the stroke of four they all arrived back. It was a bit like ringing a school bell.

Instructing was not popular. Pupils had a habit of flying their instructors into hills or into the ground, and tended to over-value their skill so that they lost control and crashed as they tried illicit aerobatics.

It was part of Dicken's job – a heritage of that almost forgotten ambition to be a radio operator at sea – to make sure that they were instructed in the mysteries of wireless. Most of them only wanted to fly and it was clear they regarded their instructors as outdated, outmoded and out of fashion. Because of his record and the number of medals he wore, they were more respectful with Dicken but still found it hard not to believe that *they* were the ones on whom the future depended.

While at Upavon, Dicken met a man called Whittle who had entered the RAF as an apprentice at Cranwell and was now on an instructor's course. He was at work on a new kind of power plant and when the weather was unfit for flying liked to discuss the principles he had in mind. Most people seemed to consider him mad because his idea was to produce an engine that provided its power not by a propeller but by whirling fans inside a tube which would force hot air out behind. More than once his theory was laughed at but Dicken remembered Henry Ford's ideas only too well.

Because of his signals background, he found himself in command of an experiment with speech radio. The sets had to be adjusted by their operators to a high degree of sensitivity, so that conversations from air to ground or air to air always remained doubtful and resulted in lost aircraft wandering about the country and exercises being cancelled because of misunderstood messages. One pilot, receiving a message to patrol Halton at 15,000 feet from an airman who had a habit of dropping his aitches, spent the next hour patrolling Alton, a hundred and fifty miles away. It was decided very quickly that place names on a map were useless.

But flying had changed. A pre-flight check was no longer a twang on the wires, a wiggle of the rudder and a kick at the tyres, but a scientific inspection following laid-down rules, checking the minutest details by the book. Pupils not only had to learn to fly but also had to understand navigation, rigging, controls, the engines that powered their aircraft, bomb sights, and the workings of machine guns and parachutes, and had to go solo after ten hours or be dismissed.

It didn't always work and occasionally there were funerals when the pupils, purple-faced in boots and puttees and well aware that the next time it could be one of them, went through the rigmarole of the slow march, their faces expressionless as the chaplain recited the service and the bugler blew the Last Post. Everyone had to attend to put on a show for the grieving parents and as Dicken retired to his office from one such event and hung up his cap, he turned to see Hatto sitting in his chair.

'Willie! What are you doing here?'

'Come to see you, old lad. They told me you were busy.'

'Yes. Sealed and weighted coffin, because there wasn't really enough to bury. Bit awkward when loving mothers insist on seeing their son for the last time. What are you up to?'

'Got a job for you.'

'Not another bloody signals posting, for God's sake! I'd like to go back to flying.'

'All in good time,' Hatto said. 'These days people like you and I have to accept that our job's to leave the dangerous business of flying to youngsters. Youth's gone, old lad. Long since. You try going up to 20,000 feet without oxygen. We did it regularly during the war – when we could get that high, that is – but I tried it recently with a crew of twenty-year-olds. They were fine but I had problems.'

'And the job?'

'I'm at the Ministry at the moment and my chief's learned that the German Air Service, which is supposed to be defunct, is anything but. They've created a secret air section of the Reichswehrministerium and a hundred and eighty-six ex-air force officers have been judiciously planted throughout the ranks of the army, and they've been training men south-east of Moscow at Lipezk.'

'I could have told you that ages ago.'

Hatto looked startled. 'Then why didn't you?'

'I put in a paper. It never saw daylight.'

Hatto frowned. 'You speak German?' he asked.

'I learned it when I was flying for Lord Ruffsedge. It was useful for picking up girls.'

'And where did you get this information of yours?'

'Erni Udet. When he was in his cups.'

'Know him well?'

'Very well.'

'That's what we heard. How about going and have another chat with him? We're thinking of sending you as temporary air attaché to the embassy in Berlin.'

*

Berlin hadn't changed much. It still had a lunatic atmosphere of indifference but now there was also an underlying element of bitterness, frustration and despair.

The one thing the Germans found hard to accept was the weight of the reparations which had been loaded on them by the French, who, forgetting Napoleon's depredations, had insisted that never again should the Germans be allowed to rampage through Europe. The Berliners were able to accept the loss of their colonies, even the provinces of Alsace and Lorraine, but they couldn't accept that the reparations they were expected to pay were to continue until 1988.

'It means,' the elderly German who stoked the boilers at the embassy told Dicken, 'that not only will I pay them, but also my children and grandchildren when they grow to adulthood.'

The one word on everybody's lips was 'Zeitgeist', the quality of life, but the German capital's idea of what constituted quality was strange.

'Wie schön ist es hier zu leben,' Dicken was told more than once. 'How good it is to live here.' But happiness seemed to consist of pushing morals to their very limit. At night, places like the Café Josty, the Café Luitpold, the Café Stefanie and the Romanische Café on the corner of the Tauentzienstrasse and the Budapestherstrasse were full of avant garde writers, critics and thinkers who, in their attempts to be ahead of their time, favoured all the things that had been frowned on for generations – sexual promiscuity, drugs, marital infidelity, pacifism, pornography, even incest and pederasty. Out to shock, they seemed fascinated by ugliness and lack of harmony.

'Kunst ist Scheisse,' Dicken heard. 'Art is shit.'

Udet hated the lot of them for their views. 'This isn't Germany,' he growled. 'Any more than the view that vas put over in the last century of plump, contented husbands mit their hausfraus, children and bocks of beer. Ve exist somewhere in between, like all other nations, mit the good and the bad among us. Here in Berlin at the moment, the bad has come to the top like froth on beer. Fortunately, they won't last long when the National Socialists get power.'

'Will they get power?'

Udet shrugged. 'The Nazis believe in a way the English never do in *Rassenstolz* – pride of race – and they've sworn to rebuild the Fatherland. And when they do, I shall be behind them – in spirit if not politically – because I'm a German.'

'They're not strong enough to gain power for years.'

'Don't you be too sure, my friend. They're in favour of *Nazionalgeist* – regeneration of the Fatherland and the rekindling of German patriotism. And Germany is tired of the theoreticians and the November criminals who signed the Armistice in 1918. The Nazis are well aware that the people who're running the country now are intellectuals and Social Democrats, and they know that Germany wants things to happen, not just to talk about them happening. They're tired of Leftism and the unemployment that's dragging us down. I've made and lost half a dozen fortunes because of the state of the economy. Everybody's suffering from an inferiority complex and they intend to change all that when they get power.'

'*Will* they get power?' Dicken asked again.

Udet shrugged. 'I give them a fifty-fifty chance,' he said. 'If only because they're the only party which knows what it wants. This Hitler – they'll shove him out of the way when they get power, of course, but they've got some muscle behind them. Ludendorff favours them. The Ruhr industrialists favour them. The army favours them. Several of our lot are vith them.

Bodenschatz, who vas adjutant to the Rittmeister, Goering, who took over after the Rittmeister was killed, von Greim, von Schoeneberg, Richthofen's cousin, Wolfram, Jeschonnek, Loerzer, Milch, Osterkamp. All fliers, my friend, who want their place in the sun. If the Rittmeister – the Rote Kampf-flieger – had been alive he'd have probably joined them, too, and for the same reason.'

Dicken listened quietly. Udet had had too much to drink and was in a talkative mood. 'They're backed by the aircraft manufacturers,' he pointed out. 'Heinkel, Junkers, Messerschmitt – who see money in it for themselves, and, believe me, my old friend, *they*'re not thinking of biplanes. Their minds are on monoplanes – all-metal monoplanes with retractable under-carriages, like darts with wings. You and the Americans are still wallowing in memories of the last war. When I was last in the States they even produced some guy I'd shot down in 1918. Pure sentiment. Germany is not sentimental.'

'Will *you* join them, Erni?'

Udet smiled and shook his head. 'Goering tried to get me to join the party. He said I belonged with them but I told him that politics didn't interest me. But then he said "Not politics, aviation," and there he had me because aviation's the one thing I want out of life. He said that things were changing and that they needed men like me and could he count on me vhen the time came?'

'What did you say?'

Udet shrugged. 'I said, "Yes, sure, he could." But I didn't mean it. I wasn't serious. I was just trying to get rid of him because he always talks too much. If they do get power I hope he forgets.'

'What about the Jews?' Dicken asked. 'We read stories of them getting beaten up. Do you go along with that?'

Udet was a simple, kind, shallow man. He liked his pleasures and lived for flying, and his reply was unequivocal.

'Werner Voss was a Jew,' he said. 'I could never see much wrong with Voss. He was only tventy and he shot down forty-eight of your boys before he vas killed.'

It seemed to sum up Udet's entire attitude to politics. Voss was a flier so, whatever was said about Jews, to Udet Voss was all right.

176

'All the same,' he went on slowly, 'Germans have noticed that Jews are in key positions everywhere – in politics, industry, entertainment.' He shrugged. 'Because they are cleverer, I suppose. But it leads to anti-semitism. The politicians stir it up and the generals feed everybody the theory that they did not lose the war but were stabbed in the back by Socialists and Jews who remained at home during the fighting and destroyed the will to continue.' He seemed faintly depressed. 'They say that Germany's become a Judenrepublik – a Jewish republic – and the people begin to feel they have too much influence.'

'Do you?'

Udet grinned. 'I'm never here. I've built aeroplanes and lost the money I made from them. I've won races and lost races. I was once out of cash in Italy so I borrowed a saw and gave a musical entertainment on it to raise enough to get me home. Publicity's my bread and butter and I have some good friends. I've lost a few, too. Paul Baumer was killed diving into a lake. Berthold was strangled with the ribbon of his own Blue Max by the Marxist bastards who tried to run the country in 1918. I flew with Thea Rasche – Rash Thea they call her in the States. I've written a book on flying filled mit my cartoons. I'm making films, doing the flying for Leni Riefenstahl. *Pitz Palu* was good and I'm in the money again. So why should I worry about politics? It won't last long so I'm going to enjoy it while I can.'

2

In the RAF, even senior officers were killed occasionally in crashes and, returning to England, Dicken found that Hatto's chief was one of them. Hatto himself had left to command a squadron of troop-carrying Vickers Victorias in Iraq – 'Back to gooly chits,' his note said – and nobody else seemed to have the slightest interest in what Dicken had to say. It was puzzling, particularly as only now, eleven years after its birth, was the RAF, its much publicised efforts abroad saving it from extinction at home, beginning to walk on firm legs.

'The Allied Control Commission's well aware of what's going on,' he was told as he tried to recount what he'd learned in Berlin. 'But they simply close their eyes. At least we know about it and if we tried to stop the Germans, they'd only do it somewhere else. The first batch of pupils in Russia were ex-wartime pilots on a refresher course.'

'They're not now,' Dicken said. 'And they're being taught on machines that fly at two hundred.'

'My dear chap, don't get in such a flap. We know they're building aeroplanes. We haven't got our eyes closed. And we know they belong to the League of Nations and preach peace and disarmament while they're secretly thinking of the next war. After all, the press is on to it. *The Times* long since suggested there might be a secret clause attached to the Russo-German Treaty, even that there are other secret bases. One for training tank crews, another for gas warfare.'

Almost as if he'd become an embarrassment, Dicken was given a temporary job with the Directorate of Staff Duties at Adastral House, the RAF Headquarters in Kingsway, where he found himself working with Tom Howarth on plans to be put into operation in the event of a war and a general mobilisation.

'You needn't bother much, of course,' he was told. 'Because there isn't going to be a war.'

Having listened to Udet, Dicken wasn't so sure. 'I know exactly why this country always starts her wars by nearly losing them,' he growled. 'It's sheer lack of the right equipment because of the Ten Year Rule.'

Howarth smiled. They'd all heard of the Ten Year Rule. Every officer involved in trying to foresee the future was thwarted by it. It had been laid down as Treasury policy that expenditures must be governed by the assumption that no major war would break out within ten years.

'It was probably a good idea when it was laid down,' Howarth said. 'At that time no major war *was* likely to break out within ten years.'

'It's different now,' Dicken growled. 'And the bloody thing's self-perpetuating. At the end of every year, it starts again, so that war's always officially ten years away. And, Tom, I'm not so bloody sure that war *is* ten years away.'

There seemed a total lack of realism. It was well known that the embryo German air force, still secret and still expanding, had accurate models of all RAF aircraft while the RAF had none of theirs, and, driven to bring it up at a conference, Dicken pointed out that there wasn't even a draughtsman at the Air Ministry to make drawings, let alone models.

Diplock was sitting at the opposite side of the table. 'There's no establishment for a draughtsman,' he pointed out.

'Then let's call him a mapmaker,' Dicken snapped. 'We're surely entitled to that.'

'He'd have to take a mapping course.'

There was a long silence and Dicken burst out angrily. 'Then let him! Who's operating clandestinely? Us or the Germans? *Their* activities are understandable. They're trying to build up their air force without anybody knowing. But surely *we* don't have to justify ourselves'. The only way we can find out anything about the Germans is by reading *Flight* and *Aeroplane* and looking at the illustrations in Continental magazines.'

Quick to criticise out-of-date methods, he pointed out that while the Americans were using full aerodrome floodlighting for night-time landing, the RAF were still using paraffin flares but his report came back with the comment in Diplock's

179

handwriting that flares were mobile while floodlighting was not. The same attitude existed in the navy, and one of the Lords of the Admiralty appeared, to give an address that still doggedly denied that aircraft could be a danger to a battleship. 'Their Lordships,' he announced solemnly, 'do not consider that any warship competently handled is in danger from aerial attack.'

'Pity we can't challenge the bugger with a few big bombs,' Dicken muttered to Howarth.

Because Hatto was in Iraq, Dicken occasionally made a point of seeing his wife. He had known her almost as long as he had known Hatto and she was the same Hon. Caroline he and Hatto had taken to *The Maid Of The Mountains* and the Ritz with her friend, the Hon. Maud, before departing for France in 1917 to fly 1½-Strutters. She was still beautiful, still slender, still gentle. Occasionally, the Hon. Maud appeared. The fact that Dicken had ended up in her bed on the night they had gone to the theatre with Hatto and the Hon. Caroline didn't seem to matter much any longer because she had married a colonel in the Guards, whom she'd left within a year, and was now married to a man who made motor cars. But it soon became clear that she hadn't changed much. She was still stunningly beautiful and always managed to stay close to Dicken. Dining out with her and her husband, Dicken was just considering the absence of Zoë and wondering whether he ought to grasp the opportunity the Hon. Maud was clearly offering when the waiter slipped a card on to his plate. He recognised the writing on the back at once.

I'm coming round to your flat afterwards. See you later. Zoë.

The words leapt out at him as if they were underlined in crimson and, swinging round, he searched the crowded tables behind him. But there was no sign anywhere of his wife and, excusing himself as they left on the grounds that the card had been a summons back to duty, he hurried to his flat and poured himself a drink with a trembling hand.

'For the love of God!' Furious that the thought of Zoë appearing brought him to this pitch of excitement, he crushed out his cigarette. She didn't deserve his interest. She had never in the whole of their marriage done anything to warrant his faith in her. Her outburst when Harmer's plane had crashed had convinced him finally that they had been lovers and he suspected even that there had been others, yet he was still eager for a sight of her face.

At the tap on the door, he almost leapt across the room to fling it open. She was standing in the corridor outside, dressed in the sort of evening clothes that only a wealthy woman could afford.

'In the name of God,' he said, 'why do you always turn up when I'm least expecting you?'

She grinned in the old forthright way that had once enchanted him. 'I arrived just in time,' she said. 'I saw you eyeing that old bag at your table.'

He was aware of a guilty flush crossing his face. 'What do you expect? It's months since I saw you.'

'I telephoned your mother,' she went on coolly. 'She was a little stiff with me – '

'She probably felt she had the right to be.'

She shrugged. 'But she told me where your flat was. Aren't you going to invite me in?'

He held the door open and she stepped inside.

'How did you get here?' he demanded. 'I thought you were still in the States.'

'I was. But I had to go to Paris.'

'And now?'

'You'll have heard of Alan Cobham. He was knighted a couple of years ago.'

'Of course.' Everybody had heard of Cobham. He had been advancing aviation with meticulous long-distance flights ever since 1921.

'He's thinking out a technique for refuelling aircraft in flight.'

'I thought you didn't believe in it.'

'I do now. He gave me a lift to London. I know him well.'

'You move in exalted circles these days, Zo.'

She eyed him calmly. 'So could you, if you wished. With your record and skill. He's interested in air-to-ground communication.'

'The RAF have been experimenting with it for some time. Me in particular. Because of that bloody radio certificate I took in 1914.'

'He's a good man to work for.'

He eyed her for a moment. 'Is this another stunt, Zo? Like the

Dufee Derby and those bloody awful aeroplanes Harmer built?'
She gave him an icy look. 'It's stunts that further aviation,'
she snapped. 'Not your stuffy RAF flying by the book.'

'It was the RAF who pioneered the routes you civilians are so
smugly flying these days,' he snapped back. 'And the day will
come when *all* flying will be done by the book.'

Within minutes of meeting, they were at each other's throats,
both of them prickly because they had always seen aviation
from different viewpoints.

Zoë's expression was one of contempt. 'You haven't even
started using monoplanes yet,' she said. 'In the States monoplanes are everywhere. Lockheed, Fokker, Ford, Travel Air.
They're all flying single-wingers these days. All the records that
are being broken are being broken by monoplanes.'

'Are *you* breaking records?'

She gave him a cold look. 'I'm thinking of having a go. So are
other women. There's a girl here in England. From Hull. Amy
Johnson. But she's short of cash. I'm not.'

'Who's doing your navigating? You couldn't navigate across
a football pitch.'

Her look became an angry stare. 'I can afford to hire
navigation now. The best there is. I'd like to fly to Australia.
Amy Johnson likes the idea, too, so I've got to get a move on.'

For a moment there was silence. Then Dicken spoke.

'And why are you here now? Apart from the lift you got from
Cobham?'

'I wanted to see you.'

'You surprise me.'

'I need you, Dicky Boy. You might not realise it – '

'I might not.'

There was another silence and it occurred to Dicken that
every time he and Zoë met the silences grew longer.

'Aren't you going to ask me to stay the night?' she asked.

'I can't stop you. As you've just pointed out, I'm your
husband, so that makes you my wife.'

'Dicken, I love you.'

He didn't say anything and she tried once again to explain. 'I
do, Dicken. It's something I can't explain. I'll show it to you if
you'll melt a little and give me a chance.'

Their love making was fierce and passionate but somehow,

despite what she said, Dicken knew something was missing. The following morning, he made coffee but, as he took it in to her, she eyed him warily, as if expecting him to launch another attack on her.

'Well?' she asked.

'Well what?'

'Doesn't this satisfy you? I've shared your bed.'

'There's nothing odd about that. The only strange thing is that you share it so rarely. What happens now? Do I get a larger flat?'

She sipped the coffee. 'I shouldn't,' she said. 'I'm going back to the States.'

'When?'

'End of the week.'

'Why did you come?'

'To see you.'

'To do what?'

'To get you to run Toshack Air Travel. I have three Avro Tens. You'd be surprised, now that Imperial Airways are operating regularly to Paris, how many people have become air-minded. A businessman wanting to go to Glasgow from London is prepared to fly these days. We have cabins. Big enough for seven people and a steward to supply them with brandy to calm their nerves. I could do with someone to run it. George Peasegood's all right for the garages but he's not big enough for this.'

'You hated my guts when Harmer was killed.'

'That's forgotten.'

'I'm not a businessman, anyway. I can't even read a balance sheet.'

'You could soon learn.' She seemed to be making an appeal. 'Dicky Boy, can't you see? Love isn't just being in the same house together and sharing the same bed.'

'It goes a long way.'

'It demands mutual respect, mutual allowance for the other person's wishes.'

'Getting me out of the RAF and into business doesn't seem to indicate it.'

'That's different.'

'How?'

'Dicky Boy, people are making fortunes from flying.'

'If that's what you want, we seem to be different. I'm really not very interested in making a splash, old love.'

'Come in with me.'

'Why should I, Zo? For God's sake, why? Of your own choice, you spend your life as far away from me as you can, but then you tell me, after announcing once more that you've no intention of staying with me, that you need me. I find it hard to believe.'

She went into a long rambling explanation. It was confused, almost incoherent. As far as Dicken could make out her need was for acceptance, for people to regard her as a normal woman and not as a freak who knew nothing of anything except aeroplanes. She felt she was different from everybody else, but was still prepared to disappear back to the States. She seemed to want her bread buttered on both sides.

'If I gave up the RAF now,' he pointed out quietly, 'I'd have wasted the last ten years of my life. I've not moved as fast off the mark as others – Arthur Diplock, your beloved brother-in-law – has made sure *his* place in the hierarchy's secure – but the higher ranks are open to me now and I don't want anything to do with commercial flying. I tried it once and I didn't like it.'

She was silent for a moment and he saw there were tears in her eyes. 'I've *got* to go back to the States,' she said. 'I've got to. Won't you come, too? Just to be with me?'

He kissed her gently on the cheek, affectionately but not with passion. 'I think it's most unlikely,' he said. 'I've put in for a posting abroad.'

3

He had expected India and when he was ordered to a squadron flying Handley Page Hyderabad bombers he decided someone in Personnel had got his wires crossed.

Zoë was back in the States now trying to find an aeroplane. 'Miss Zoë Toshack,' the *Daily Mail* announced, 'is preparing for her proposed record-breaking trip to Australia.' 'Miss,' Dicken noticed, not 'Mrs'. And 'Toshack,' not 'Quinney.' 'She is at the moment in the States, looking over likely aircraft. She is considering a Lockheed Vega like Amelia Earhart or a Stinson Detroiter capable of carrying five passengers. She claims she would prefer a British machine to anything else.'

And there she was again, smiling at the camera, so that Dicken's heart jerked uncomfortably at the sight of her.

But he knew it didn't really matter any more and he'd finally even been to see a lawyer about a divorce. Unfortunately, the following day a letter had arrived begging him not to abandon her and, calling himself a fool, he'd dropped the whole business.

They were an unlikely couple, he decided, with differing temperaments, different aims, different demands on life, and what had held them together for so long he didn't know. He suspected it was nothing more than familiarity, and that, had he met anyone else, he might have done something about it. But since Nicola Aubrey there never had been anyone with whom he could imagine living the rest of his life so he'd always let things slide, suspecting he'd always be there when Zoë became frightened at her growing wealth and fame and needed a shoulder to cry on.

He was grateful to be flying again, aware of the brightness of the upper air which glowed in a way earthbound mortals could never conceive, aware once more of that feeling of being one of

God's chosen few because he felt the sun before it reached other people, because he'd acquired the skill to support himself in the sky in the way man had always wished to since the Middle Ages. He wasn't sure what to make of the Hyderabads, however. They were big and clumsy, but surprisingly responsive with their two Napier Lion engines, so that sometimes he was inclined to bank them too steeply on the tight turns.

He had always been basically a fighter pilot and at first he didn't fancy the prospect of flying with a crew but suddenly he realised he'd been missing something and found an unexpected compensation in the team spirit and comradeship. Especially at night, when the rest of the country was asleep and the sense of loneliness was relieved by the tightness of the little group of men in their black machine high above the earth.

Then Zoë reappeared like a ghost from the past in a paragraph in the newspapers. She was far too photogenic not to have her picture in regularly and she had a gift for getting her personality across. Considering she'd broken only one rather unimportant record which had added nothing to the future of flying, it was almost as if the newspapers were falling over themselves simply because she photographed well.

This time it was because she'd finally decided to buy a British machine for her attempt to fly to Australia, and was debating between one of her Avro tens and a new type of De Havilland.

The Hyderabads began to bore Dicken a little because he felt at times little better than a chauffeur for a group of men whose tasks were more important than his own, which was simply to deliver them from one place to another, but then a squadron leader at RAF HQ in India was killed when a DH9 flew into a mountainside near the Khyber Pass and, with no one of sufficient rank and experience to take his place, Dicken found himself on a ship ploughing through the Mediterranean with a draft of men heading for Egypt.

They left the ship at Alexandria where he was able to visit Tom Howarth who, by this time, was working on a new training scheme in the Middle East and they ate dinner in Cairo, watching the dahabiyas drifting past on the Nile.

'Egypt gets under your skin,' Howarth observed. 'Egyptians bumping their foreheads on the ground to the priest's chanting, the face of the Sphinx, sunset on the Nile, the silhouettes of the Pyramids at dusk.

'There are disadvantages, of course. Water has to be filtered and dosed with chlorine – considering the corpses of animals floating in it, Sweet Water Canal's a complete misnomer – the heat makes the engines erratic, and the windsock's always in danger of being stolen by the Arabs to make clothing. But the desert can be incredibly beautiful and there are always the Gezirah Club, cocktails on the terrace at Shepheards', and polo at Heliopolis.'

The journey that followed was an anti-climax – the Red Sea, so calm the sea melted into the sky and there was no horizon in the heat, then the brown sun-baked coast of India. The journey from Bombay by train was monotonously khaki-coloured and heavy with dust, but Delhi was a civilised city, though the formality had to be seen to be believed.

Appointed Squadron Leader Air Staff, Dicken was responsible to his immediate superior, who turned out to be Cuthbert Orr, bigger and more hearty than ever. He welcomed Dicken like a long-lost brother and made their position clear at once. 'Out here,' he said, 'Trenchard's influence carries no weight whatsoever. The Indian Army runs the show and we're short of spares – tyres and radios especially – and it's not so damned long since we announced that for all intents and purposes the RAF in India was non-existent. Out of seventy aircraft only seven were serviceable and half of 'em were 1918 vintage and still had patches sewn over the bullet holes they got in France. All squadrons are up in the North-West Frontier Province but at last they're sending us two new ones – the first post-war machines we've had. Westland Wapitis. Know anything of 'em?'

Dicken smiled. 'Yes, sir. They had a lot of spare parts for the DH9s so they designed the Wapitis to use 'em up.'

Orr pushed a packet of cigarettes across. 'Only part of the Frontier Province is administered by us, of course,' he pointed out. 'The rest's controlled by independent tribes who owe us no direct allegiance and live in what's known as tribal territory with their own laws and customs. We let 'em get on with it, so long as they don't raid into British India. It's only six years since one lot attacked an officer's home at Kohat, murdered

187

him and his wife and kidnapped his daughter. There's one other snag. We're expecting trouble in Rezhanistan.'

'Does it affect us? It's not part of India.'

'We have an embassy there. The King made a tour last year of Turkey, Iran, England and a few other places and was so impressed with the emancipation of women he came back determined to carry out reforms in Rezhanistan. Unfortunately religion there goes a bit deeper than it does at Stow-on-the-Wold on a sunny Sunday morning and just lately, the mullahs have been as restless as a lot of fleas. They're not interested in the King's lectures at the palace, or the pictures of Lindbergh he put up and it's surprising no one's taken a potshot at him. But he's still opening new schools and demanding that young ladies wear short skirts and have their hair bobbed as they do in London.' Orr grinned. 'I think the thing that irritates his ministers and tribal leaders most, though, is that he expects them to wear top hats and tail coats. I saw them once. They looked like a lot of out of work undertakers. I reckon they'll explode any day now.'

*

Dicken's arrival coincided with the move from Delhi to Simla in the foothills of the Himalayas for the hot months of the year. It was a dreadful period for those wives and families who were in India only on a short-term tour and had to worry about how to live within their means. His job was to be responsible through Orr and the Chief of Staff to the Air Officer Commanding for operational policy and intelligence, sharing responsibilities for the preparation of the RAF budget, organisation and re-equipping and the provision of answers to parliamentary questions sent from England. One such asked the number of bombs dropped on the frontier since 1919, the number of people killed and the value of the property destroyed by bombing. It took one minute flat to answer. For the number of bombs, he wrote 'Sixty-five,' which was the first number that sprang to his mind. For the number of people killed, he wrote 'One,' adding that it was impossible to be certain as bombing usually took place in conjunction with army operations and it was therefore difficult to differentiate between those killed by guns and those killed by bombs. For the value of property destroyed, he wrote 'Unknown, since there is no value placed on a mud hut, and there are no house agents on the frontier.' Orr considered it good enough to buy him an extra drink.

Zoë continued to crop up. She had decided finally to buy a machine nobody had ever heard of, its only qualification being, it seemed, that it was British. It was called a Munson Ghost, and there she was in *The Times of India*, standing alongside a high-winged monoplane with a pair of Gypsy I engines mounted on a single crankcase. She had hired an ex-Merchant Navy officer called Angus Packer, who had transferred to flying and was considered to be an expert navigator. He had flown the route more than once with British Airways and was considered unlikely to make mistakes.

Dicken's stay at headquarters was short because Almonde, who had been commanding a squadron of DH9s at Kohat went down with jaundice and it was necessary for someone to take over. Since it was a single-squadron station it was a good job because it meant Dicken would also be the station commander, and as the squadron was working with the army in Waziristan it offered a chance of action.

The frontier area was divided into two adminstrative sections, each with its own provincial government responsible to the government of India. The North-West Frontier Province was roughly four hundred miles long and a hundred miles wide, with Peshawar – known to everybody there as 'Pshah' – as its capital. The dominant note about the country was its size. To the north were vast silent mountains cloaked in eternal snow, wild glacier-born torrents, cruel precipices and pastureless hillsides, all the colour purged away by the glare of the sun. Very little was cultivated and, dwarfed by the limitless expanse of rock, glacier and mountain, the fertile patches were the only relief in the monotonous grey-brown of the vast slopes of shale and shingle, while the willows and plane trees and the soldier-like poplars marching across the valleys were the only points of coolness after the fierce light and dust on the hillsides. The cantonment in which they lived was surrounded by barbed wire and patrolled by Indian sentries. All movement in or out of the camp was forbidden after sundown and if a married officer was away on duty for a night it was automatic to place an armed guard on his home.

Looking for the Signals Section to send a signal to Simla indicating his arrival, the first person Dicken saw was Babington, who had flown with him in Iraq. He was now a corporal and gave him a grin of delight, while, sitting at the Signals Officer's desk, was Handiside, a flight-sergeant once more, a little redder in the face these days but still wearing the same grin.

'The Signals Officer's gone down with jaundice, sir,' he said. 'It seems to be catching. I'm running the show till he gets back.'

It was Handiside as much as anyone who filled Dicken in about the squadron. It had been a long time in India and its machines were as old as its pilots were young. They had all joined since the war and, with many of them inexperienced, it was Dicken's job to start a series of exercises in bombing, navigation and gunnery.

Despite being operations officer as well as CO, whenever active operations were in swing he managed to take part. His chief task was to impose a blockade day and night on a section of the Bohmand country where difficult tribesmen were living. It was a small area adjoining that of friendly tribesmen, so the blockade called for a high standard of map reading and very careful briefing. Flying mostly at night or at midday when weather conditions were uncomfortably rough and bumpy, he knew that more sensible men were taking it easy and that nobody objected to him flying their aircraft.

Below him the countryside was inhabited by some of the toughest fighting men in India. Moving columns through their mountains was a specialised form of warfare in which inexperienced units could suffer heavy casualties, and the RAF and the army had worked out a system of close support. If trouble was expected, the RAF kept one or more aircraft over the area throughout the hours of daylight, and there were times when they bombed and shot up the tribesmen within thirty yards of an army outpost.

The work went along without serious harm to either side until a man called Shimi Par, who was well known as a troublemaker, appeared in the area. A Persian by birth, he had arrived in India via Karachi and made his way to Waziristan where he had made a reputation for himself as an orator in the mosques. Gradually it became noticed that he was preaching a jehad, a holy war, against the government of India, and suddenly all the tribes in the area were on the move.

There was a hurried exodus further south of families and government officials from Peshawar, and Orr flew in from Simla with orders.

'We can't get land forces up to the front in time,' he said. 'We'll have to run the show. We're to drop messages warning the tribes to return to their villages within forty-eight hours with the threat of air action if they don't.'

Two days later, Dicken took off with another aircraft, to make sure the tribes had disappeared. He could see no movement below him and was on the point of giving up the search when he caught sight of a cloud of dust moving along a narrow valley two and a half miles south of Kat. The country they were flying over provided good cover, and with the tribesmen moving at speed, it was important that they be stopped before they broke into open country.

'Get a message to Group Headquarters,' he warned Babington who was flying with him. 'Give map references and ask for instructions. It's not our job to start a war.'

For a long time the aircraft circled, while Babington struggled with his set, but it was impossible to raise Group.

'The ball's in our court,' Dicken decided and, indicating to the other aircraft to follow him, pushed his nose down and headed for the moving tribesmen.

Swooping along the valley, one behind the other, they dropped their bombs, and as they lifted, Babington's gun began to clatter. Swinging round, they strafed the column again and again, the howl of the engine echoing back off the craggy slopes of the gorges. By the time they had finished, the column had scattered in both directions, some riding ahead, others hurrying back the way they had come, men on foot scrambling up the slopes to crouch behind rocks to fire defiant shots at them.

Before first light, the aircraft took off again, five of them this time, and found the tribesmen grouped together round their camp fires. As they returned, more aircraft took off to keep them moving and when Dicken went up again in the evening, it was clear Shimi Par had given up his invasion and his men were straggling homewards.

As he landed, the telephone went and he lifted it, expecting

Orr's congratulations. The message was somewhat different.

'It's started,' Orr said.

'What's started, sir?'

'Rezhanistan. The bloody place's risen in rebellion and the whole place's become a battlefield, with the British Legation smack in the middle.'

4

It was the girls in their summer dresses who had caused all the trouble. Young Rezhan females dressed in European style passing through tribal country to Peshawar to be educated in the European manner had stirred up the resentment of the Amwaris, a backward and fanatical tribe who had never paid taxes, and they had risen as one man prepared to forfeit their lives rather then send a quota of their daughters on some ungodly journey such as had been ordered. To unveil their women was against their religion and, in a country where religion was the dominant feature of life, the bitterness spread, and the Amwaris, joined by other tribes, had taken up a position astride the main road that ran from Ambul, the capital of Rezhanistan, to the Khyber Pass and the safety of India. All road communication along the route was cut, and the tribesmen, joined now by Bohmands and other Pathan tribes, had invaded Ambul, blowing up bridges en route and raising to revolt the tribes in the southern half of the state. The British Legation was cut off and left with the Ambul wireless station as their only communication with the outside world – and that very doubtful because thousands of armed Rezhans were marching on the city.

In Peshawar and stations along the frontier, Intelligence and Equipment Officers hurriedly began going through their papers to find out what they knew about Rezhanistan. The Rezhans were Pathans, speaking Pushtu, and virtually a law unto themselves. Every man was armed with a long rifle or a jezail, which could shoot further than a normal British rifle, and they had all been taught to fight from childhood. Their faith in Islam far outweighed all their earthly possessions and they were devoted to their religious leaders. Their country was a desolation of great peaks and deep valleys, of precipitous gorges and rushing grey rivers – barren and beautiful in the intense sunlight, and when the shadows lengthened and the peaks turned gold, pink and mauve in the setting sun. Every road and path and pass of it was said to be soaked in blood.

The rebel leader was a man called Bachi-i-Adab, the son of a water carrier. British Intelligence knew him as a bandit and the hero or villain of every fantastic story that came out of the bazaars. His quarrel was only with the King of Rezhanistan and he was not interfering with ordinary travellers, but a force of the King's cavalry sent to deal with him had deserted to him. By this time, disaffected Kohistanis, Afridis and Waziris, to say nothing of supporters of Shimi Par, had joined him and forts to the north-west of Ambul had been captured and the whole yelling horde of fanatics was camped to the west of the British Legation, their bullets knocking in the windows as they fired on the King's troops to the east. The possibility of a massacre was only too great and preparations were made in case a decision was taken to evacuate the women and children.

*

Dicken was among the officers called to a conference by Orr. The commanding officers of all squadrons were present, as well as the Air Officer Commanding in India and staff officers from Peshawar and Simla, among them, Dicken noticed, Diplock, representing his chief, Air Commodore St Aubyn.

'This operation,' the AOC began, 'is going to fall entirely on the RAF. The army can't get through because all bridges have been blown up and the casualties could be enormous because the Rezhans would initially resist such an invasion. However, if we're to bring these people out, we're going to need far more aeroplanes than India can provide and I've asked for Victorias to be sent from Baghdad.'

There were a few sidelong glances. Though the Victorias could carry twenty soldiers and their kit, their range left something to be desired.

'That's a distance of nearly three thousand miles, sir.' The voice was Diplock's.

'Two thousand eight hundred to be exact,' the AOC said

mildly. 'They'll need refuelling en route. But it's the only course open to us. They can reach Karachi in two days. There's only one question in doubt: Is the Victoria able to take off with a heavy load in Ambul, which is 6000 feet above sea level, and climb to a height of 10,000 feet to cross the mountains. Last year it was decided they could do no such thing.'

'We can take everything off them that's not needed,' Orr offered.

'We can try,' the AOC agreed. 'There's also a Hinaidi heavy transport in Iraq, waiting to take the Foreign Secretary home from India. The total evacuating power, therefore, consists of twenty-four DH9s and two Wapitis, with, two thousand eight hundred miles away, a number of Victorias and the Hinaidi. I'd like to know your views, gentlemen.'

'It can't be done,' Diplock said. 'It's impossible,'

'Quetta's the same height above sea level as Ambul,' Dicken pointed out, 'Why not carry out tests there? If the Victorias can get off from Quetta, they can get out of Ambul.'

The AOC looked round at the assembled officers. 'I think we should try,' he said.

*

Five days later, the first Victoria arrived, piloted by Hatto, and Dicken flew down to Quetta with Orr to see how it was behaving.

It was a huge machine, dwarfing the Tiger Moth alongside it. With its biplane tail, four hugh wheels and two enormous wings, it looked far from easy to manoeuvre.

Hatto greeted them cheerfully. 'Had to land at Bandar Abbas for fuel,' he said. 'We found we'd lost the weight off the trailing aerial so we used a tin of bully beef, but the wife of the local agent saw it and, as she'd eaten nothing but mutton for months, she persuaded us to change it for an old flat-iron.'

His manner was optimistic but he was worried. 'She'll stagger off in four hundred yards with a weight equal to that of twenty passengers,' he said. 'Then she'll gain just enough height to fly not over but through the passes to India. Thank God it's the cool season. In the summer heat, we couldn't do it. We'll be operating in conditions for which the Victorias were never designed and the engines'll be labouring at full throttle all the time. However, with everything, even the wireless operator, out of the machine, I reckon we can just reach Ambul and return with a maximum number of passengers, though we'll be dusting the snow off the mountains with the wingtips.'

'The crews'll be unarmed,' Orr pointed out. 'The British Minister in Ambul's asked for it. The rebels are accustomed to indiscriminate bombing by the Rezhan Air Force and it's felt it'll reassure them. We'll provide the usual gooly chits.'

As he climbed inside the Victoria to decide what else could be removed from its fitting, Hatto took Dicken to one side.

'She's due off any day, old boy,' he said quietly. 'Did you know?'

'Zoë?'

'Yes. She's expected at Baghdad. She hopes to make good time to Aleppo. They're refuelling there and making it a rest stop. This chap Packer's expected to bring her in bang on the button.'

Dicken said nothing and Hatto looked at him curiously. 'Perhaps if she pulls this off,' he said, 'she'll settle down.'

That same night a faint message was received at Quetta from Ambul. The British Minister was known to have a small personal transmitter-receiver and, when the Rezhan wireless station went off the air, he had been forced to use it. The message was faint but it was possible to understand it '. . .Request reconnaissance aeroplane as soon as possible.'

There were no more messages, no request for an evacuation, only silence, a silence that was hard to accept because everything was ready. The engines of the DH9s were run up every morning and Hatto's Victorias were awaiting the call. They already knew the conditions for landing at Arpur, the aerodrome just outside Ambul, but without permission from the Rezhan authorities they couldn't even contemplate a rescue.

That day *The Times of India* erupted in a shout of delight to the effect that Zoë Toshack and her navigator, Anguş Packer, were expected very soon in Karachi in their Munson Ghost.

'Everything,' they reported, 'is reported as going exactly to plan. They will fly from England in five days and the 1550-mile trip from Baghdad, with one stop for refuelling at Bandar Abbas, will be completed in just over twenty-four hours. From

Bombay, they will fly to Karachi. After that starts the more difficult part of the journey over a wild unpopulated country with few facilities for aircraft, then the last stretch across the Java and Timor Seas to Darwin and on to Brisbane.'

It was beginning to look as though Zoë might pull it off and get her name in the annals of flying at last and Dicken even found himself hoping she'd succeed.

He was still studying the newspaper when Orr appeared. 'We've decided to send up one of your machines,' he said. 'The AOC's unhappy about the silence and we've got to try to re-establish contact by dropping a Popham panel.'

The Popham panel was an ingenious apparatus like a Venetian blind which had been devised for ground-to-air communication. When closed it showed dark because the tops of the slats were painted green, but, held closed by strong elastic, the slats could be opened by a cord to show the white on the other side, so that it became a simple device for sending morse.

The following day Diplock flew in. His attitude was that, in view of the danger, one of the younger pilots should be sent because he could best be spared.

Orr's heavy brows came down. 'That's a damn-fool idea,' he snorted.

Diplock's face tightened. 'It's Air Commodore St Aubyn's considered opinion,' he said.

'Then it's a bloody stupid one!' As usual, Orr was pulling no punches, even to the point of making enemies. 'If anyone goes, it should be someone with experience.'

'The Air Commodore – '

'The Air Commodore's not running this show!' Orr snapped.

'Sir – !' Diplock tried again and Orr rounded on him, his face red, his moustache bristling.

'Who the devil *are* you?' he snapped. 'I've seen you before. You seem to make a profession of arriving like a prophet of doom to veto every damn thing I suggest! Let the Air Commodore look after the little bits of paper on his desk and leave the flying to me. He was always better at flying desks than aeroplanes, anyway!'

As Diplock disappeared with a flea in his ear, Orr turned to Dicken. 'I'd like *you* to do the trip,' he said. 'The panel's got to be dropped close to the Legation building and, because you've got to have enough petrol for the return flight, you're going to have no more than fifteen minutes overhead. They'll also probably shoot at you and there'll be no landing in the mountains on the way back. You'll need a good wireless operator. We have to get them all out. You must make that clear.'

Choosing Babington because he knew he was good and quite unflappable, Dicken took off the following morning for the hundred-and-forty-mile flight to Ambul and back. For the first forty miles, they climbed over the featureless plain that constituted the north-west corner of India but, as they drew near the Khyber Pass, the scenery changed to the foothills and lower ranges of the Hindu Kush. Because they hadn't reached their maximum height, they threaded their way through the valleys, rugged mountains towering on either side to eight or nine thousand feet, snow-covered and contrasting sharply with the blackness of the gorges and valleys between. After an hour they approached the Boragil Pass, where twin peaks 10,000 feet high looked like sentinels guarding the route. At the other side of the pass the terrain levelled off as it debouched on to the plain of Ambul, a stretch of land sprinkled with villages and cultivated plots 6000 feet above sea level.

'There it is, sir!'

The white Legation building lay just outside Ambul and they could see the Union Jack still flying from the roof. Putting the nose down, Dicken dropped to five hundred feet and began to circle.

'Message down there, sir!'

As they banked low over the building they read the words, made up from white towels and strips of material laid out on the lawn: 'FLY HIGH. DO NOT LAND. ALL WELL.'

Despite the message, there was no sign of life, no movement, no hands waving from windows.

'Better drop the two halves of the panel separately,' Dicken advised. 'And we'll see if anybody comes out to collect it.'

Flying low over the building, they managed to land the first half-panel right on the doorstep. No one came out to pick it up.

'I'm going to fly low,' Dicken said. 'See if you can see any light in the building, or any faces at the windows.'

But the windows had been boarded up, and dark figures moved among the trees near the surrounding wall with more groups along the heights overlooking it and near the royal palace, clearly firing at the aeroplane.

'Drop the other half,' Dicken ordered. 'One half's no good to anybody.'

As Babington leaned over the side of his cockpit, there was a bang from somewhere in front of Dicken who was immediately covered with hot black oil. As Babington turned to report that the panel had gone, his eyes widened.

'Christ, sir,' he said. 'You all right?'

'I'll have to land!'

Babington was as unflappable as ever. 'Get some height first, sir,' he said. 'I want to send a message.'

Pulling back the stick, Dicken began to climb so that the little propeller on the wing which worked the generator could force out enough voltage for Babington to transmit. As the engine began to splutter and finally died, the wireless operator lifted his head.

'Got it away, sir,' he said.

Arpur aerodrome lay several miles away so, finding a patch of flat land between the rocky hills, Dicken sideslipped off height and floated in to land. But the tyres were shot through and the machine stood on its nose. As he scrambled clear, barely able to see for the oil on his face, he saw there were bullet holes in the machine, one of them in the engine sump.

As they were examining it, from among a group of rocks a head popped up, then another, and another, and within minutes they were surrounded by a mob of heavily-armed shouting tribesmen. Then an ancient Ford Tin Lizzie appeared, clattering over the ground, its front wheels wobbling and shaking on the stony surface. It seemed to have no driver but there were rifles sticking out from the sides. As it stopped near them, six or seven dark-skinned men with unshaven faces wearing balaclava helmets climbed out and walked slowly towards them, their rifles at the ready. One of them, obviously an NCO, halted the others and advanced on Dicken. At the last moment, he lifted the rifle quickly and fired it in the air. The bullet whistled past Dicken's nose.

The NCO grinned. 'Prisoner, sahib,' he said.

*

Within minutes the men from the car had become a mob, all of them waving rifles or knives. They were speaking Pushtu and, since Dicken could only speak Urdu, they were not able to communicate.

He produced his blood chit hurriedly but nobody could read, though after a while a man wearing a military-looking great-coat arrived who claimed to be a brigadier in the royal army. Though he wasn't hostile, he clearly didn't set much store by the blood chit, and it appeared that while he and his fellow countrymen associated khaki with the British, because of the winter season Dicken and Babington were wearing blue.

Since they were carrying no arms and the bomb racks were empty, the Rezhans found nothing more aggressive than a Very pistol, so that their hostile manner changed. Trying to explain the peaceful nature of their mission, Dicken persuaded the brigadier to post sentries on the wrecked machine, then they were led down the slopes to a stony village where they were given tea and chupattis. That night they spent crammed together with a dozen malodorous tribesmen round a charcoal fire in a very small farm building entirely devoid of ventilation.

For two days they remained there, making up crosswords and playing draughts with matchsticks on a board drawn in the dust, then on the third morning a decrepit Chevrolet van appeared which brought wheels and tyres for the damaged machine. It was explained that the Rezhan air force also flew DH9s.

The damaged wheels were replaced and, using the mob which was still hanging around out of curiosity, they turned the DH the right side up, hitched the tail to the back of the van, and set off for the airfield with the armed guard, twenty-three men aboard a vehicle designed to carry twelve.

The Rezhans at the airfield were not hostile, merely curious, until they saw Dicken studying their old DH9s. They were in a dreadful condition. They had no instruments and where the altimeters should have been there were just holes. The pilots were Russians who were refugees from the Revolution and the annoyance they showed, Dicken suspected, came less from hostility than from shame at the condition of the machines.

The commanding officer was a large fat Rezhan who wore a pale green jersey, the same balaclava helmet as the rest of them, and a bandolier stuffed with bullets. Since he was the commander of the whole Rezhan air force, he was conscious of his importance and had a little office at the end of the landing strip where he took off his bandolier and invited them to sit down to lunch with him. The meal was curried goat and there was a sentry on the door with a rifle but, halfway through the meal, the sentry propped his weapon in a corner and sat down alongside Babington and started to eat with them. While they were eating, one of the Russian pilots appeared, demanding bombs, so the commander wiped his mouth on his sleeve, and opened a large safe in his office to take out a very rusty-looking Cooper 20-pounder. The Russian disappeared with it in a suitcase.

During the afternoon, they were told they were to be taken to a hotel and, climbing into a car, they trundled off the airfield to a shabby-looking building. It was a two-storeyed affair with a single room downstairs, where battered armchairs were grouped round a few potted palms. They climbed to an outside balcony from which led several bedrooms. The room they were given matched the shabbiness downstairs, with two sagging beds covered with grey-looking sheets, what appeared to be old army blankets, and a threadbare bedspread covered with pushtu symbols. The door was locked behind them and they knew there was a sentry outside because they could hear him hawking and spitting and clicking the bolt of his rifle.

During the night they were awakened by shouts and screams and the banging of doors, but, deciding not to get involved, they went back to sleep. The following morning they saw the door was open and, scrambling out, they saw the sentry lying in a heap, minus his rifle and obviously very dead.

There were more bodies on the stairs and in the hall, and they learned that Bachi-i-Adab's men had got through the lines the previous night and broken in to ransack the place before the King's troops could push them out again.

*

The Legations of other foreign powers in Ambul were nearer to the city than the British Legation so, during the next two or three days, they tried to make contact with them to find out what was happening. They were successful with the French

Legation, but the French knew nothing, though they believed there had been no casualties, and, bombarding the Rezhan commander with questions, they learned that the British Legation was still displaying signals on the lawn advising against landing either at Arpur or anywhere else.

Though allowed a certain amount of freedom, they were always watched carefully by an armed guard led by a small sergeant with black curly hair, a black toothbrush moustache and large flat feet who became known to them as Charlie Chaplin. Learning that the Rezhan wireless equipment had been repaired, Dicken insisted on seeing the Rezhan Foreign Minister. Charlie Chaplin clearly had no idea what a foreign minister was but, after a long argument, he produced a boy who had lived in India and spoke some English, and, explaining what he wanted, Dicken saw that the boy understood.

The following day the boy returned with a safe conduct pass and they were led to a fort on the edge of the town which was also the King's palace. The Rezhans clearly had little idea of hygiene, and refuse had been flung into the alleys and left to the scavenging birds, while the ground, dusty in summer, was at the moment a quagmire of mud, spattering the walls of the palace, blurring the expert filigrees of Pathan craftsmen and dulling the colours of foliage and clothing. The Foreign Minister's quarters contained chipped furniture, and neglected wood carvings rubbed shoulders with threadbare drapes and unrevered ornaments, the mud walls visible through gaping holes in the panelling.

The Minister, one of the King's unwilling converts, was a short thickset man with a three-day-old beard, wearing a shabby European suit that looked as if it had been sent on the back of a camel from an Indian bazaar. His tie was worn without a collar and on his head was a European felt hat which he didn't bother to remove. Though he was full of smiles and apologies, it was clear immediately that he was giving nothing away.

The people in the Legation were still alive, it seemed, but there had been little communication with them and the Foreign Minister obviously didn't intend to risk his neck between the firing lines to find anything out.

'Then may I get into contact with India, via Peshawar,

perhaps also via Quetta, using the Rezhan wireless station?'

The Foreign Minister agreed, but, escorted to the room at the top of the palace where the wireless station consisted of several elderly British army radio sets, Dicken's requests were met with blank stares. In the end, Babington persuaded the wireless operators to let him have a go and he bent over the set, frowning heavily. 'We'll be lucky to get in contact with anyone across the road with this lot,' he muttered.

However, to cries of wonder from the Rezhan operators, he finally got the set working, though they were unable to raise either Peshawar or Quetta.

'We can always have a go with the set from the machine, sir,' he suggested.

But when they tried, the accumulators ran down quickly and they were again unable to make contact.

'How about getting permission to send a message by land line to Peshawar?'

To their surprise permission was granted at once and, with the aid of the English-speaking student, they made out the message and sent it off.

During this period, the Rezhan air force was constantly in the air, dropping on the rebels bombs which were doubtless all carried by suitcase from the commanding officer's safe. Every time they took off, they were met by a fusillade of fire from the area round the British Legation and in the end one of the machines went out of control and crashed within a few hundred yards of where they stood and burst into flames. Immediately, thousands of insurgents poured forward to cut the throats of the crew but, as they spread in a huge cloud of running figures, the King's troops opened fire and, with a wail, they scattered, leaving several of their number lying silently alongside the blazing aircraft.

*

There still seemed to be no contact with the British Embassy and Babington began to grow irritated.

'What they need in there,' he said, 'is a good wireless operator.'

The air force commander offered to find them a guide, but by this time shells were falling in and around the Legation and they heard that several people had been hit and cut with glass or flying splinters of wood.

Eventually, a Rezhan dressed in long white robes, a waistcoat and a fez, appeared, and said he was bearer to Sir Andrew MacAllister, the Minister.

'The sahibs must not let anyone see their uniforms,' he warned. 'The King's Russian pilots wear uniforms very similar and have been bombing the rebels, and if you fall into their hands they will think you are Russian and –' he drew his finger across his throat.

The ancient Chevrolet appeared after dark and they drove away through the streets of the town. In the villages near the Legation, there were bodies everywhere, their stomachs swollen, and the houses were charred, the stonework black and oily. Leaving the car and groping their way in the dim light of a torch, they pushed into the shadows, the bulk of the buildings faint against the sky. There was a stink of death and several times they heard rats squeaking among the rubble and their claws castanetting over the stones.

Eventually the Rezhan guide held up his hand and they sank down in the shadows of a wall which they realised surrounded the garden of the Legation. It had a large scorched hole in it.

'Rebel field gun misfire,' the Rezhan said. He gestured to left and right. 'Here are Bachi-i-Adab's army. Here are King's army. We must wait.'

A lot of firing was going on and they could hear the whack-whack of bullets. Among the trees huge fires were blazing. There was no sign of life from the Legation, a large rambling white building full of arches and colonades to catch the cool winds during the hot summer. In the moonlight, it looked a little like the Parthenon in Athens. Nearby was a large house obviously belonging to one of the Legation staff, but it had been hit by shells and one end had collapsed.

The guide pointed to the Legation. 'I will go first. When firing stops, next one go.'

A breeze had got up and it was cold enough to make them shiver. The guide tapped Dicken on the shoulder and slipped away and a moment later they saw him running across the lawn, with his head well down. Eventually he vanished into the shadows alongside the Legation.

'You next, Babington.'

Babington's teeth flashed as he grinned and, ducking his head, he slipped through the hole in the Legation wall and began to run as the guide had run, his head down and following a zigzag route. As he disappeared, the firing swelled up and Dicken had to crouch down lower against the shattered wall.

After a while he heard voices and, sinking into the shadows, became aware of rebel soldiers nearby. As they moved in and out of the trees in the moonlight, he could see they were armed to the teeth. They obviously suspected something was afoot and were searching the undergrowth. Dicken could hear them talking to each other and occasionally a burst of laughter, then they disappeared, except for one who remained watching the Legation.

For a while, Dicken waited. A light flashed abruptly from the Legation then went out and he guessed they were encouraging him to make a dash for it, but the rebel soldier was still there and he could smell the rancid smell of sweat and woodsmoke that came from his clothes.

Finding a heavy stone in the undergrowth, Dicken flung it towards where he had seen a pebbled pathway. At the clatter, the soldier lifted his head and began to run in the direction of the noise. As he vanished, Dicken scrambled through the hole in the wall.

The firing started again at once and the chances of being hit seemed dangerously high. Instead of being a hundred and fifty yards, the distance seemed to Dicken more like a hundred and fifty miles, even like a run in a nightmare – going backwards as he tried to go forward. As he reached the blackness of the verandah, he paused to get his breath, then took several stumbling steps forward and raised his hand to push against a glass-panelled door. As he did so, it opened in front of him and, caught off balance, he fell inside into the darkness.

As he sat up, he heard the clash of curtain rings and someone slamming the door, then a light went on. In front of him was a circle of men, all incredibly handsome, all immaculate, as if their nationality and profession called on them to be so. Among them was the guide, and alongside him, grinning, Corporal Babington.

And – Dicken's eyes widened – holding two children just behind Babington was Nicola Aubrey!

5

The room was crowded and as everybody pressed forward the face vanished, so that Dicken felt he'd been seeing things.

They were in the billiard room of the Legation and under the wide table were children's toys. As Dicken scrambled to his feet, a tall, good-looking man stepped from among the other tall, good-looking men. He was impeccably dressed.

'I'm Sir Andrew MacAllister,' he said. 'The British Minister in Ambul. How do you do? How kind of you to come.' He was all charm, as if they were meeting at a party. 'You can see it's a bit of a mess here.'

Dicken glanced around him, his eyes alert for that fugitive face he had seen so briefly.

'I came, sir, with the intention of arranging an evacuation,' he said.

MacAllister ignored him. 'It's been rather a noisy day here today,' he pointed out. 'Following an unrefreshing night when they kept us all awake. We spend most of our time in the billiard room because it's the safest place. I spend most nights walking round the corridors and sleep during the day. What weapons we have I keep in my bathroom. You'd better meet my wife.'

In a daze, Dicken found himself being introduced to a middle-aged woman as calm and attractive as the Minister himself. He'd often read of besieged Britishers behaving as normally as if the enemy were hundreds of miles away and he suspected they probably still dressed for dinner every evening.

'The Bachi came to the gate yesterday,' MacAllister went on calmly. 'He knew we had white women here but he promised they'd come to no harm. As a matter of fact, I think he meant it but, of course, it's impossible for him to answer for every man in

206

his forces, any more than it is for the King, who's also promised us no harm. Fortunately the Rezhans are all dreadful shots but we've lost a lot of windows and chimney pots, and we've been hit by over fifty shells. The children spend most of their time in the cellar.' He sounded like a Vicar recounting what had been done with the proceeds of the Belfry Fund.

Once again Dicken tried to explain why he was there but MacAllister seemed so absorbed with his thoughts he didn't appear to hear him. 'The place is full of rebels, of course,' he went on. 'We watched them taking the forts to the north-east. Then they began marching towards Ambul and began to collect outside the gates here. We locked them for safety but our Rezhan guards dropped their rifles and all vanished within twenty-four hours.'

It seemed to Dicken that the whole affair was being handled in far too leisurely a manner. 'I think we ought to make some attempt to contact Peshawar, sir,' he said, but MacAllister waved a hand.

'I have the Bachi's word,' he said. 'I met him at the gate.'

'You were very brave, dear,' his wife interposed.

MacAllister shrugged. 'He made an impassioned speech, saying the King was an infidel and must be dethroned. I explained that was *his* affair but that I expected him to respect the Legations. He said he would. In the meantime everybody moved here from their homes for safety.'

There was a curiously dreamlike quality about the situation and Dicken was handed over to another tall handsome man who was equally unruffled.

'Their troops came past the Legation,' he said. 'Standards. Mullahs on horses. That sort of thing. Took the Shirira Fort and the Riding School. Spasmodic firing all the time. Got all the bedding and mattresses into the Legation building, y'know. Thought it safer.'

'Look – ' Dicken was growing angry '– I came here with the express intention of organising an evacuation. The machines are ready and so are the crews. They only want the Minister's word. But when I mention it he doesn't seem to be listening. Is he deaf or something?'

The new speaker, who turned out to be the Minister's Secretary and seemed to be trying to ape the Minister with his neatly-cut breeches, box-cloth gaiters and cravat, smiled. 'Oh, no,' he said. 'He's just very conscious of the dignity of the British Empire.'

'Dignity won't help much if that lot out there run amok.'

'They'll never do that! They tried once or twice. The Minister always manages to calm them down.'

'Perhaps one day he won't be able to.'

The Secretary offered a gold case and, lighting a cigarette, continued leisurely. 'My dear chap,' he said. 'You don't evacuate a Legation just like that. This is British territory, you know. I don't think the Minister's even considered it.'

The Minister and his wife had vanished by this time and Dicken suspected they were wandering round the building somewhere, bolstering up everyone's courage with their calm demeanour.

'Lots of activity between the Lalu Pushta and the forts still,' Dicken's guide continued. 'Still fairly safe in the garden, though, and we continued to come and go. Then Henry's kitchen and George's lounge were hit and a lot of those damned Russian aviators dropped bombs. Rotten shots. Battle's all round us now. German Legation and French Legations have been in touch. Got the wind up a bit. Wondered if they could join us. Said yes, of course. Got to help foreigners, what? Shell burst on the lawn yesterday. Rebels want to burn down the Nau Burja and came begging for oil. Pretended to be a bit stupid and gave 'em some in a saucer. When they said they wanted our lamp oil, we told 'em we use electricity. Put 'em off a bit. Minister's decided that if they break in we're not going to fight. Just keep calm. By the way don't undress. Sleep in your clothes. Safer.'

The Legation looked like a colander. On the wall opposite the windows upstairs, Dicken counted forty bullet holes.

'One singed the Minister's moustache,' the Transport Officer, another of the calm handsome young men, said. 'And a shell missed his head by inches. Lots of VC work going on here, you know. But the Bachi's behaving jolly well.'

Babington and Dicken looked at each other, both faintly bewildered.

'Don't you think, sir, since you're on such good terms with the Bachi,' Babington suggested, 'that I ought to get my wireless set out of the aircraft? It'll be better than the one you've got.'

The idea was put to the Minister who pooh-poohed it gracefully. 'Can't afford to lose you, my boy,' he said. 'Perhaps the Squadron Leader would do the job. Have to be careful though. Scotty was shot in the leg yesterday. Most inconvenient.'

Within three hours of arriving at the Legation, Dicken found himself outside again. The Transport Officer went with him and they led two horses.

Arriving at the aerodrome, the Transport Officer shook hands with the aerodrome commandant, who was more than willing to help and, detaching the generator and the heavy T21 and TF long wave sets from the aircraft, they roped them across the horses' backs. As they returned towards the Legation there was a lot of artillery fire and the Transport Officer explained that the Bachi had captured several old Turkish field guns belonging to the King but, since no one knew how to aim them, there was no telling where the shells might go.

His eyes still on the look-out for that face of which he had caught such a fleeting glimpse, Dicken helped Babington to carry the sets and the generator up the stairs to the highest part of the house. Neither of them had slept properly for days but to Dicken there seemed rather more urgency than the Legation staff seemed willing to admit.

There were a Rolls and a Crossley tender in the garage, so they disconnected the batteries and carried them after the wireless sets. The highest point of the house turned out to be the Minister's bedroom but his wife agreed that they should use it and they screwed the sets to her dressing table. The T21 was a long range set that needed a big aerial, and climbing to the flat roof in the moonlight, they studied the flagpole against the moving clouds and the whiteness of the snow on the surrounding mountains.

Babington had just climbed the pole and was attaching a loop to the top when the clouds moved away from the moon and they heard the whack-whack-whack of bullets. Babington descended so quickly he landed on top of Dicken and they both collapsed at the foot of the pole. Diving for cover trailing the lead, they disappeared down the stairs to the bedroom and began to connect up. Within half an hour, Babington was tapping out morse and within minutes he gave a yell of delight.

'We're through, sir! We've been picked up by somebody in Miranshar. They're going to pass on anything we wish to send.'

*

The following day was a Sunday and Dicken and Babington found themselves at a service conducted in the little chapel attached to the Legation. There were bullet splashes in the plaster above the altar and one of the windows had been blown in to allow a cold draught to blow through so that everyone wore coats and gloves. To Dicken's surprise when the priest arrived it was Father O'Buhilly, bearlike as ever, a red woollen scarf round his neck and a pair of green mittens on his hands.

MacAllister sat at the front with his wife. Behind them were the Secretary and his wife and children, then the Transport Officer with, behind them, ranged in order of precedence, the rest of the Legation staff, including Rezhan and Indian servants and their families. Dicken's eyes roved among them as O'Buhilly moved in front of the altar, searching all the time for the face he'd seen so briefly at the moment of his arrival.

As everybody began to file out, he felt himself grasped by the shoulder, then O'Buhilly swung him round and gave him a bear-like hug.

'Me boy,' he beamed. ''Tis simply not possible that it's yourself! I was hardly able to keep me mind on me job when I saw you sittin' there. I heard we'd had visitors but, sure, it never entered me mind that it would be me ould fellow-prisoner from China.'

'What are *you* doing here, Father?' Dicken asked.

'Simple, me boy. It seemed to me it wouldn't be long before we were all chucked out of China. So I came here.'

'But Rezhans are Moslems.'

Father O'Buhilly shrugged. 'I'm not a crusader, me boy. I just look after the women and children. There is a lot of poverty here and the women are badly used. When trouble looked likely, the Anglican padre suddenly discovered he was sick and bolted for India and I was asked if I'd oblige by joining the staff. Nobody seems to mind that I'm a Catholic and I conduct an ecumenical service that suits everybody.'

'We should be thinking of getting out of here, Father.'

'That we should.' O'Buhilly smiled. 'But I think Himself's read about Gordon at Khartoum,' he said. 'It is failin' the British Empire he'd be if he were to consider leavin'.'

He led the way to his room, which seemed as bare and empty as the room he'd had in Shanghai. As he produced a bottle of Irish whiskey and a packet of cigarettes, it seemed to Dicken to be time to enlist his help to identify the face he'd seen.

'Look, Father – that girl. The one with the children. There wasn't much light. Only candles. I thought I was seeing things. Who is she?'

'She's governess to the Minister's Secretary's children. Why?'

'I've got to talk to her, Father.'

Father O'Buhilly studied him with a faint smile. 'She's pretty, me boy,' he said. 'What are y'intending?'

'I know her, Father. You remember how we talked when Lee had us as prisoners.'

'I do indeed, me boy. Is she the one?'

'She is, Father.'

'I thought you were married.'

'I am. And I shan't forget it. But I must talk to her. Can you arrange it?'

'I think so, me boy. This evening, I should think.'

*

There was a lot of talk during the day about the prestige of the Union Jack but Dicken suspected that they were all being heavily over-optimistic. Pathan tribesmen were no respecters of persons and, if it suited them, they could easily sweep over the Legation and butcher everbody inside. The Minister was still against aircraft trying to land, however, because the rebels were shooting at anything within sight.

When Babington sent a message asking for another aircraft to fly over, the words that came back startled them. 'Squadron Leader Quinney to return at once – repeat at once – to Miranshar,' it read. It was signed 'C. A. Diplock, Wing Commander.'

MacAllister, who had appeared as soon as the set had started to cheep, shook his head immediately.

'Oh, no,' he said. 'That's not possible! We need you here. If we have to evacuate we shall need every single man.'

'*Are* we going to evacuate, sir?'

MacAllister gave him a mild reproving look. 'We represent His Majesty's Government and we don't leave until it becomes absolutely necessary.'

'Not even the women and children?'

'I have the Bachi's word that no harm is intended to them.'

It was a little like arguing with a gramophone record.

*

In the expectation of an aeroplane appearing overhead, Dicken and Babington lugged a large looking-glass to the roof in the hope of using it as a heliograph. Outside, the fighting swayed backwards and forwards all day. Troops rushed a two-storeyed house nearby and captured a few insurgents who were shot on the spot, but they were then pinned down themselves by fire from near the Legation gates. During the afternoon, the Legation gardener was shot through the head, and during the evening, the men isolated in the captured house managed to escape and fled through the Legation garden, starting another storm of firing as they went.

The face of a large clock in the hall fell to pieces and the hospital stores were moved upstairs for safety in case the rebels forced an entry and started looting. Later in the evening a machine gun began to rake the walls, another window fell in, and a chair collapsed under the Transport Officer as its leg was shot away. Finally the lights went out.

As candles were brought, Dicken looked round for Nicola Aubrey but there was no sign of her and he grabbed Father O'Buhilly's arm.

'Where is she, Father?'

'Steady, me boy. Steady. She was on her way up when the firing started and it was decided to keep the wives and children in the cellar. 'Tis the only really safe place.'

Bolting for the stairs, Dicken almost fell down them. The cellars were dimly lit and the women were sitting patiently with their children. The girl Dicken had seen was in the far corner, quietening a fretful small boy. As she looked up, somehow she looked different from how he remembered her, slimmer, with larger eyes, and incredibly young for a woman approaching thirty.

'Hello, Dicken,' she said, giving him a grin.

It was unbelievable. Eleven years before, while flying Camels in northern Italy, he had fallen heavily in love with Nicola Aubrey, and he found himself wondering what she was doing here in Ambul and what had happened to her religion. If her Catholicism, which had been such a stumbling block between them, hadn't allowed her to marry him as they'd both wished, what was she doing in the household of a man who was quite obviously an Anglican?

'I did see you then,' he said. 'That first night. Where have you been?'

'There's been a lot of shooting going on,' she replied calmly. 'Most of my time's been spent with the children. They're not quite as unafraid as their father.'

'You must have known I was here.'

'I knew you wouldn't be going away. None of us are. At least not until the Minister decides we can do it without letting down the British Empire.'

'But Nicola – !'

She shook her head. 'Not Nicola!'

Dicken stopped dead. 'You *are* Nicola Aubrey?' he said. 'Right?'

She grinned. 'Wrong,' she replied. 'I'm Marie-Gabrielle.'

6

For a long moment, Dicken stared at her, understanding at last the differences he had noticed, the bigger eyes, the apparently everlasting youth. Like all the Aubreys she was good-looking, beautiful even, and it was little wonder he'd mistaken her identity because her parents, also both blessed with fine features, had looked like brother and sister, and their children were almost identical in looks, colouring and stature.

'Marie-Gabrielle,' he said slowly. 'The youngest in the family!'

'We all looked so alike, you remember,' she laughed. 'People said mother and father didn't make us in the usual manner, but had us stamped out by a machine.'

A slow smile began to spread across Dicken's face and he was just about to bombard her with questions when there was a tremendous double crash and the place was filled with dust. As the women began to shriek, he leapt for her and, pulling her down, crouched on the floor with his arm across her.

The rebel artillery had started to fire over the Legation but their aim was bad and within minutes every member of the staff was in the cellar, because the shells were reducing the upper rooms to rubble. Babington crouched nearby, talking to a stout turbanned Indian official, while MacAllister seemed to be conferring in the corner with all the handsome young men of his staff at once.

His arm round the girl, his mouth close to her ear, Dicken put his questions between the crashes. As a child Marie-Gabrielle had been one of his favourites. She had climbed on his back, sat on his knee, swung on his arm, never involved in family squabbles, sunny-natured, good-tempered, gregarious, cheerful and friendly.

'How did you come to be here?' he asked.

'Not very difficult,' she said briskly. 'Father died in 1927. Heart attack. He was only sixty. Mother, who was French, you remember, went back to Paris to live and the family split up a little. George became a missionary, as he said he would, and went to China. I worked as a nanny for a year and was in London wondering what to do with myself when I saw an advertisement in the Personal Column of *The Times*: 'Will Miss M. G. Aubrey please communicate at once with Mr Basil Forsythe with a view to looking after his four small sons. Please write The British Legation, Ambul, Rezhistan.' "

'Did you know him?'

'Never met him in my life. But he'd known my father in India, while I was in England at school. I arrived early in the year. The whole Legation staff were on the lawn to greet me. Then on December 12th the rebels came pouring down from Sihar and bullets started flying and the fort on the Bagh-i-Bila was taken by tribesmen from Kohistan. There must have been three or four thousand of them. They say the King changed his uniform three times in an hour and rushed into the street, pushing rifles at both men and women and shouting "Save me, save me!" If the Bachi had pushed his attack then the whole thing would have fallen apart but I think he was more surprised by his success than anybody.'

She paused, looking at him while the roaring of shells above drowned her voice. When they stopped she continued. 'We were collecting flowers in the garden when Mr Forsythe came rushing out. "Come quickly, Auby," he said. "There's trouble," and we all went into the Legation and all the gates and doors were locked. I had no idea what was happening so I went up on the roof. All I could see was a solid mass of humanity, all waving guns and shouting. Then the Bachi stopped at the gate and promised no harm should come to us but as soon as he left the shooting started again.'

'What about the rest of your family?' Dicken asked.

'Bernadette and Marguerite are married – Bernadette to an Italian – and Cecilia's engaged to a Frenchman. If you remember, we were rather a cosmopolitan lot. Mark joined the army. He's in Khanpur, which was one of the reasons I decided to come to India too.'

215

'What about Nicola?' By this time, Dicken was sure, she was either married into a good Roman Catholic family, a nun or a missionary.

'Oh, she's old,' Marie-Gabrielle said with the cheerful contempt of the young. 'Twenty-nine now, and married to an American diplomat. A Baptist.'

'A Baptist!' Dicken stared at the laughing face a few inches from his own. 'When *I* wanted to marry her she was afraid of ex-communication because I was an Anglican.'

'It doesn't seem to bother her so much these days,' Marie-Gabrielle said cheerfully. 'I can only think she wasn't as much in love with you as she thought. Personally, I thought she was potty. *I'd* have married you. Any time, church or no church. I remember I asked you, even. I was nine at the time.'

Suddenly it all seemed funny.

'A Baptist?' Dicken said. 'For God's sake, a Baptist! That's about as far from Catholicism as you can get. What about her husband?'

'He was supposed to agree to the children being brought up as Catholics, of course, but somehow it's been overlooked and I understand they all go together to the Baptist Church in Washington.'

For a long time, aware of the crack and rattle of bullets outside, the occasional thump of a shell, and the slow trickle of sand and dust through a crack in the wall, Dicken was silent, wondering how he could have suffered such agonies of love to no avail.

'Why did she never write to me?' he asked. 'I wrote to her.'

Marie-Gabrielle managed a shrug. 'She thought you'd let her down.'

'Why?'

'Because you went away.'

'There was a war on! If you remember the Austrians were trying to break through to Venice. I was sent with the rest of the squadron from Capodolio where you lived to Schia Piccola to help stop them.'

'I don't think she managed to take that into account. She was always inclined to be romantic and never managed to see much sense.'

'But your parents? Why didn't they write?'

216

'*I* wrote.'

'You weren't very old at the time, if you remember.'

'I think they thought you'd quarrelled and that love affairs between young people were best left alone. I tried to make it up.'

'You forgot to include your address.'

'I wondered why you never wrote back to me.'

He suddenly realised they were thinking only of the past, about something which was dead and finished with.

'What about you?' he asked. 'You're not married. Are you engaged?'

'No.'

'I'm surprised.'

'Nobody asked me. At least, nobody I ever wanted.'

'Who did you want?'

'I wanted you,' she said bluntly. 'I did when I was nine. And I don't think I've ever come across anyone since whom I preferred.'

They were silent for a moment then she went on with disarming frankness. 'My father was ten years older than my mother and Nicola's Baptist is ten years older than she is.' She gave him a smile. 'It seems to run in the family. Perhaps that was what was wrong with you for Nicola. You weren't old enough. I've often thought about you.'

'For ten years?'

'First impressions are important ones. I thought you were handsome, brave and honest. It's obvious you still are. I think when the Minister finally gets around to having an evacuation – and I suppose he will some time – I'll persuade them to let me stay in Peshawar until you arrive. I'm sure they wouldn't dream of allowing the men to go until all the women and children have gone first. They're terribly fussy about that sort of thing. Then when you arrive, I hope we'll talk again.'

'About what?'

'About me marrying you.'

Dicken gave a hoot of laughter. 'I remember you telling me once that you had a wasting disease. You coughed for my benefit. You sounded remarkably healthy. And you were always tormenting Nicola about the way she changed her clothes every time I appeared. You were always fooling about.'

He became aware that she wasn't smiling. 'I wasn't fooling about *that*,' she said. 'I'm still not fooling.'

Dicken was just digesting what she had said when MacAllister's secretary appeared. For a change he was neither immaculate nor unmoved. He was covered with dust and flakes of plaster from a fallen ceiling and he looked alarmed.

'The King's troops are breaking down the gates, Minister,' he said. 'I think you'd better come.'

MacAllister rose and, followed by his gaggle of staff, hurried up the stairs. Dicken glanced quickly at Marie-Gabrielle then scrambled to his feet and followed. By the time they arrived at the gate, the Rezhan soldiers were already inside the garden and heading for the house. As MacAllister moved to meet them, one of them raised his rifle and Dicken snatched it away.

'You must leave this property.' MacAllister's voice was calm as if he were talking to the gardener. 'Under international law, this is British territory and you have no right to be here.'

Whether they understood him or not was hard to say but they certainly seemed to be impressed by his demeanour. It took an hour to clear them all out, however, and the women and children were sent back to the cellar. A few minutes later one of the King's DH9s appeared overhead and there was a twitter of nerves in case the insurgents suspected double-dealing.

It was quite clear the situation was becoming worse rather than better but during the night the usual signal was put out on the lawn – 'Don't land. All's well.' It seemed to Dicken that MacAllister was being unduly optimistic because the next day the gates were pushed open again, this time by the rebels. Once more they all hurried to persuade them to leave and once more there was the rigmarole of pointed rifles and threats and the possibility of an eruption of anger. MacAllister dealt with it in his normal urbane fashion, then headed for the house to draft a signal for Babington, requesting a radio to be dropped by parachute.

'It seems to me, sir,' Dicken pointed out, 'that instead of a radio, we ought to be requesting an evacuation by air.'

'I have grave doubts that it can be done,' MacAllister said. 'It's never been done before.'

'There are machines waiting at Peshawar.'

'Would they be able to land?'

'Yes, sir. At Arpur.'

'How do we get the women and children to Arpur?'

'We could walk, sir. I'll be willing to try to arrange a safe passage.'

MacAllister seemed tempted. 'Do you think it can be done?'

'Sir, I've already been through the lines three times. Once when I came here and twice when I went to fetch the radios.'

'I hate giving up the Legation.'

'Sir, you might have to!'

There were a few more questions then MacAllister nodded, convinced. 'Very well,' he said. 'I have to admit that I have grave doubts about the Bachi *or* the King being able to control their men much longer. These people like fighting and they know there's a possibility of loot in the legations.' He sighed. 'It goes against the grain, you know, being forced to evacuate my post but perhaps, after all, we'd better try. I'm beginning to think that if we don't go willingly we shall be forced to go unwillingly and that's something I can't think about with the women and children. How soon can it be arranged?'

'If we can get a message through, the aircraft can be here tomorrow.'

MacAllister considered for a moment, then he nodded. 'I'll go and ask the ladies to pack,' he said.

*

That night, while Babington was struggling to contact Miranshar, there was a clatter on the French windows. As they rushed to open them the firing outside swelled up again and two men fell in.

'Von Rotow, sir,' one of them announced breathlessly. 'German Legation. We have come to request evacuation.'

MacAllister's eyebrows shot up. 'We haven't arranged our own evacuation yet,' he said.

'Nevertheless, Herr Minister, we have heard you intend to. So also have the French Legation.'

During the night, as the rebels made another attempt on the Palace and the city, the fighting flared up and, as servants appeared one after the other with requests for help, it began to be clear that everybody in Ambul who was not a Rezhan had somehow heard of MacAllister's decision and decided it might be better to bolt for India. More requests, brought by bearers, came from the Persian Legation and from individual British Indians and Rezhans. When they added up the figures it came to over three hundred.

'My dear chap – ' MacAllister seemed startled that Dicken didn't panic '– we can't remove *that* lot by air.'

'I think we can, sir,' Dicken said. 'If five troop-carrying machines come in at a time, we can remove them in bunches of a hundred. It would require several trips but it'll take less than five days. They'll work round the clock at Peshawar.'

*

They were unable to raise Miranshar again. Babington checked the set carefully and Dicken and the Transport Officer headed for the garage where the batteries had been recharging, struggling under the weight of the old ones. The night was dark but by the light of a torch, they saw that an unexploded shell had passed through the wall and gone straight through the Minister's Rolls Royce. It hadn't damaged the recharger, however, and as they struggled back with the fresh batteries, Babington began the vigil once more, tuning and retuning, patiently tapping out his call sign and that of the Miranshar station.

Almost unnoticed Christmas had crept up on them. Somebody had erected a small tree in the billiard room and hung a few decorations made from coloured paper on the branches.

'When the firing dies down,' MacAllister said, 'we'll send for the children to come and see it.'

It had started to snow heavily. The sky had darkened rapidly until it looked like lead, and the snow, coming down in huge flakes, whirled through the valleys between the mountains and began to settle. It didn't stop the fighting, however, and during the evening after a long bombardment the King's troops stormed a hill to the south of the Legation. The hill dominated the forts held by the Bachi-i-Adab's men who had also captured forts at a village called Pangam. By diverting the stream which supplied power for the hydro-electric plant in the city, they had plunged Ambul into darkness and the royal arsenal and the other small factories which depended on it had come to a standstill. The Legation was once again hit by shells. Most of the windows were now knocked out, the stables had been destroyed and the horses killed, and the tank in the water tower had been perforated so that they were now reduced to rationing the water. On the credit side, however, a messenger arrived from the Rezhan Foreign Office with the information that the airfield at Arpur would be ready to receive the British when they decided to leave.

It was not until late in the evening when the firing finally died away that they were able to send for the children to see the Christmas tree. Forsythe and his wife had arranged one or two candles round it and everybody had searched through their belongings to find a few small gifts.

With the firing quiet, MacAllister ordered champagne to be served to celebrate Christmas Eve and the Indian servants began to hand round the glasses in the dim glow of the candles. As everybody began to chatter, he drew Dicken aside.

'Will your operator be able to get through?' he asked. 'Because we've had still more requests. They include twenty-two women and twenty children from the Turkish Legation, Australians, Swiss, Syrians and several more Rezhans who are in fear of their lives.'

'We can stuff them in somewhere, sir.'

As they were talking the door opened and the small children were ushered in. Marie-Gabrielle was bending over them, her head down and Dicken was just going to bombard her with questions again when the door opened again and Babington appeared.

'Sir,' he yelled. 'I got through! They got every word of the message. The first machines will arrive tomorrow morning!'

7

There was immediate confusion as everybody rushed off to pack. The children were whisked away and Marie-Gabrielle vanished, as abruptly and completely as she had the first time.

Dinner was more of a buffet supper with everybody helping themselves in between bouts of packing, but more champagne was opened and a few toasts were given in an atmosphere that was electric and not far from hysteria.

In the early hours of the morning, the women with children began to gather in the billiard room dressed in warm coats and sensible shoes. Some of them, determined to leave nothing behind, wore two coats and were wrapped in long scarves and shawls. Just before daylight a company of the King's troops arrived outside the gates to escort them to the airfield, swarthy-faced, unshaven men muffled to the eyebrows and wearing Russian-type cloth caps with the flaps down over their ears. They had brought pack animals and as they were loaded with luggage, MacAllister appeared, splendid in a fur-collared over-coat and grey felt hat. He was carrying a gold-topped walking stick and was escorted by an Indian servant.

As they began to move, Dicken brought up the rear, a revolver concealed inside the pocket of his flying suit. Alongside him was Father O'Buhilly carrying a remarkably heavy-looking staff.

Slipping silently through the gates, they began to move quietly through the semi-darkness. At the battle lines, they saw dark faces watching them and more pointed hats among the trees. Desultory firing had started near the Legation and MacAllister hesitated.

'This is where I must leave you,' he told the women. 'Because I must remain at my post. The Italian Legation's just over there, safely away from the fighting, and the Italians have promised to accord you every facility for rest until the arrival of the aeroplanes.'

A second company of soldiers materialised among the misty trees and as the Minister kissed his wife and began to head back towards the Legation, the party set off again with Dicken and Father O'Buhilly carrying two of the smallest children. The villages were the same ones Dicken and Babington had passed through not so long before, but the bodies had been cleared from the pathways and a lot of the litter of battle had been removed.

The Italian Legation provided coffee and rolls, and the women, many of them laden with treasures and tired after the long walk, sank down in the armchairs. Arranging to send a messenger back, Dicken set off alone for the airfield.

After the snow, the skies had cleared and it had become intensely cold and he could see the King's Russian pilots having difficulty starting their engines. Two hours later he heard the sound of the first aeroplane arriving. It was a Westland Wapiti, roaring over the field. All its guns had been removed and it swept overhead, the black spider of its Jupiter radial rumbling and poppling, to touch down bang on the stroke of nine o'clock.

As it swung, its engine ticking over, the propeller turning gently, Dicken climbed on to the wing.

'Keep your engine going,' he warned. 'Or you might never get it started again.'

Ten minutes later three DH9s touched down and lined up alongside the Wapiti. Following them came the reassuring bulk of a Victoria.

The Italian Legation had placed a car at Dicken's disposal and as the last machine rolled to a stop, he ordered it off with a message for the evacuees to be sent on. His pilots were pleased to see him and advanced on him, grinning.

'Thought they'd got you, sir,' one of them said. 'We were jolly glad to hear young Babington on the air. Your wife's arrived in India. Did you know?'

They were still talking when Hatto appeared and shooed them away. 'Push off, you lot,' he said. 'We have things to discuss.'

'Thanks, Willie,' Dicken said. 'Is she really here?'

'Arrived in Karachi two days ago and preparing now to fly on to Calcutta. She's resting there a couple of days before starting the last leg of the flight to Bangkok and down to Singapore where she stays a day before going on to Australia. It looks as though she's going to make it.'

He gestured at the Victoria. The cabin had been stripped of everything except the canvas seats and there was a pile of blankets to protect the passengers against the intense cold of the journey over the mountains. Hatto had also brought short wave radios for easier communication, a propeller, wheels, radiator and sump for Dicken's machine, blocks and tackles to hoist them into position, a corporal fitter and rigger to do the work, a spare pilot to fly it back when they'd finished, and Flight Sergeant Handiside and a wireless operator to handle the radio traffic from the airfield.

'No orders for me to return?'

Hatto laughed. 'That was Parasol Percy. We were picking up your radio even though we couldn't get through, and you were being mentioned too many times in MacAllister's messages. Diplock didn't like it. When this is over, old son, the AOC's determined there are going to be a few gongs flying around, if only to show the army and the navy that the RAF has its uses. After all they've said, he's determined to rub it in, and Diplock was afraid you'd get a gong and he wouldn't. Orr was livid when he heard.'

As the cars began to arrive, the sandbag ballast was removed from the rear cockpits of the DH9s and people and luggage stuffed in its place. As the Victoria lumbered slowly round to face the wind, the airfield was a blinding sheet of snow. The tail came up and it lifted into the air, climbing slowly but steadily for the hills. The DH9s began to take off after it, followed finally by the Wapiti. As they vanished the snow began to fall again.

*

It was harder getting back into the Legation that it had been getting out. At the Italian Legation, where they were also now considering evacuation, a company of the King's troops were waiting to escort them to the lines but, as they reached them the rebels started firing heavily and they learned it was because Bachi-i-Adab had been wounded the previous evening and was losing control of his men.

The snow was falling heavily now but the blizzard conditions were a help because the firing dwindled and eventually stopped, and they made their way through the outposts until they reached the hole in the Legation wall.

MacAllister was there to greet them. 'We saw the aircraft leave. Is all well?'

'They should be landing in Peshawar about now, sir,' Dicken said. 'If they haven't already landed.'

MacAllister indicated the weather. 'Thank God we got the children away,' he said. 'This will end the evacuation.'

'Don't let's shout "Abandon ship" till she starts sinking,' Father O'Buhilly boomed. 'I'm more than willin' to try to get the Foreign Minister to lend us troops to clear the landing area.'

They passed on the news of the Italians' decision to evacuate and the danger of the Bachi losing control of his troops.

'There were a lot in the outskirts of the city,' Father O'Buhilly pointed out. 'And there were flames. If they set it on fire, it will not be possible to remain here. They're still comin' in and the Italians have identified Shinwaris, Bohmands, Khogianis and Waziris, and they're wanting to take over the airfield.'

It was decided the evacuation should continue, despite the snow, and messages were sent off to the other Legations to make ready. The Italian Legation, the closest to the airfield, would be the last to close.

During the evening, a Tin Lizzie Ford carrying a white flag wobbled along the stony road past the gates, but as it did so the rebels opened fire on it and the flag fell. Several figures toppled out of the car, which clattered to a stop, leaking steam, and a horde of black figures burst from among the trees brandishing knives and swords. There were a few screams and then silence.

'I think we'd better get away the rest of the women,' MacAllister said.

'Together with the Secretary's governess,' Dicken pointed out. 'She wasn't among the first party.'

MacAllister frowned. 'A very determined young woman, my boy,' he said. 'She speaks excellent Italian, it seems, and she insists on staying behind in case she's needed.'

Marie-Gabrielle was in the cellar with the remaining wives and children and she put Dicken straight at once. 'I'll go when you go,' she said.

There was an intensity in her manner that troubled him. 'Marie-Gabrielle,' he said, looking at her young serious face, 'I'm married. My wife's Zoë Toshack, the airwoman. At this moment, she's probably taking off from Calcutta to fly to Darwin.'

She became silent. The news was clearly unexpected. 'Oh,' she said. 'I see. I didn't know.'

'In other circumstances I might have given your suggestion careful consideration.'

'Now *you're* joking,' She stared at her fingers for a moment. 'Do you love her?' she asked quietly. 'Your wife, I mean. Some men don't love their wives.'

He paused before answering, and found he honestly didn't know the answer. Between himself and Zoë there was undoubtedly something, but over the years it had become like a thread stretched taut which could be broken without much heartache to either of them.

'No,' he said slowly. 'Not any more.'

'Did you once?' She seemed earnest and very concerned.

'Yes. But she's gone her own way and she's crazy about flying. She fell in love with it the same day I did.' He shrugged. 'I think if I'd known in 1919 where your family were, I'd have *demanded* that Nicola married me. But you were the only one who wrote, and you didn't send an address.'

She looked up at him, her face sombre. 'Poor Dicken,' she said. 'Poor me. Why don't you divorce her?'

'It's not as simple as that.'

'You don't love her.'

He managed a smile. 'Things aren't always very clear-cut. I think she needs me a little – in the background.' He could see that in her youth she was finding it difficult to understand. 'I expect when she arrives in Australia she'll be famous and she'll turn up on the doorstep again. She's very beautiful, Marie-Gabrielle.'

'As attractive as me?'

She sounded very young and Dicken smiled. 'About the same,' he said.

'*Would* you divorce her, if you found someone else?'

'I never have.'

There was a long pause. 'There's me,' she said quietly.

He looked at her, still unable to believe she was serious.

'When I first saw you, with all your medal ribbons,' she went on slowly, 'I felt I'd never met anybody like you ever before in my life. I hadn't, of course. I wasn't old enough. But, somehow, the impression remained. Every boy I met seemed so inadequate by comparison.'

'I'm not really all that exciting.'

'You always were to me. After you disappeared I kept your photograph on my dressing table and when I went home to school it was in my Bible. I always thought I'd meet you again and, knowing that Nicola was married to her American, that it would be all right.' She sighed. 'Girls think like that when they're young, you see.' She managed a smile. 'And here you are at last. You haven't changed much. Just a bit older, a bit more self-assured. But that's all.' She looked at him with her frank young eyes. 'I still think I was right.'

*

It was silent outside now but as MacAllister and his staff sat round the billiard table discussing their plans, there was a shout from the stairs.

'Your Excellency – ' it was one of the Indian servants ' – the Rezhans are breaking in!'

Scrambling to his feet, Dicken reached for his revolver and they all raced for the stairs. A crashing of glass and the splintering of woodwork came from the back of the Legation and, through a gap in the boards that barred the broken windows, they could see moonlight and the sheen of snow. Then the door flew open and framed in the opening they saw half-a-dozen heavily-armed men wearing tall Kabul-made caps and carrying rifles and swords.

As the light caught the men inside, the intruders stopped dead, clutching their weapons, then MacAllister stepped forward, and began to address them in Pushtu. Previously his appearances had been sufficient to quell both rebels and King's men, but this time it didn't work. These men looked like strangers and one of them yelled something, and lifted his rifle. A shot whistled across the room, so close that MacAllister involuntarily ducked his head. At the second shot one of the handsome young men behind the Minister clutched his forearm and cried out, but they all remained in a group, looking vaguely like the pictures Dicken had seen of General Gordon and his followers facing death on the steps at Khartoum. Suddenly the whole thing irritated him.

'This is bloody silly!' he snapped and pulled the trigger.

The man who had fired disappeared backwards through the doorway as the rest surged forward. A huge double-barrelled pistol appeared and for a moment Dicken found himself staring at what looked like twin cannons, then there was a flash and a crash. Only one barrel had fired but the heavy bullet hit the table, sending up splinters and scoring a groove before striking a decanter, and Dicken reeled away, his face specked with red where splinters had struck him. As he did so, however, the handsome young men came to life at last. One of them picked up a heavy chair and brought it down with a crunch on an unprotected head. Another picked up a dropped rifle and started swinging it by the barrel. The man Dicken was wrestling with had his feet kicked from under him and somebody hit him with a heavy bronze candelabrum. The last intruder was about to run off when Father O'Buhilly's great fist felled him like an ox.

Dicken stared round angrily. 'It took you long enough,' he growled.

*

MacAllister, still standing in a heroic posture with his chest out, one foot forward, one arm across his chest, suddenly came to life and turned away with a frown. His secretary, Forsythe, brushed his sleeve and smiled. 'The old blazing eye and stiff upper lip technique seems to have run out of steam,' he said.

He gave a bark of laughter as though the break-in had suddenly made them all shed the icy British diplomat image.

'We'd better get rid of these people,' Forsythe said briskly, indicating the limp forms at their feet. 'If their friends find out what's happened to them they'll probably come back, and the Pathans like their blood feuds too much. Henry – ' he gestured at the Transport Officer ' – go to the bathroom and bring some of the weapons down. Arthur – ' one of the other young men stiffened, as if he were on parade ' – I'll leave it to you to barricade this door again. Lionel, will you be so kind as to inform the ladies that there's nothing to be alarmed about. Squadron Leader – ' he looked at Dicken ' – I think we should get the rest of the women and children to the airfield at once. I think the Minister would be glad if you'd ask for aeroplanes tomorrow morning.'

*

MacAllister's young men, their diplomatic coolness gone, were suddenly behaving resolutely, calmly and briskly. With Babington upstairs by the transmitter, they up-ended a heavy table against the door and Dicken turned away, his hands still red with blood, to see Marie-Gabrielle staring at him with wide horrified eyes.

Making him sit down, she carefully arranged a circle of candles round him and began to pick splinters from his cheeks. Her eyes were glistening with tears.

Babington appeared. 'Every aircraft they can raise'll be coming in tomorrow, sir,' he said. 'I've informed them that we expect the Legation to be overrun and that the palace, the city and the airfield might fall in the next few days.'

They assembled the remaining women, British, Indian, American, Syrian, Swiss, Afghan, Rezhan, as well as an unexpected Roumanian who had turned up from somewhere, then, with MacAllister's young men properly armed at last, they prepared to leave. The remaining donkeys were brought from the dairy where they'd been housed when the stables were destroyed and the radio sets lashed on their backs.

MacAllister looked round. He was wearing his heavy fur-collared overcoat and grey homburg and carrying his gold-topped stick. As they were preparing to leave he disappeared and there was a momentary panic until he returned carrying the Legation's flag. He studied the women. Some of them looked enormous with several layers of clothing because, although it had been stipulated that no luggage should be carried, no one had said anything about how many clothes might be worn.

'Shall we go,' he said.

With servants leading the donkeys and Babington hovering near to make sure his precious sets came to no harm, they set off in a long straggling file, the men on the outside and all armed.

For the first time, Dicken felt they could look after themselves. As he walked alongside Marie-Gabrielle, he felt her slip her hand into his. As they passed the German Legation they were joined by the German contingent, and then, as they passed the French Legation, the French contingent. There were enough of them now to look like a regiment on the march. On the outskirts of the city, there was another group waiting for them, guarded by a company of the King's troops – Persians, a Syrian, several Afghans and a few terrified Rezhans. A long dark file of frightened human beings stumbling in the snow, as they neared the Italian Legation a group of cars passed them, heading north.

'That's the King, sir!' The voice was Forsythe's. 'I saw him quite clearly! He's bolting!'

As they drew closer to the Italian Legation, a fleet of horse-drawn 'growlers', such as had graced London's streets at the turn of the century, passed them, carrying officials in frock coats and top hats but without ties, the last traces of the King's modernisation campaign.

The Italians added their fleet of cars to the procession and they set off again through the snow. The aircraft were flying in even as they arrived, four Victorias and the Hinaidi and half a dozen DH9s. One of the top-hatted, frock-coated tieless diplomats was arguing with MacAllister. The King had bolted with his luggage, two of his wives and their children and the Foreign Minister and his family, leaving the rest of his harem and their children and his agonised officials to face the mob.

The Hinaidi was just turning as they reached her. The pilot had a rim of ice attaching his moustache to his scarf but with a grin, he produced a bottle of beer which he'd brought for Dicken. It had frozen on the way, however, and they had to break it with a spanner and distribute the pieces of iced beer to anyone who wanted one.

The airfield was several inches deep in snow, so, threatening, arguing, disputing, pleading, Dicken, Hatto, MacAllister and Father O'Buhilly and all the young men persuaded everybody who could walk to tramp up and down the landing strip to flatten it for aircraft to take off. Even the top-hatted ministers added their weight and soon there was a horde of people moving up and down.

The King's harem left first. They were shrouded from head

to foot, not even their eyes showing, and they climbed into the interior of the Hinaidi like a troop of ghosts, not speaking, doing exactly as they were told. They refused the proffered blankets and sat in silence like huddled bundles of dirty washing. When they were all aboard there was room for two more so the German Minister, who was very fat and had a history of heart trouble, was pushed in after them with his wife. They were enormous under the layers of clothing they were wearing, the minister's wife even wearing three hats, one on top of another, and the door seemed to be an insuperable obstacle but, with the aid of a shoulder behind them, they were successfully injected inside.

As the women began to enter the Victorias, Marie-Gabrielle refused to leave Dicken's side but the machines finally took off full, leaving only thirty of the women behind until the next day. The top-hatted ministers were stuffed with their luggage into the rear cockpits of the DH9s and the fleet of aircraft began to manoeuvre round the field, until with a roar, the engines opened up and they slid away over the tightly packed snow to lift off one after the other and head for the hills.

The night was very dark because the moon was late rising and they made a point of fortifying the few sheds near the hangars in case of an attack, but, with the King gone, the rebels had poured into Ambul, looting, raping and murdering. Part of the city was in flames, the strong breeze wafting the fires across the ancient, wooden-framed buildings. From midnight until the next morning, they could hear firing going on, long rattles of musketry and machine gun fire as the King's troops, knowing what their fate would be, tried to hold out.

Dicken spent the whole night sitting next to Father O'Buhilly with his revolver in his hand, his arm round Marie-Gabrielle. She said nothing, merely huddling against him until she fell asleep. They were awakened by the sun in their faces and almost at once they caught the low hum of aircraft and soon afterwards saw the first Victoria appear over the mountains to the south.

'This time you'll have to go,' Dicken said as it landed and swung to face the breeze.

Marie-Gabrielle nodded. 'Yes. I understand. I'll go now.' She turned and, putting her hands on his shoulders, kissed him on the mouth.

He watched her climb into the Victoria and saw her take a seat where she could look through the window. Other women were pushed aboard and the door slammed. The idling engines roared, the tail swung and the window framing her pale face disappeared. Seconds later the Victoria was roaring off the ground and heading south.

As Dicken stared after it, a hand gripped his shoulder. It was Father O'Buhilly.

'I think you'd better pray for me, Father,' Dicken said quietly.

The Rezhan air force commander was looking nervous by this time because he'd heard that the Bachi's troops, having destroyed the city, were now heading for the airfield. They watched anxiously, one eye on the south, the other on the road from the city. People were moving in the distance and they could even make out their individual shapes, black against the snow, when the first of the Victorias reappeared.

As soon as it touched down, MacAllister gestured to twenty of the refugees to be ready. As it swung round and the door opened, the twenty clambered aboard, and as it started to move again, a second Victoria arrived. As it did so the mob appeared on to the edge of the field, surrounding one of the sentries. In a moment they were hammering him with rifle butts and they finally started tossing him into the air and catching him on bayonets as he came down. His screams died as MacAllister signalled to the second batch of refugees.

'Let's hope,' one of his young men said, 'that none of the aeroplanes conks out.'

When the last Victoria arrived, there were still over thirty of them left, Dicken, Babington, Handiside and the ground staff, MacAllister and his young men, the airfield commander who was clearly taking no chances, and several of his pilots. The pilot this time was Hatto and he didn't hesitate. 'Shove 'em all aboard,' he said. 'We'll manage.'

The mob were streaming across the field now, their chests criss-crossed with bandoliers of bullets, and they halted in a long straggling line about a hundred yards away. Agitators were shrieking abuse and demanding that they attack the aeroplane, but the mob stood watching, the line broken now into scattered groups.

There was a gap in front of them and Hatto shouted out. 'Hold your hats on,' he said.

As he opened the throttles and the Victoria began to gather speed, Dicken found MacAllister clutching the Union Jack he had rescued and looking at him with apprehension.

Dicken managed a smile. 'The usual procedure at a time like this, sir,' he said, 'is to cross all disengaged fingers and hope.'

The Victoria was rumbling towards the scattered line now, until it seemed it was going to plough into them, but at the last moment, realising what would happen if one of the whirling propellers hit them, the mob began to scatter, yelling with fright. A few slow movers flung themselves flat and one of the agitators flung a stick. It bounced off a strut then the rocking wings steadied, and, as the tail came up, Hatto pulled back on the control column.

For a minute the wheels continued rumbling beneath them and Dicken could see the end of the field with the hangar rushing towards them. Then as the shaking stopped, he realised they were airborne. For a long time, Hatto held the machine down, allowing it to build up speed until it seemed they were going to fly straight through the hangar, then Dicken felt it lift, agonisingly slowly until the roof of the hangar flashed past beneath them, no more than a few feet from the wheels. There was a yell from the cockpit and Hatto's voice came, elated and joyful.

Looking back, Dicken saw the mob had reached the ancient DH9s belonging to the Rezhan air force. The remaining Russian pilots were in a group, clearly intending to defend them, but the mob swept over them and the sticks, swords and guns rose and fell as the mob surged over them. Fragments of clothing flew through the air, then the bloody wreckage of what had been men was hoisted up on the bayonets and he could see the open mouths of the howling mob.

MacAllister's face had grown stiff and taut, as though he were watching the end of a world, a world of grace where the prestige of the British Empire had been important enough to stop a war and protect its citizens. For a while it had worked, then it had all fallen apart, and the butchery seemed to go to his heart like a dagger thrust.

233

8

It was wonderful to feel the warmth of the Indian sun as they stumbled out of the fuselage. They had been shockingly cramped for the hour and a half flight, so many of them packed inside the fuselage they could barely move. An airman, counting them as they appeared, looked at Hatto.

'My God, sir,' he said, 'where did you put 'em all?'

Hatto shrugged. 'You might well ask.'

As Dicken appeared, his grin died and he slapped him on the back.

'Nice to have you home, old lad,' he said quietly. 'I expect they'll be sending me back to Iraq now that the job's done. Perhaps they'll even give us leave and send us home.' He paused. 'What'll *you* do?'

Dicken looked up, unable to thrust from his mind the incredible conversations he'd had with Marie-Gabrielle. 'Go and find Zoë, I suppose,' he said.

Hatto frowned and was silent for a moment. 'Dick, old lad,' he said. 'Didn't you get my message?'

'What message was that?'

Hatto looked uncomfortable. 'Someone should have told you. A message was sent, I know. I expect it was overlooked in the panic. She went missing between Singapore and Java.'

Dicken was silent, uncertain what to say. 'She'll be all right,' he said slowly. 'She's always all right. She's got the luck of the devil.'

Hatto sighed. 'Not this time, old lad, They fished the wreckage out of the sea two days ago. They were still inside.'

*

234

For a long time, watched by curious airmen, Dicken walked slowly about the airfield. Babington approached him, then, seeing the expression on his face, turned away and Dicken guessed that someone had told him the news.

What had happened, he wondered? Had Angus Packer, the navigator, been another of Zoë's bad choices, like Charley Wright and Harmer and George Peasegood? He tried to avoid the thought of her struggling in the water, her hair plastered across her face, blood on her cheek, her eyes wild and afraid, gasping as she fought for breath. It was too painful and as it kept returning he brushed it away with a movement of his hand. He'd never see her grin again, or hear that blunt forthrightness that had captivated him as a boy and hurt him so often as a man. Drowning was a wretched way to die and the thought of her struggling in the water came back again, stark and nauseating, so that he had to put aside the image of her terror as the water filled her throat and nose and eyes and nostrils.

When he returned to the headquarters building, he found a message waiting for him from Diplock, insisting that he write a report on what had happened. It was marked 'Urgent' and stressed the importance of immediacy. He recognised it as another of Diplock's ploys to irritate him and simply tore it across and threw it into the orderly room waste paper basket.

Curiously, though, it seemed to start him from his mood and he decided to look up Father O'Buhilly. He found him in a hotel in a poor part of the city. His room seemed as bare as all his rooms. The moment he entered them, it seemed as if the furniture flew out of the window, leaving nothing but an iron bedstead, a chair and a table.

'I heard what happened, me boy,' the priest said. 'I've said a prayer for her soul.'

'Thank you, Father. What shall I do now?'

'In what way, my son?'

'For ten years I've been chasing her round the world. I even started a divorce. Now she's gone. For ten years Marie-Gabrielle was chasing *me*. Ought I to try to find her?'

'What do you intend?'

'I don't know. Just talk, I think. I could do with someone to talk to.'

'Will not I do, me boy?'

235

Dicken smiled. 'She'd perhaps be better, Father.'

Father O'Buhilly smiled back. 'Then why not? God's grace is about us and He's more understanding than people realise. I think you should.'

'So soon after – ?'

'Now, me boy. Do you wish any help?'

'No, Father. I'll be all right.'

Returning to RAF headquarters he found, as he expected, that the sergeant clerk in the orderly room had a typed list of everybody who'd been brought from Ambul. The air force was at its efficient best with lists. You could always rely on a list being made and you couldn't carry anything from anywhere to anywhere else without someone insisting on setting it down on paper. It was one of the exercises Diplock was so good at.

He wondered what Annys would have to say in the inevitable note she would send about Zoë. The usual platitudes, he supposed. But what else could you offer for a death except platitudes?

He found the name, 'Marie-Gabrielle Aubrey, spinster, 20, governess to Major Basil Forsythe,' and placed his finger against it.

'This one, Sergeant,' he said. 'Where's she staying?'

He didn't know what he wanted, except sympathy, and he felt that Marie-Gabrielle, young as she was, could give it to him, saying little, just reassuring him with her silences.

The sergeant was looking at him, a worried frown on his face. 'She wouldn't tell us, sir,' he said. 'She just said she wanted to go away.'

'Where to?'

'She didn't say, sir.'

'What about the Forsythes? Where are they?'

'They're staying with Major and Mrs Harvey, Army Medical Corps, sir. Some relation, I believe. Everybody's offering help until they can be found somewhere to go.'

'Do you have the telephone number?'

The sergeant did and Major Harvey brought Forsythe to the telephone.

'Hello, old man,' he said briskly. 'We have you flying chaps to thank for our lives.'

Dicken was brusque. 'Have you got Miss Aubrey there?'

'No, old man.' Forsythe sounded worried. 'We met her when she landed, of course. Expecting her to join us. But she said she didn't want to and that we'd better get an ayah for the children. It was damned odd.'

'Does your wife know where she is?'

'I'll ask. Hang on.'

Forsythe's wife didn't know. Several hours later, having checked everywhere in the cantonment and the hotels, Dicken had found out only that she'd stayed long enough to sleep one night in the city and had then caught a train south to Delhi.

Putting the telephone down for the last time, he was suddenly aware how tired he was. It would be impossible to find her in the teeming millions in Delhi, especially since he didn't for a moment imagine she intended staying there. By this time, she could even be somewhere on the high seas heading for England, Australia or China.

He lit a cigarette and nodded his thanks to the sergeant.

'No luck, sir?'

'I'm afraid not.'

As he walked outside, almost the first person he saw was Babington heading for the wireless section. He grinned and slammed up a tremendous salute.

'I don't think we let anybody down, sir,' he said.

Dicken returned the salute. 'No, Babington,' he said. 'I don't think we did.'

Only me, he thought, as he headed for the sunshine. Only me. Only me and Zoë and, above all, Marie-Gabrielle.

Max Hennessy is the pseudonym of John Harris, author of many acclaimed historical novels, including *The Sea Shall Not Have Them* and *Covenant with Death,* and the *Lion at Sea* and *Soldier of the Queen* trilogies, written under the name of Max Hennessy. Ex-sailor, ex-airman, ex-newspaperman, ex-travel courier, he went to sea in the Merchant Navy before the war, and during the war served with two air forces and two navies.